THAT ALL MAY SEE

That All May See

Scott Buchanan

@DisciplesStorehouse

Published by a storehouse of disciples.

Email: disciplesstorehouse@gmail.com

YouTube: @DisciplesStorehouse

"And to make all see what is the fellowship of the mystery, which
from the beginning of the ages has been hidden in God who created
all things through Jesus Christ."

Ephesians 3:9

"That they may see and know, and consider and understand
together, That the hand of the Lord has done this, and the Holy
One of Israel has created it."

Isaiah 41:20

"till we all come to the unity of the faith and of the knowledge of
the Son of God, to a perfect man, to the measure of the stature of
the fullness of Christ"

Ephesians 4:13

Holy Bible New King James Version

TABLE OF CONTENTS:

It was out there in Belize in 2015 the Lord brought Scott Buchanan and his wife Melissa our way as we taught the word of God in a conference, as we were pursuing the revival labour in Belize. They encountered the cross of Christ afresh and it marked the turning point in their lives and marriage. Scott and Melissa have been so drawn to the word of God that they would not miss any of our meetings in any part of the US, and they came severally for the MLR (Ministers Leadership Retreat) in Gboko, Nigeria.

He and his wife came to Nigeria for MILERT (Ministers Leadership Refresher Training) and Scott, at a great cost, came to stay with us in Gboko for an intensive discipleship training and traveled about with me wherever I went to preach the word of God then. During an intensive training of trainers' session we had in Gboko in January 2020, Scott excitedly said to me, "Brother Gbile, now I see and know what I need to pursue and do when I get back to the US. Our nation is in dire need of this message and of genuine discipleship." I saw a man with hunger in his heart and with a burden to make Christ known. He cried profusely about what he had done wrongly, having been ignorant of the finished work of Christ at the cross and the mystery of Christ. Since he left back home at the brink of Covid-19 Pandemic, the passion in his heart has been, "That I may know Him" and he and his wife gave themselves to studying the word of God.

The second unquenchable passion in his heart is "That all may see this mystery and be ushered into this life." A little flock of couples began to desire this truth and Scott and Melissa have been labouring over their lives and pouring into them in a concerted discipleship relationship. Reading through this book, you will meet a brother whose yearning and commission is to do all that lies within him to labour in the word of God that all may see this mystery of Christ. Scott, working assiduously with Melissa has written from his heart and you can feel the passion in every page of this book. I count it a great privilege given to me by God to stand with this brother and his wife, to watch them grow in the grace of God in Christ Jesus and to be able to labour with them and see them walk into the good works for which Christ captured them. To be asked to write a foreword to this book, I count it a grave responsibility and yet a joyful one.

The book begins with a very incisive instruction on "Preparing to Pursue the Mystery of Christ" as no one can receive anything from the Lord, unless the Father in heaven gives to him. The right preparation of the heart is indispensable unto having any insight into the mystery, for it is only he who seeks that finds, the one who asks that receives and to him who knocks, will the door be open.

Chapter two gives the rationale, the burden and the charge on brother Scott to engage this elaborate study of the mystery of Christ as it pertains to our deliverance from the old sinful nature. Actually, Christ is God's message to mankind, and He is the message all prophets were trying to convey. He is the only message of the entire scripture and to progressively understand the mystery of Christ is a worthy venture for any and every child of God. *"And this is eternal life: [it means] to know (to perceive, recognize, become acquainted with, and understand) You, the only true and real God, and [likewise] to know Him, Jesus [as the] Christ (the Anointed One, the Messiah), Whom You have sent."* John 17:3 AMPC

Chapters three and four come with an elaborate study exploring the treasure embedded in Christ Jesus, for it pleased the Father that in Christ, all fullness should dwell. All of God is packaged in Christ. All who would know the only true God can only do so through Him and by knowing Him. All the fullness of the godhead bodily dwells in Him. The length, the breadth, the height and the depth of the riches of God in Christ Jesus, which is actually bottomless and unsearchable is what these chapters try to unveil. Knowing Christ, the mystery of God, is a life-long pursuit, but this book provides for us a starter!

And the goodness of our Great God and Father who desires for all to be saved by coming to repentance, who so loved the world that He gave His Only begotten Son as a ransom for us to have life and have it abundantly is the emphasis of Chapter five. It gives us an insight into the heart of the Father who sent Jesus Christ into the world.

Despite all that God in His eternal goodness packaged in Christ Jesus for us, there is still a disconnect, causing so much misery in the lives of men and even in many who have come to the Church. What made God to drive the first man from his glorious estate still cuts men short of the glory of God today. In Chapters six and seven, brother Scott took the bull by the horn to deal with the problem of sins, of the heart of stone, the sinful nature and of lack of knowledge of the truth that sets men free. Unless sin is confessed, out of deep convictions, forsaken and uprooted by the axe God will lay on its root, all God provides for us remains inaccessible. These chapters carefully point to the only way out, as the next chapters delved into examining God's provisions for our deliverance: the Blood of Jesus Christ for the cleansing of sins committed, the cross of Christ as the means for terminating the old sinful nature, and the new life by His resurrection.

Chapters eight, nine, ten and eleven are the very pivot of this book. The mystery of the blood of covenant and cleansing flood, its efficacy in dealing with every stain, purifying our conscience, and as a weapon to overcome the accuser of the brethren is x-rayed for us in Chapter eight. The mystery and ministry of the cross for taking away the old for God to bring in the new, taking away the first, so as to make a way for the second, its power to dislodge the principalities and powers, and its daily application to release the new life has been the exposition of the word in Chapters nine and ten. And the mystery of His resurrection that we might rise and be translated to live and walk on a new plane of life together with Him and to give us access to His very life at work in us is the focus of the eleventh chapter. The two chapters on the cross of Christ brought fresh insight into our baptism into His death. As it were, He drank us into Himself, so as to terminate our sinful nature in His own body at the cross. You will have to read this section over and over again until these mysteries become personal realities in your own life. The victory Christ wrought for us at the cross is once and for all time. It is a daily victory you can and should have over sin, over self, over the world system and over Satan, the ruler of this world. His Resurrection gives us His life to dwell in us by the Spirit and so we bear about in our mortal body His own life and this is greater than he that is in the world. This is the treasure we carry around in an earthen vessel, that the excellency of the power may not be of us, but of God.

Even though Christ was born of the Spirit and not of the flesh, and walked in an unbroken communion with His Father, He needed to be endued with power from on high for the life and the ministry He had to discharge while on earth. He would not send forth His disciples to do anything for the kingdom unless He had given them power over all the unclean spirits. He actually commanded them to wait for the Promise of the Father before they could be witnesses unto Him. Only those so born of the Spirit can have the holy oil poured upon them. The anointing oil must not be poured on the flesh. To conclude this incisive book, and to send you forth bearing this mystery of Christ in you, the hope of glory, Scott, being led of the Spirit, has drawn us to look into this necessary power for living the resurrection life and for preaching Christ and Him crucified. It is always as it was with our Lord and Master, "Not by might, nor by power, but by My Spirit, says the Lord Almighty."

But to grow this life of Christ and walk in this mystery, the Lord has also made a provision, and this is the matter of discipleship. Brother Scott in pursuit of this mystery that all may see has also come into looking into this means of growing in the life of Christ to become like Jesus. In the final chapter you will note all that the resurrection of Christ provides us to be a joint heir with Christ will only become accessible as we grow into Him in all things. To take His yoke upon you, learning of Him is the way to become conformed to His likeness from one degree of glory to another. The journey to Christ likeness continues and I dare charge you to embrace the genuine discipleship that will fashion and grow you into His very nature and stature.

I heartily recommend this book to you.

Gbile Akanni
Peace House, Gboko
October 2025

INTRODUCTION

📖 ***2 Corinthians 11:2-3 NKJV***

"For I am jealous for you with godly jealousy. For I have betrothed you to one husband, that I may present you as a chaste virgin to Christ. But I fear, lest somehow, as the serpent deceived Eve by his craftiness, so your minds may be corrupted from the <u>simplicity that is in Christ</u>."

Jesus Christ—nothing more, nothing less. Our God has made it that simple for us. However, it appears much of the body of Christ has deviated from the simplicity that is in Christ. As a result, our churches are filled with people whose lives and character bear little resemblance to Jesus, who are dissatisfied with their Christian walk, and who have little effect in establishing the kingdom of God on earth as it is in heaven. We are flooded with crafty teachings of men that lack much substance, which have caused God's people to be famished, without victory over sin, and lacking the understanding of all God accomplished and provided for us in the Gospel of Jesus Christ—the mystery of Christ and Him crucified. God's people are distracted and divided over many theological topics and teachings, and we are not united in the faith and the intimate knowledge of the Son of God. Christ, in whom God put all things, is not actually the center and focus of it all. The Lord intends to bring His people back to the simplicity that is in Christ Jesus, and to open our eyes of understanding to manifest the Son of Man to us afresh. Many members of the body of Christ have become desperate to find something that will work in their lives; something that will last. There is a cry in the heart of God's people saying, "God, please help me, there has got to be more to this Christian life than what I am experiencing." In His mercy, God hears us!

📖 ***Isaiah 41:17-20 NKJV***

"The poor and needy seek water, but there is none, their tongues fail for thirst. I, the LORD, will hear them; I, the God of Israel, will not forsake them. I will open rivers in desolate heights, and

fountains in the midst of the valleys; I will make the wilderness a pool of water, and the dry land springs of water. I will plant in the wilderness the cedar and the acacia tree, the myrtle and the oil tree; I will set in the desert the cypress tree and the pine and the box tree together, <u>that they may see</u> and know, and consider and understand together, that the hand of the LORD has done this, and the Holy One of Israel has created it."

Not knowing the truth blinds and cripples the believer. It handicaps us from encountering the fullness of all God has done and created for our deliverance in Christ Jesus. It is not an issue of honestly, genuinely trying to do good, serving in church, or giving money away, but of not knowing accurately and intimately the Person of Jesus Christ and the Way of God which is in Him. Many of God's people are sincerely trying their best but frustrated with the way their lives are turning out, and the lives of those around them. Churches are splitting, marriages are falling apart, children are going astray, sin is prevailing, and disappointment and despair are settling in. The solutions of men are not providing the answers of the heart. Many love the things of the world, the things of self, and satisfying their own appetites and pleasures rather than desiring to satisfy God. But God, in His love and mercy, desires to revive us and reveal the way of Christ and Him crucified to us, so we can practically experience the reality of His salvation, and the victory and purpose He has planned for each of us. We humbly present this book to you in the belief that God can unveil the mystery of Christ to you and enable you to see the Lord Jesus more vividly than ever before. He Himself is the Way, the Truth, and the Life!

📖 ***John 14:6 NKJV***
"Jesus said to him, 'I am the way, the truth, and the life. No one comes to the Father except through Me.'"
📖 ***Isaiah 30:21 NKJV***
"Your ears shall hear a word behind you, saying, 'This is the way, walk in it," whenever you turn to the right hand or whenever you turn to the left."

If you don't understand and know all God designed the blood of Christ for, you will never be able to live your life in the fullness of that provision. If you don't know all Christ accomplished in His body on the cross at Calvary, you will be missing out on the practical experience of your complete deliverance. And if you are hazy or blind to the reality and purpose of the resurrection provision, you will seldom be able to experience the power that flows from it. The time is now for God to open our eyes to see Jesus and to help us understand His will for our life with Him. Because the Kingdom of God is at hand, He wants to help us walk in wisdom and make the most of the time He has given us on earth.

 📖 *Ephesians 5:15-17 NKJV*
"See then that you walk circumspectly, not as fools but as wise, redeeming the time, because the days are evil. Therefore do not be unwise, but understand what the will of the Lord is."
 📖 *Ephesians 5:15-17 GNT*
"So be careful how you live. Don't live like ignorant people, but like wise people. Make good use of every opportunity you have, because these are evil days. Don't be fools, then, but try to find out what the Lord wants you to do."

Do you want to find out what the Lord wants you to do? As we travel these pages together, we invite you to make use of every opportunity to learn Christ and gain understanding of the will and purpose of God in Him. We will examine the Scriptures and let the Holy Spirit lead and teach us the mystery of Christ, and we will ask God to unfold His word to us and give us the light of understanding and revelation in the knowledge of Him.

 📖 *Psalm 119:130 NKJV*
"The entrance of Your words gives light; it gives understanding to the simple."
 📖 *Psalm 119:130 AMPC*
"The entrance and unfolding of Your words give light; their unfolding gives understanding (discernment and comprehension) to the simple."

As you read, please do not pass over the Bible verses that have been included. This book is composed in such a way that it is critical you read everything (in order) for the development of full understanding and comprehension, which will translate into life transformation as you practice and learn to walk in it. We use the New King James Version as our primary Bible to draw our study from; however, we also use many other translations to help give further insight to whatever truth is being looked at. Finally, you will see that we use the terms "man" and "men" often to refer to mankind as a whole (which includes men, women, children, etc).

Are you hungry for the truth? Are you desiring to know Jesus more personally? Are you longing to gain a deeper understanding of how to walk in the Way with Him, and how to practically experience the fullness of the calling of God on your life? We commit this book into your hands, not trusting man, but the word of God and the supply of the Holy Spirit to do a wondrous work in your heart. I want to let the words of Jesus encourage and admonish us before we enter the first chapter.

📖 *Mark 4:24-25 AMPC*
"And He said to them, 'Be careful what you are hearing. The measure [of thought and study] you give [to the truth you hear] will be the measure [of virtue and knowledge] that comes back to you- and more [besides] will be given to you who hear. For to him who has will more be given; and from him who has nothing, even what he has will be taken away [by force].'"

Whether you are a seeker of truth, a new Christian, an elder in the Church, or at any stage in your development with the Lord, I encourage you to be attentive to the words you read and prayerful in interacting with the Lord along the way. God has something He wants to impart to you, and much He wants to reveal to you. The measure of thought and study you give to the truth you hear will be the measure of the virtue and knowledge of His life and His Way that will be coming back to you. And because God is so wonderful, to those who are really hungry and thirsty to see and know Jesus, He will cause that measure of revelation to be even more abundant than what you put in.

 1 Thessalonians 5:24 NKJV
"He who calls you is faithful, who also will do it."

✝

May God Himself open your eyes to see the mystery of Jesus Christ and Him crucified. May He grant you a hunger and thirst to learn the Truth and the Way of God more accurately. And may He bless you as you pass through the pages of this book. Father God, we ask You to release an abundance of grace on every soul that reads this book. Please help them to get wisdom and to get understanding in the knowledge of You, the only true God, and of Jesus Christ whom You have sent, and of the Way of God You have located in Him. Please cause ALL TO SEE what You want them to see and let Your will be fully done in their lives. Thank You, Father, for hearing us, for we are praying to You in the name of Jesus Christ. Amen.

PREPARING TO PURSUE THE MYSTERY OF CHRIST

As we begin our pursuit together to know and understand this wonderful mystery of Jesus Christ and Him crucified, we need to consider a few key issues that will help us to be better prepared and successful in our quest.

The Issue of Progressive Revelation in the Knowledge of God

📖 *Luke 8:9-10 NKJV*
"Then His disciples asked Him, saying, 'What does this parable mean?' And He said, 'To you it has been given to know the mysteries of the kingdom of God, but to the rest it is given in parables, that 'Seeing they may not see, and hearing they may not understand.'"

📖 *Luke 8:10 AMPC*
"He said to them, To you it has been given to [come progressively to] know (to recognize and understand more strongly and clearly) the mysteries and secrets of the kingdom of God, but for others they are

in parables, so that, [though] looking, they may not see; and hearing, they may not comprehend."

Revelation knowledge is the divine opening of our understanding, as we look into the Scriptures, which enables us to see something that naturally we would never be able to see on our own. It is where the Spirit of God breaks open the word of God and gives us an insight into the truth we are reading, causing us to understand and know God (and His Way) in a deeper manner. This revelation imparts life into our spirit, understanding into our mind, brings immediate help into our life, and draws us into a more personal, intimate *knowing* of the Lord as we live according to it. God has set things up for us to receive revelation knowledge of Him in a progressive manner, by His Spirit, as we continue with Jesus.

For example, I meet you for the first time and learn your name is John. I have come to an initial *knowing* of you, but I don't really know you. I have only learned your name and observed and engaged you on this particular occasion. Even if you wrote a great book and I read it, and was fascinated by you because of it, I still don't know you. I have only read what you wrote and come to know *about* you a bit more. For me to really get to know you, I would need to come and spend time with you. Then, day by day, from one interaction to another, as I connect with you, relate with you, and learn of you, I will progressively be growing in knowing you—more accurately, more personally, and more fully.

> *Revelation knowledge is the divine opening of our understanding...to see something that naturally we would never be able to see on our own.*

It is the same way in our everyday walk with the Lord Jesus Christ. God's design is to reveal and teach His children one truth at a time, and to build upon each truth in a progressive way as they continue with Him. It's like a child passing through his early education years. That child must learn certain foundational principles and concepts of mathematics before additional insights and concepts can be added. Each year of learning (and successful testing for correct application and success in life) is dependent upon the previous year's principles being fully understood and practiced by the student. This progressive process helps the student to learn well and prepares them for soundness in mathematics and its application to daily life. This is God's own method of teaching and revealing the knowledge of Himself and His Way to His children. He builds understanding one step at a time for maximum learning and effective application according to His word and His will.

> *This is God's own method of teaching and revealing the knowledge of Himself and His Way to His children. He builds understanding one step at a time for maximum learning and effective application according to His word and His will.*

📖 *Isaiah 28:9-10 NKJV*
"Whom will he teach knowledge? And whom will he make to understand the message? Those just weaned from the milk? Those just drawn from the breasts? For precept must be upon precept, precept upon precept, line upon line, line upon line, here a little, there a little."

God makes Himself and His Way known to us *progressively* (in stages) in our relationship with Him. It is God who knows the plans He has for us, and it is only God who can build our lives according to those plans as we walk with Him, seek Him, and place our faith and hope in Him and in His Christ.

📖 *Jeremiah 29:11-13 NKJV*
"For I know the thoughts that I think toward you, says the LORD, thoughts of peace and not of evil, to give you a future and a hope. Then you will call upon Me and go and pray to Me, and I will listen to you. And you will seek Me and find Me, when you search for Me with all your heart."
📖 *Psalm 127:1a NKJV*
"Unless the LORD builds the house, they labor in vain who build it;"

3

Consider a building being built out of cinder blocks. Though there are architectural plans for the layout of the entire building, from start to finish, it can only be built one block at a time, each block connected to the one next to it by mortar. That is how God builds our lives and reveals Himself to us; precept upon precept, line upon line, here a little, there a little, until He has completed His work; block by block. For us, the mortar that holds it all together is the understanding He gives us in the truth He reveals to us. Then that understanding and knowledge of Him (and His way) allows further construction to happen as we practically apply (and obey) it in our daily walk. Receiving revelation in the knowledge of Him happens progressively as we walk with Him, study His word, and follow His Son, Jesus Christ.

> *That is how God builds our lives and reveals Himself to us; precept upon precept, line upon line, here a little, there a little, until He has completed His work; block by block.*

The Issue of Personal Valuation

To gain the mystery of Christ, it will come to you as you persist and persevere in your pursuit of the true knowledge of God. *And* it will only come to you in accordance with your personal valuation; how much YOU value it. *Valuation* is an estimation of the worth of something; to consider something or someone to be important or beneficial.

📖 *Matthew 13:44 NKJV*
"Again, the kingdom of heaven is like treasure hidden in a field, which a man found and hid; and for joy over it he goes and sells all that he has and buys that field."

This man was searching in a field and discovered a treasure hidden in it. He assessed and valued the treasure as being more valuable to his life than everything else he owned, so he sold it all to buy the field it was in. This kind of conviction (which compels decisive action) can only come to someone who has *personally* evaluated the treasure and *personally* determined what they think it is worth. It does not matter what someone else thinks or tells them it is worth. This is the concept and principle of personal valuation. A person will not give up or release something valuable they possess, to acquire something they think is worthless, or at least is not worth the price it is being offered to them for. With this in mind, what is it that we possess which we use as currency in our everyday life to acquire the things we want? It is our time, our mind, our attitudes, our energy and strength, our financial resources, and our heart (to name a few). Every day we make decisions, and conduct transactions with these possessions, which reveals what we really value, and what we are trying to acquire in our life. The value we place on something is the extent to which we will exchange what we possess to get it.

Nobody, in their right mind, will give up what they possess for something they deem inferior, unworthy, or not valuable enough to surrender their assets to acquire. That is why we have to search the Scriptures, seeing and hearing the word of God, and receiving revelation knowledge of Christ. It is to increase our personal valuation of Jesus and our faith toward Him, so we

> *The value we place on something is the extent to which we will exchange what we possess to get it.*

can walk with God the way He purposed for our life. Many Christian lives are in disarray because they have not seen or understood much of the treasure of Christ. Therefore, the life they are living gives little evidence that Jesus Christ is their highest pursuit; little evidence that knowing Him is more valuable to them than everything else they possess; and little evidence of the victorious life God intended for them. As a result of not knowing Jesus very well, Christians become unwilling to exchange their time to be with and learn from Him, their thoughts to acknowledge and think with Him, their energies to follow and obey Him, and their desires in order to devote their lives to Him. Other things become more valuable, and time and resources are spent in cultivating and acquiring those things rather than Christ. Personally, I don't believe it is reasonable to tell someone to forsake all and follow Jesus and expect them to drop everything they are doing to follow. Not if I don't deliberately labor to help them see the value of Jesus and what they would gain. Knowing the concept of *personal valuation* compels me to work hard to reveal Christ to them by the word of God and the help of the Holy Spirit. This is so they see and experience Him personally and come to know and value Him in a way so as to decide to count all things loss, in exchange for the priceless privilege of the knowledge of Him.

As we prepare our hearts to discover the mystery of Christ, let's look at this issue of personal valuation in the life of Peter, before he became a disciple. One day Jesus was teaching some things many of His disciples considered to be difficult sayings. Some became disgruntled, they began to complain, and many of those disciples went back and walked with Him no more. Their personal valuation of Jesus and their knowledge of Him was not high enough to compel them toward complete obedience and following of Him. They chose to walk away from Him rather than to continue with Him and be His disciples. They didn't value Him. Then Jesus turned to His twelve disciples and said, "Do you also want to go away?" This is what Peter replied.

> *As a result of not knowing Jesus very well, Christians become unwilling to exchange their time to be with and learn from Him, their thoughts to acknowledge and think with Him, their energies to follow and obey Him, and their desires in order to devote their lives to Him.*

📖 *John 6:68-69 NKJV*
"But Simon Peter answered Him, 'Lord, to whom shall we go? You have the words of eternal life. Also we <u>have come to believe and know</u> that You are the Christ, the Son of the living God.'"

📖 *John 6:69 AMP*
"We have believed and confidently trusted, and [even more] we <u>have come to know</u> [by personal observation and experience] that You are the Holy One of God [the Christ, the Son of the living God]."

6

This reflects progressive revelation knowledge which causes a man to "come to know" and become persuaded of the treasure of Jesus Christ. This is the statement Peter was able to make after many experiences, exposures, and interactions with Jesus. He was not always this confident in Christ. It came as a result of being with Jesus, learning from Jesus, and observing Jesus in everyday life situations as he followed Him. He was progressively coming to know Jesus and growing in confidence of who He truly was. This produced in him an authentic, personal valuation that compelled him to say, 'Lord, to whom shall we go? You have the words of eternal life.'

In His ministry with souls, Jesus operated with the mindset of knowing these key issues of progressive revelation and personal valuation. He labored in the word and with His life, hoping they would make personal decisions, of their own free will, to forsake all and follow Him according to the will and word of God. Let's look at the Bible to see where Peter made that decision in his own life.

In the gospels of Mark and Matthew, we have similar accounts of this story so we will read these together.

📖 *Mark 1:16-20 NKJV*
"And as He walked by the Sea of Galilee, He saw Simon and Andrew his brother casting a net into the sea; for they were fisherman. Then Jesus said to them, 'Follow Me, and I will make you become fishers of men.' They immediately left their nets and followed Him. When He had gone a little farther from there, He saw James the son of Zebedee, and John his brother, who also were in the boat mending their nets. And immediately He called them, and they left their father Zebedee in the boat with the hired servants and went after Him."

📖 **Matthew 4:18-22 NKJV**
"And Jesus, walking by the Sea of Galilee, saw two brothers, Simon called Peter, and Andrew his brother, casting a net into the sea; for they were fisherman. Then He said to them, 'Follow Me, and I will make you fishers of men.' They immediately left their nets and followed Him. Going on from there, He saw two other brothers, James the son of Zebedee, and John his brother, in the boat with Zebedee

their father, mending their nets. He called them, and immediately
they left the boat and their father, and followed Him."

If we were only to read Matthew and Mark's account, we would look at Simon (called Peter) as an amazing man of great faith. I mean, who abandons everything they are doing to leave all and follow Jesus, just because He said, "Follow Me?" How could a man make such a drastic decision without having any knowledge of Jesus? Is this just blind faith or is there more to this story? In these passages we see that Jesus came up to Peter and Andrew as they were casting a net from the shore into the sea. He said, 'Follow me," and they immediately left their nets to follow Him. Then Jesus approached James and John to find them sitting in the boat, with their father, mending their nets. Jesus called them, and they immediately left the boat to follow Him. If that were their first encounter with Jesus Christ, this would be an great story of the faith of these men. However, this is not everything that happened on that day. Their personal valuation of Jesus was not just because He walked up to them and said, "Follow Me," and they, in that brief encounter, valued Him to be someone or something important. To discover what created the kind of valuation that compels men to leave all to follow Jesus, we have to dig into the Scriptures and see what Luke's account reveals as well.

When we don't search the Scriptures *well* (and diligently) to discover truth and to receive revelation from the Lord, we can make mistakes in our assessment of the Way of the Lord and how to walk in it. Let's take a closer look at what was happening around Jesus on the day Peter decided to follow Him.

> *When we don't search the Scriptures well (and diligently) to discover truth and to receive revelation from the Lord, we can make mistakes in our assessment of the Way of the Lord and how to walk in it.*

📖 *Luke 5:1-11 NKJV*
"So it was, as the multitude pressed about Him to hear the word of God, that He stood by the Lake of Gennesaret, and saw two boats standing by the lake; but the fishermen had

8

gone from them and were washing their nets. Then He got into one of the boats, which was Simon's, and asked him to put out a little from the land. And He sat down and taught the multitudes from the boat. When He had stopped speaking, He said to Simon, 'Launch out into the deep and let down your nets for a catch.' But Simon answered and said to Him, 'Master, we have toiled all night and caught nothing; <u>nevertheless at Your word</u> I will let down the net.' And when they had done this, they caught a great number of fish, and their net was breaking. So they signaled to their partners in the other boat to come and help them. And they came and filled both the boats, so that they began to sink. When Simon Peter saw it, he fell down at Jesus' knees, saying, 'Depart from me, for I am a sinful man, O Lord!' For he and all who were with him were astonished at the catch of fish which they had taken; and so also were James and John, the sons of Zebedee, who were partners with Simon. And Jesus said to Simon, 'Do not be afraid. From now on you will catch men.' So when they had brought their boats to land, they forsook all and followed Him."

Now there is more to the picture for us to see. Jesus was standing by the Lake of Gennesaret (also called the Sea of Galilee) with a great crowd pressing about Him to hear the word of God. We see the two boats standing by the lake (having come ashore) with men outside of the boats washing their nets. At this first point, Jesus didn't walk up and say, "Follow Me," but we see He climbed into Peter's boat and asked him to put out a little from the land. Can you picture it? Peter is out of his boat (which is in the shallow water by the beach) cleaning a net after a long night of fishing with no success. Jesus climbs in and asks Peter to put the boat out a little, so Peter gets in the boat and does it. Then Jesus sits down, faces the multitude standing on the shore, and begins to teach them and speak the word of God to them.

We don't know the duration of His teaching, but it was not likely short if we base it on other teachings of Jesus recorded in the Scriptures. Either way, Peter was there, Andrew, James and John were there, and they were all hearing the word of God proceeding from the mouth of Jesus. When Jesus stopped speaking, we see Him turn to Peter and instruct him to launch the boat into the deep and let down his nets for a catch. This further helps us understand they were still in the shallow water near the land, so the people could hear the word of God. Peter told Jesus of the failed night of fishing, BUT added, "nevertheless at Your word I will let down the net." Why would a man, who is a professional fisherman, who understands that lake inside and out, and who spent the entire night fishing with all his expertise (catching nothing), agree to go out and do it again, just because this Man, Jesus asked Him to?

This wasn't Peter's first exposure to Jesus. In John 1, it is recorded that Andrew brought Peter to Jesus one day and Jesus looked at him and said, 'You are Simon the son of Jonah. You shall be called Cephas.' But on that day, Peter did not leave all to follow Jesus, and Jesus did not say to him, "Follow Me." Also, before this particular day at the lake, it is noted in Luke 4 that Jesus came to Peter's house. It is recorded that Simon's wife's mother was sick with a high fever and Jesus stood over her, rebuked the fever, and it left her. Once again, on that day, Jesus did not say to Peter, '"Follow Me," but it was yet another exposure to Jesus for Peter. Finally, on this occasion at the Lake of Gennesaret, Peter had just spent all that time on his boat with Jesus, observing Him and hearing the word of God proceeding from His mouth. *All* these experiences were increasing his personal valuation of Jesus, in his own heart, as he was gaining revelation in the knowledge of Him. He was even willing to override what was logical in his mind, concerning his unfruitful night of fishing, and launch again into the deep.

> *Peter, by His exposures to Jesus, came into a revelation in the knowledge of his sinfulness as he was on his face before the Lord Jesus Christ. Jesus looked at Peter and said, "Do not be afraid. From now on you will catch men."*

Continuing, we see that when Peter and Andrew got the boat out into deep waters (with Jesus in it) and let down their nets, according to the instruction of Jesus, an abundance of fish filled their nets. So much so that they called their partners in the other boat (James and John) to help them with this great catch. Both boats were so filled they started to sink. Wow! Four professional fishermen, not able to catch anything all night, with all their training, abilities, and experience, and now they simply did what Jesus told them to do, and the result was miraculous and supernatural. Peter, after considering this great catch, fell down at Jesus's knees and said, "Depart from me, for I am a sinful man, O Lord." Peter, by His exposures to Jesus, came into a revelation in the knowledge of his sinfulness as he was on his face before the Lord Jesus Christ. Jesus looked at Peter and said, "Do not be afraid. From now on you will catch men."

Then they brought the boats back to the land. Jesus didn't invite Peter to follow Him until He was on the land according to the Matthew and Mark accounts. On the boat, Jesus didn't say, 'Follow Me, and I will make you become fishers of men,' He said, 'Do not be afraid. From now on you will catch men.' One was an encouragement to a repentant and believing heart; the other was the invitation for following. The reality was there

> *One (statement) was an encouragement to a repentant and believing heart; the other was the invitation for following.*

was a massive cargo of fish they brought back which had to be dealt with. Normal operating procedures for fishermen would be to process and prepare the fish they caught, and to clean and mend their nets. So, at some point in that process, after the boats were brought back to land, we see (from Matthew and Mark) that Jesus came to Peter and said, "Follow Me," and he forsook all to follow Him.

This encounter with Jesus, on the boat listening to the word of God that Jesus was teaching, and out in the deep witnessing the huge catch of fish that Jesus predicted, caused Peter to see more of the fullness of the unsearchable riches of Christ. Peter saw Jesus in a new light. Peter heard Jesus in a new light. Peter experienced Jesus in a new light. Jesus became less mysterious to Peter. His eyes of understanding were being enlightened, and his personal valuation

11

of Jesus was increasing as he was experiencing progressive revelation in the knowledge of Him. So, when Jesus finally came and said, "Follow Me," he was ready and fully persuaded to decide to do it. Where are you?

As we've put this book together, we have asked God to release to us an abundance of revelation in the knowledge of Him unto all who read. Now, as we deliberately pursue knowing God and the mystery of Jesus Christ, we need to ask God to increase our personal valuation of Him so we can persevere, persist, and press deeper to know Him. Are you ready to do that?

Lord God, may You grant us mercy and help us to receive an abundance of revelation in the knowledge of You, of Your Son, Jesus Christ, and of Your plan and purpose for our life in Him. We ask You to prepare and enlarge our hearts for pursuing and discovering the mystery of Jesus Christ. Please increase our personal valuation of the treasure You have put in Him. Please open our eyes to see Jesus and grant us personal encounters with Him like You did with Peter, no matter how far we've already come. Thank You, Father, for hearing us, for we are praying to you in the name of Jesus Christ. Amen.

THE MYSTERY OF JESUS CHRIST

Mystery is something difficult or impossible to understand or explain; a religious belief based on divine revelation, especially one regarded as beyond human understanding.

T he Bible speaks of a *mystery* numerous times and in various ways. It speaks of the mystery of the kingdom of God, the mystery of God's will, the great mystery, the mystery of the faith, the mystery of iniquity, the mystery of godliness, the mystery of the gospel, the mystery which has been hidden from ages and generations, and the mystery of God. The aim of this book is *that all may see* that those mysteries are actually one; wrapped up and fulfilled in the revelation of Jesus Christ and the Way of God in Him. Many Christians are trying their best to follow and serve God but struggling to understand why their lives are the way they are and why they don't experience much of what the Bible says is available. What I have discovered in my own journey of faith is that this can always be traced back to a lack of intimately knowing Jesus and the unsearchable riches God has located *in Him*; by progressively growing in the knowledge of Him and walking with Him **according to His**

way. There is more to this Jesus than most people know: a great mystery from God meant to be searched out, discovered, understood, and applied to everyday life for the glory of God.

There Is a Mystery to Be Discovered

📖 *Ephesians 3:1-4 NKJV*
"For this reason I, Paul, the prisoner of Christ Jesus for you Gentiles -if indeed you have heard of the dispensation of the grace of God which was given to me for you, how that by revelation He made known to me the mystery (as I have briefly written already, by which, when you read, you may understand my knowledge in the mystery of Christ),"

> **There is more to this Jesus than most people know; a great mystery from God meant to be searched out, discovered, understood, and applied to everyday life for the glory of God.**

The apostle Paul was given, by the Holy Spirit, an abundance of revelation in the knowledge of what the word of God calls the *mystery of Christ*. This revelation impacted him so much that he resolutely committed the rest of his life to personally knowing Jesus, and to making known to souls nothing else but the message of Jesus Christ and Him crucified. He concluded everything else in his life was rubbish in comparison to gaining the knowledge of Christ.

📖 *Philippians 3:7-8 NKJV*
"But what things were gain to me, these I have counted loss for Christ. Yet indeed I also count all things loss for the excellence of the knowledge of Christ Jesus my Lord, for whom I have suffered the loss of all things, and count them as rubbish, that I may gain Christ."

When Paul (known as Saul) encountered the Lord Jesus Christ on the road to Damascus, he came into an initial revelation in the knowledge of Him as Lord. But that was only the beginning of a journey of progressive revelations of Jesus, which would alter everything about his life and ministry. Listen to Paul's recounting of what Jesus told him on that day.

📖 *Acts 26:15-16 NKJV*

"So I said, 'Who are You, Lord?' And He said, 'I am Jesus, whom you are persecuting. But rise and stand on your feet; for I have appeared to you for this purpose, to make you a minister and a witness both of the things which you have seen and of the things which I will yet reveal to you.'"

📖 *Acts 26:16 AMPC*

"But arise and stand upon your feet; for I have appeared to you for this purpose, that I might appoint you to serve as [My] minister and to bear witness both to what you have seen of Me and to that in which I will appear to you,"

Paul came into an initial revelation (a *seeing* with understanding and knowledge) of Jesus. In his first exposure to the Lord, he didn't see or know everything there was to know about Jesus. He received a glimpse, which began a relational journey with Him of progressive revelations in the knowing of Him. In this book, we will deliberately search and consider the Scriptures to discover Jesus. We will trust God to uncover this mystery to us and help us acquire more and more of the unsearchable riches God has placed in Him. And we will also trust God to explain to us and give us insight (from the Scriptures), into what the *fellowship* of this mystery is, and how we can actively participate in it, like Paul did.

📖 *Ephesians 3:8-9 NKJV*

"To me, who am less than the least of all the saints, this grace was given, that I should preach among the Gentiles the unsearchable riches of Christ, <u>and to make all see</u> what is the fellowship of the mystery, which from the beginning of the ages has been hidden in God who created all things through Jesus Christ;"

Paul was so moved by what God showed him, he devoted his entire life *that all may see* the riches and glory and fellowship that is in Christ Jesus. He was called to bear witness of what he had seen of

Jesus, and what he was going to see, as Jesus revealed Himself to him in their walk together. It became Paul's only message to declare to the world; this apostolic message of Jesus Christ and Him crucified, which the Holy Spirit calls *the testimony of God*.

📖 **1 Corinthians 2:1-2 NKJV**
"And I, brethren, when I came to you, did not come with excellence of speech or of wisdom declaring to you the testimony of God. For I determined not to know anything among you except Jesus Christ and Him crucified."

📖 **Colossians 4:3 NKJV**
"meanwhile praying also for us, that God would open to us a door for the word, to speak the mystery of Christ, for which I am also in chains,"

> *It became Paul's only message to declare to the world; this apostolic message of Jesus Christ and Him crucified, which the Holy Spirit calls the testimony of God.*

This is the testimony of God, Jesus Christ and Him crucified. This is what God talks about, and what Paul encouraged brethren to pray and ask God to open doors for. This revelation of Christ (and the message of the cross) was so impactful to Paul that he realized and determined he could make nothing else known to souls. He could not waste his time preaching or teaching anything else from the Scriptures. Jesus Christ is who God desires "to make all see," and the fellowship that is in Him God desires to make known to *you*. How well do you know Him and the un-searchable riches God has put in Him? Have you come to experience (in your life) the power that God has located in this message?

📖 **1 Corinthians 1:17-18 NKJV**
"For Christ did not send me to baptize, but to preach the gospel, not with wisdom of words, lest the cross of Christ should be made of no effect. For <u>the message of the cross</u> is foolishness to those who are perishing, but <u>to us who are being saved it is the power of God</u>."

We praise God for the blood Jesus shed to save us from our sins which grants us forgiveness and a new life. That is a wonderful gift in itself, but there is much more to this Jesus. What He *fully* accomplished at the cross is critical for *all to see*. There is power (from God) embedded in this message. If a Christian has confessed and forsaken his sins, believed on the Lord Jesus, and received Him in their heart but their life is still plagued by sin, anger, anxiety, depression, fear, faithlessness, defeat, etc., what has their knowledge of Christ gained them? Do you ever wonder to yourself saying, 'There has got to be more to the Christian life than what I am experiencing'? I am here to humbly declare that there is. The Holy Spirit will reveal it to you (by the word of God) if you want to see and are willing to ask Him and agree with Him. It is not based on the wisdom of man to discern and discover, nor his charisma or works, but by the wisdom of God and the aid of His Spirit.

📖 *1 Corinthians 1:22-24 NKJV*
"For Jews request a sign, and Greeks seek wisdom; but <u>we preach Christ crucified,</u> to the Jews a stumbling block and to the Greeks foolishness, but to those who are called, both Jews and Greeks, <u>Christ the power of God and the wisdom of God.</u>"

Do you ever wonder to yourself saying, 'There has got to be more to the Christian life than what I am experiencing'?

Jesus is the power and wisdom of God. The fullness of what He did at the cross is a mystery to most people. This mystery extends into all He accomplished: by leaving heaven and living the life He lived on earth; by shedding His blood as a life sacrifice for sins; and by dying on the cross and being resurrected from the dead. The depths of this mystery, when seen, understood, believed, and experienced, brings deliverance and peace through practical application in everyday life. In Ephesians 3:4, we saw the word say, "when you read, you may understand my knowledge in the mystery of Christ." We are going to read, explore, and dig into the word of God to search out this mystery and trust the Holy Spirit to reveal it to us. We will ask Him to give us understanding, which brings forth the effective working of

Christ's life (and power) in and toward us who believe. Do you want that power in your own life? Has the Gospel (you believed) *practically* delivered you from the power of sin, the powers of darkness, the power of this world system, and even from your own self? Listen to how Paul prayed in the beginning of his letter to the Ephesian Christians.

📖 *Ephesians 1:17-19 NKJV*
"that the God of our Lord Jesus Christ, the Father of glory, may give to you the spirit of wisdom and revelation in the knowledge of Him, the eyes of your understanding being enlightened; that you may know what is the hope of His calling, what are the riches of the glory of His inheritance in the saints, and what is the exceeding greatness of His power toward us who believe, according to the working of His mighty power"

God wants you to have revelation of His Christ in abundant measures. He wants to give it to you so you may know (practically, with understanding) the hope of His calling for your life in Christ Jesus. He wants you to know (practically, with understanding) what are the riches of the glory of His inheritance IN the saints. And He wants you to know (practically, with understanding) the exceeding greatness of His power toward you who believe. Our God wants you to experience the peace, rest, and freedom that comes from knowing Jesus more intimately, and walking in His way more consistently with understanding.

> *Our God wants you to experience the peace, rest, and freedom that comes from knowing Jesus more intimately, and walking in His way more consistently with understanding.*

In my own story, God saved me from an awful, sin-filled life. He caused me to be born again when I repented, believed on Jesus, and received Him into my heart. Early on, God gave me a hunger and desire for the word of God, and I memorized much Scripture by His grace. For years, I grew in ministerial leadership duties and tried my best to teach and lead people to God. My wife and I were even missionaries in a foreign country. I was completely sincere in my love for God and my love for people. I was whole-heartedly trying *hard* to serve God and to serve people. But some-thing was missing. I saw, in the word of God, a different kind of experience (and power) than what I was having. My marriage was suffering, and I didn't understand why. Sin was still plaguing my life and dismantling the things God wanted to do through me. I was easily angered and didn't know how to overcome the difficulties I was facing, and the emotions, pain, and confusion I was experiencing. I used to cry out to God and say something like this, "Father, is this all there is? Am I always going to be this way? There has got to be more to this life than what I am experiencing; please help me."

> *But something was missing. I saw, in the word of God, a different kind of experience (and power) than what I was having.*

By the mercy of God, our Father in heaven began opening our eyes to see more of Jesus Christ and the message of the cross. In His good-ness, He connected my wife and I with disciples who labored in the word of God with us. They helped us to discover the hidden wisdom of God which God ordained before the ages for our glory.

📖 *1 Corinthians 2:7-8 NKJV*
"But we speak the wisdom of God in a mystery, the hidden wisdom which God ordained before the ages for our glory, which none of the rulers of this age knew; for had they known, they would not have crucified the Lord of glory."

The scripture said, 'for had they known, they would not have cruc-ified the Lord of glory.' So, the mystery of Christ has much to do with what was done at the cross when Jesus was crucified. What hap-pened at the cross was so hidden that the devil himself would not have let Jesus be crucified if he would have known what God was doing. Do you know why? We will search and discover why in the chapters to come.

19

A mystery is a secret that is to be discovered, or that is intended to be hidden from understanding until an appointed time of revelation. It is important to note it is a part of the character and nature of God to conceal valuable things, in order that they may be discovered by those who love Him and want to diligently search for and seek Him.

> *It is important to note it is a part of the character and nature of God to conceal valuable things, in order that they may be discovered by those who love Him and want to diligently search for and seek Him.*

📖   *Proverbs 25:2 NKJV*
"It is the glory of God to conceal a matter, but the glory of kings is to search out a matter."

📖   *Deuteronomy 29:29 NKJV*
"The secret things belong to the LORD our God, but those things which are revealed belong to us and to our children forever, that we may do all the words of this law."

📖   *1 Corinthians 2:9-10 NKJV*
"But as it is written: 'eye has not seen, nor ear heard, nor have entered into the heart of man the things which God has prepared for those who love Him.' But God has revealed them to us through His Spirit. For the Spirit searches all things, yes, the deep things of God."

All things belong to God! The things everyone sees, and the things concealed in secret; they all belong to God. By His Spirit, He reveals the secret (valuable) things which He has prepared for those who love Him. Revelation in the knowledge of the mystery of Christ is reserved for those who want to pursue a deeper relationship with Him and are willing to dig with Him in the word of God to discover the treasure of Christ Jesus.

Even creation bears witness to this principle. All precious metals, gems, and minerals are hidden inside the earth, in the mountains and in the seas. They are not laying around on the surface for just anyone to acquire but are buried for the diligent to discover and possess. It takes deliberate searching for them, putting in the work to discover them, and laboring on them until they become a precious possession in your life.

Are you wanting to seek after the treasures He has reserved for YOU? You have to ask Him to show you, then begin to seek with all your heart, and keep on knocking until He opens to you fresh revelation in the knowledge of Jesus, which will bring transformation to your life. Look at what Jesus gave as instructions to His disciples and what the word of God says about asking, seeking, and believing God.

Revelation in the knowledge of the mystery of Christ is reserved for those who want to pursue a deeper relationship with Him and are willing to dig with Him in the word of God to discover the treasure of Christ Jesus.

   📖 *Matthew 7:7-8 NKJV*
"Ask, and it will be given to you; seek, and you will find; knock, and it will be opened to you. For everyone who asks receives, and he who seeks finds, and to him who knocks it will be opened."
   📖 *Hebrews 11:6 NKJV*
"But without faith it is impossible to please Him, for he who comes to God must believe that He is, and that He is a rewarder of those who diligently seek Him."
   📖 *Jeremiah 33:2-3 NKJV*
"Thus says the LORD who made it, the LORD who formed it to establish it (the LORD is His name): Call to Me, and I will answer you, and show you great and mighty things, which you do not know."

Can you please call on God, even now, and ask Him to show you the great and mighty things of Christ Jesus which you have not known to this point in your journey with Him? There are many dimensions and glorious revelations of the mystery of Christ.

And, if God has mercy on us, we will see more of the fullness of this mystery as we press on.

21

We will see:

- ❖ *The mystery* of how God made all things through Jesus Christ, put all things in Him, and what that means for us.
- ❖ *The mystery* of how man disobeyed God, and what happened to all humanity when he did.
- ❖ *The mystery* of the mercy and love of God to devise means to deal with the problems between man and Himself, and to rescue mankind after entering into sin.
- ❖ *The mystery* of how Jesus lived His life on earth as a Man who never sinned.
- ❖ *The mystery* of the blood of the cross, and what the blood provision of Jesus Christ does for us now.
- ❖ *The mystery* of all the deliverances of the cross of Christ, and what exactly Jesus crucified in His body at Calvary.
- ❖ *The mystery* of what it means to be born again.
- ❖ *The mystery* of being endued with power from on high for service to God.

BUT the riches of the glory of this mystery, the very pinnacle and highest purpose and prize of this mystery, is *Christ in you*, the hope of glory! This is the greatest treasure God can give us. His very Spirit coming to live in us, transform us, and teach us (from the inside) the ways and purposes of God, so we may succeed and prosper in His plan for our life in Christ Jesus.

📖 *Colossians 1:26-27 NKJV*
"the mystery which has been hidden from ages and from generations, but now has been revealed to His saints. To them God willed to make known what

It is by the word of God, and the comprehensive insight that comes from Him, that enables us to realize and experience the glory of God in every dimension of our lives in Christ; by the reality of Christ in us.

are the riches of the glory of this mystery among the Gentiles: which is Christ in you, the hope of glory."

Did you see that God wills (desires) to make known this mystery to us? Revelation of this mystery goes far beyond only seeing what Jesus did for the forgiveness of sins. There must be a seeing of Jesus (an increasing revelation in the knowledge of Him) that is progressively growing in us as we learn to walk with Him. It is by the word of God, and the comprehensive insight that comes from Him, that enables us to realize and experience the glory of God in every dimension of our lives in Christ; by the reality of Christ *in* us. The apostle Paul spoke clearly that he needed God's help to be able to make known this mystery in preaching the Gospel. He also said the mystery of the Gospel is the mystery of Christ. Therefore, it is of utmost importance for us to understand, know, and acquire the treasures God embedded in the Person of Christ Jesus, and in the message of Him crucified. As we search the word of God, our intent will be to discover all the hidden treasures of this mystery, and to learn how to live according to what God teaches us. Our intent is to be in an increasingly intimate union with Christ *in* us, the treasure and gift of God.

📖 *2 Corinthians 4:6-7 NKJV*

"For it is the God who commanded light to shine out of darkness, who has shone in our hearts to give the light of the knowledge of the glory of God in the face of Jesus Christ. But we have this treasure in earthen vessels, that the excellence of the power may be of God and not of us."

The power that overcomes those challenges and gives us victory is nothing other than the treasure of Christ in us (who is the power of God) being permitted to live His life in and through us.

Is the glory of God, in the face of Jesus Christ, manifesting in your marriage, in your children's lives, and in your place of business? Is the glory of God manifesting in your secret life where no one else sees? Are you experiencing the glory of

God in your battle against sin and the devil? The power that over-comes those challenges and gives us victory is nothing other than the treasure of Christ in us (who is the power of God) being permit-ted to live His life in and through us. That is the great mystery we will deliberately pursue and trust God to help us to see. Let's pray!

Our God and our Father, according to Your word, we acknowledge that we can receive nothing unless it is given to us from above, and that apart from Jesus we can do nothing. Therefore, we come humbly to ask You to have mercy on us and to make us objects of Your mercy as we travel the pages of this book. Please pour out Your Spirit upon us and grant us wisdom and revelation in the knowledge of Jesus Christ, and the message of the cross, which is the power of God to we who are being saved. Please open our eyes of understanding and draw us closer to You and show us the great and mighty things that we have not yet known. Help us to know You, the only true God, and Jesus Christ, whom You have sent, in a deeper and more personal way. Thank You for hearing us Father, for we are making these requests and believing You will help us as we are praying to You in the name of Jesus Christ. Amen.

THE TREASURE OF JESUS CHRIST
PART 1

  📖 *Colossians 1:19 NKJV*
*"For it pleased the Father that **in Him** all the fullness should dwell"*
  📖 *Colossians 1:19 AMPC*
*"For it has pleased [the Father] that all the divine fullness (the sum total of the divine perfection, powers, and attributes) should dwell **in Him** permanently."*

For mankind, the sum total of everything there is to know about God is packaged, discovered, and experienced in Jesus Christ. It was the Father's good pleasure to make it this way. He did it so that all fullness would be located *in* Jesus, and so that knowing God and the mystery of God would come through progress-ively knowing Him. As we pass through the Scriptures to discover the treasure of Jesus Christ, I ask you to be mindful of the word 'IN'— IN Him, IN Christ, IN whom, etc. It will be a key word in realizing and seeing all the particular dimensions of all the divine fullness God the Father has placed IN Jesus Christ. This chapter aims to bring you into a deeper assurance of understanding and knowing Jesus more personally and more accurately.

📖 *Colossians 2:2-3 NKJV*

*"that their hearts may be encouraged, being knit together in love, and attaining to all riches of the full assurance of understanding, to the knowledge of the mystery of God, both of the Father and of Christ, **in whom** are hidden all the treasures of wisdom and knowledge."*

📖 *Colossians 2:3 AMPC*

*"**In Him** all the treasures of [divine] wisdom (comprehensive insight into the ways and purposes of God) and [all the riches of spiritual] knowledge and enlightenment are stored up and lie hidden."*

Do you want to search and dig to discover all the treasures of divine wisdom and comprehensive insight into the ways and purposes of God? The Bible reveals that all wisdom and knowledge is found, acquired, and experienced in *knowing* the Christ of God. All enlightenment is stored up in Him and waiting to be discovered by those who want to pursue Him. We are not looking to be cheated by the wisdom and philosophies of men and their opinions but to engage the word of truth, which liberates us and sets us on a proper trajectory in the plan and purpose of God for our lives.

> *All wisdom and knowledge is found, acquired, and experienced in knowing the Christ of God.*

📖 *Colossians 2:8-10 NKJV*

*"Beware lest anyone cheat you through philosophy and empty deceit, according to the tradition of men, according to the basic principles of the world, and not according to Christ. For **in Him** dwells all the fullness of the Godhead bodily; and you are complete **in Him**, who is the head of all principality and power."*

As we progress, let us seek for God to open our eyes to see Jesus more than we ever have. Let us seek for God to help us *really* come to know Him and His love for us practically, through experience for ourselves. Let us dive into the word of God to gain Christ!

📖 *Ephesians 3:19 AMPC*
"[That you may really come] to know [practically, through experience for yourselves] the love of Christ, which far surpasses mere knowledge [without experience]; that you may be filled [through all your being] unto all the fullness of God [may have the richest measure of the divine Presence, and become a body wholly filled and flooded with God Himself]!"

Our God and our Father, we want to ask You to help us to see Jesus and cause us to know Him more practically (by personal experience) as we pass through these pages. Please open our eyes of understanding and grant us Your Spirit of wisdom and revelation in the knowledge of Him. Help us to comprehend Christ and cause us to increasingly know (in our own body) the love of Christ, and the richest measure of the divine Presence. Thank You Father, for it is in the name of Jesus Christ we pray. Amen.

The Glorious Dimensions and Features of Jesus Christ

Dimension is a measurable extent of a particular kind, such as length, breadth, depth, or height; an aspect or feature of a thing. *Feature* is a distinctive attribute or aspect of something.

📖 *Ephesians 3:17-19 NKJV*
"that Christ may dwell in your hearts through faith; that you, being rooted and grounded in love, may be able to comprehend with all the saints what is the width and length and depth and height- to know the love of Christ which passes knowledge; that you may be filled with all the fullness of God."

Imagine if God gave you a house to live your life in. In that house He has placed everything you will ever need to operate and succeed in

His purpose and plan for your life; a victorious, peaceful, abundant life. You would want to go and explore every detail of the house and discover all He has put in it for you, wouldn't you? This is precisely what He has done for us in Jesus Christ, who Himself *is* the Father's house for His children to dwell and abide in.

We are going to study some of the great provisions God has placed in Christ. We will gain understanding as we see (for ourselves), so it can become practical in our lives. You cannot apply (effectively) what you personally have not seen, understood, or come to know. If I stand in the front yard and look at that house I was given, I will have a perspective of the house which will cause me to know it in more detail. If I walk around to the side and examine it, I will have a new perspective, notice more details of the same house, and increase my knowledge of it. This will enable me to function *in* the house more fully. However, if I just stand near the house and I never enter it and search it out, looking into all its drawers, all the closets and rooms, I will be limiting my knowledge, enjoyment, and experience of that which God has provided for me to utilize in my life on earth.

> *You cannot apply (effectively) what you personally have not seen, understood, or come to know.*

This section will read as more of a study format than a book format. It is intentional so we can deliberately gaze upon, study, and consider the riches God has placed in Christ for our walk with Him. Let's begin by exploring some of the different measurable dimensions and features of all God has put **IN Christ**.

IN CHRIST: The Glory of God

📖 *Habakkuk 2:14 NKJV*
"For the earth will be filled with the knowledge of the glory of the LORD, as the waters cover the sea."
📖 *Isaiah 11:9-10 NKJV*
"They shall not hurt nor destroy in all my holy mountain, for the earth shall be full of the knowledge of the LORD as the waters cover the

sea. And in that day there shall be a Root of Jesse, who shall stand as a banner to the people; for the Gentiles shall seek Him, and His resting place shall be glorious."

These prophecies are announcing that a day is coming when the knowledge of the glory of the LORD will fill the earth. It will be Jesus, the Root of Jesse, who will declare and manifest the glory of God as a banner to the people. That is to say, everywhere Jesus is seen and heard, everywhere His gospel is declared, and His life is manifested, there will be a revelation in the knowledge of the glory of God—in seeing Jesus.

📖 *2 Corinthians 4:5-7 NKJV*

"For we do not preach ourselves, but Christ Jesus the Lord, and ourselves your bondservants for Jesus' sake. For it is the God who commanded light to shine out of darkness, who has shone in our hearts to give the light of the knowledge of the glory of God in the face of Jesus Christ. But we have this treasure in earthen vessels, that the excellence of the power may be of God and not of us."

> **The more you see, know, and understand Jesus, and all that He has done and is doing, the more of the glory of God you will experience in your life as you walk with Him.**

The knowledge of the glory of God is given when the face (the Person) of Jesus Christ, whom God sent, is revealed to a heart; either to someone who has never seen Him before, or to a believer who has only seen certain dimensions of Him. The more you see, know, and understand Jesus, and all that He has done and is doing, the more of the glory of God you will experience in your life as you walk with Him.

The greatest experience you can have of the glory of God is when you have been born again, and the Father has made it His good pleasure to reveal His Son in you. God put the treasure of Christ *in* you (who have believed) so the excellence of the power is of God and not of us. He did this so He alone will be glorified.

📖 **Colossians 1:27 NKJV**
"To them God willed to make known what are the riches of the glory of this mystery among the Gentiles: which is Christ in you, the hope of glory."

The hope of the glory of God being manifest in your inner life, your marriage, your occupation, your family, and your ministry is the reality of Christ in you being permitted to shine the light of His life through you. The knowledge of the glory of God has been set (by God) in seeing and knowing Jesus Christ, and by His very life dwelling in you. As we pass through this book, we will better understand the details of what that means. For now, let us praise God for this dimension of Christ which reveals the glory of God, and makes a way for people to experience it as they walk with His beloved Son.

IN CHRIST: The Eternal Purpose of God

📖 **Ephesians 3:9-12 KJV**
*"And to make all men see what is the fellowship of the mystery, which from the beginning of the world hath been hid in God, who created all things by Jesus Christ: To the intent that now unto the principalities and powers in heavenly places might be known by the church the manifold wisdom of God, according to the eternal purpose which he purposed **in Christ** Jesus our Lord: **in whom** we have boldness and access with confidence by the faith of him."*

A man searching for his purpose in life will only discover that purpose by being found *in* Jesus and walking with Him in complete obedience. God's eternal purpose for man has been purposed *by* God to be established *in* Christ. There is no lasting purpose outside of Christ. Every other pursuit and purpose a man engages in will fall short and could exclude him from eternity with God. It is IN Christ alone that God's plan and purpose for our life will be unveiled and obtained. *There* we will discover boldness and access to God with confidence by living in a union with Him, by faith in Christ.

📖 *2 Timothy 1:8-10 NKJV*

*"Therefore do not be ashamed of the testimony of our Lord, nor of me His prisoner, but share with me in the sufferings for the gospel according to the power of God, who has saved us and called us with a holy calling, not according to our works, but according to His own purpose and grace which was given to us **In Christ Jesus** before time began, but has now been revealed by the appearing of our Savior Jesus Christ, who has abolished death and brought life and immortality to light through the gospel,"*

The Father has a purpose for your life; a great plan and calling that He longs for you to discover and walk in. He has grace to aid you in learning that plan and entering into that purpose. That eternal purpose and grace has been deposited in Christ Jesus. It is ours to access and enjoy, as we walk with Him obediently and learn to live according to the words that proceed from His mouth.

> *The Father has a purpose for your life; a great plan and calling that He longs for you to discover and walk in. He has grace to aid you in learning that plan and entering into that purpose. That eternal purpose and grace has been deposited in Christ Jesus.*

Every part of the will of God for your life is purposely located in Jesus Christ for you to enjoy and receive. The more we study the word of God, and the more the Holy Spirit opens our eyes of understanding to know Jesus, the better we will be equipped to realize, understand, and abide in our purpose for being on this earth.

IN CHRIST: The Word of God

When it comes to the word of God, we discover three dimensions of revelation in the knowledge of Christ. These are critical understandings for us to successfully proceed in God's purpose for our lives.

1. *The Word of God is about Jesus.*

31

One day Jesus was addressing some Jewish people who wanted to kill Him because He was declaring that God was His Father, making Himself equal with God. Jesus continued explaining to them how the kingdom of God works, and then He made a statement about the Scriptures we need to catch and understand.

📖 *John 5:37-40 NKJV*
"And the Father Himself, who sent Me, has testified of Me. You have neither heard His voice at any time, nor seen His form. But you do not have His word abiding in you, because whom He sent, Him you do not believe. You search the Scriptures, for in them you think you have eternal life; and these are they which testify of Me. But you are not willing to come to Me that you may have life."

📖 *John 5:39-40 TLB*
"You search the Scriptures, for you believe they give you eternal life. And the Scriptures point to me! Yet you won't come to me so that I can give you this life eternal."

The Scriptures point to Jesus! He is the topic of the word of God from the beginning to the end. He Himself *is* the Beginning and the End. All the writings of the Bible are meant to make known Jesus Christ, whom God sent, and to manifest Him and God's way IN Him to all who want to worship God in spirit and truth. Many who read the Scriptures read primarily for intellectual acquisition, to check off a duty-list, or to get topical ideas for their life or ministry. They do this rather than reading to discover Jesus more fully and know Him more personally. Life is given *by* Him, and the benefits that come from God are acquired by being *with* Him. For example:

📖 *John 1:43-45 NKJV*
*"The following day Jesus wanted to go to Galilee, and He found Philip and said to him, 'Follow Me.' Now Philip was from Bethsaida, the city of Andrew and Peter. Philip found Nathanael and said to him, 'We have found Him of whom Moses in the law, and also the prophets, **wrote**- Jesus of Nazareth, the son of Joseph'"*

The reason God has given us the Scriptures is because they testify of Jesus and point the reader to *Him* in whom God has put all things.

All the writings of Moses, the prophets, and the disciples of Jesus point to the glorious wonders of the Person and work of Jesus Christ. Look at what Paul would use to preach Jesus from in Rome.

📖 **Acts 28:23 NKJV**

"So when they had appointed him a day, many came to him at his lodging, to whom he explained and solemnly testified of the kingdom of God, persuading them concerning Jesus from both the Law of Moses and the Prophets, from morning till evening."

> **The reason God has given us the Scriptures is because they testify of Jesus and point the reader to Him in whom God has put all things.**

When you read the Scriptures in order to commune with God and discover Jesus, you will discover (in increasing measures) the Holy Spirit opening your eyes of understanding to see Him. You will learn to receive from Him the benefits God freely gives to those who walk with His Son; those who learn to live according to the words that proceed from His mouth in a daily union. Is that the desire of your heart? Can you turn that into a prayer even now?

2. *Jesus speaks the Word of God.*

📖 **John 3:34-36 NKJV**

*"For He whom God has sent speaks the words of God, for God does not give the Spirit by measure. The Father loves the Son, and has given **all things into His hand**. He who believes in the Son has everlasting life; and he who does not believe the Son shall not see life, but the wrath of God abides on him."*

📖 **John 3:34 AMPC**

"For since He Whom God has sent speaks the words of God [proclaims God's own message], God does not give Him His Spirit sparingly or by measure, but boundless is the gift God makes of His Spirit!"

Jesus speaks the words of God. He proclaims God's message and reveals God's Way. In this passage, John said, "he who does not believe the Son shall not see life, but the wrath of God abides on Him."
So, accessing and engaging the word of God comes from reading the
Scriptures, which God has given us, and which bear witness and
point to Jesus. But it also comes in walking with Jesus and learning
to hear and do the words that He speaks directly to us. Even Moses
told the children of Israel that this Jesus would be the One in whom
God would put His words in His mouth. The One which He would
expect them to listen to and follow.

📖 *Deuteronomy 18:15-19 NKJV*

"The LORD your God will raise up for you a Prophet like me from your
midst, from your brethren. Him you
shall hear, according to all you de-
sired of the LORD your God in Horeb
in the day of the assembly, saying,
'Let me not hear again the voice of
the LORD my God, nor let me see
this great fire anymore, lest I die.'
And the LORD said to me: 'What
they have spoken is good. I will
raise up for them a Prophet like you
from among their brethren, and
will put My words in His mouth, and
He shall speak to them all that I
command Him. And it shall be that
whoever will not hear My words,
which He speaks in My name, I will require it of him.'"

**When you read the
Scriptures in order to
commune with God and
discover Jesus, you will
discover (in increasing
measures) the Holy
Spirit opening your
eyes of understanding
to see Him.**

To hear the *word* that proceeds from the mouth of God is to come
to Jesus and the Scriptures to hear what He has to say. The reason
is, God has decided to raise Jesus up to be the Prophet who makes
known God's words. No one will be able to say, "I believe in God, but
I don't believe in the teachings of Jesus Christ." God Himself says,
"whoever will not hear My words, which He speaks in My name, I
will require it of him." This is a dimension of the treasure of Jesus

Christ we need to understand and live according to for the fulfillment of God's plan for our life to be realized. Listen to Jesus:

> **To hear the word that proceeds from the mouth of God is to come to Jesus and the Scriptures to hear what He has to say.**

📖 **John 7:16-17 NKJV**

"Jesus answered them and said, 'My doctrine is not Mine, but His who sent Me. If anyone wills to do His will, he shall know concerning the doctrine, whether it is from God or whether I speak on My own authority."

📖 **John 7:16-17 AMPC**

"Jesus answered them by saying, My teaching is not My own, but His Who sent Me. If any man desires to do His will (God's pleasure), he will know (have the needed illumination to recognize, and can tell for himself) whether the teaching is from God or whether I am speaking from Myself and of My own accord and on My own authority."

If you desire to do God's will, to do what pleases Him, you will not quarrel with these truths found in the Scripture. If you really *will* to do His will, you will gain the needed illumination in order to recognize this is true, and you will be receptive to change your way of thinking and align your life to the truth that is in Jesus. Understanding the doctrine that comes from God is only discovered by understanding and knowing the teachings and Person of Jesus Christ. All truths are found within Him because He (Jesus) is the Truth.

3. Jesus is called the Word of God.

📖 **1 John 5:7 NKJV**

"For there are three that bear witness in heaven: the Father, the Word, and the Holy Spirit; and these three are one."

📖 **Revelation 19:11-13 NKJV**

"Now I saw heaven opened, and behold, a white horse. And he who sat on him was called Faithful and True, and in righteousness He judges and makes war. His eyes were like a flame of fire, and on His *head were many crowns. He had a name written that no one knew except Himself. He was clothed with a robe dipped in blood, and His name is called the Word of God."*

Jesus Christ *is* the Word of God! He is the second Person of the God-head and He is called the Word of God. He is the One God brought forth in the beginning; the One who became flesh and dwelt among us.

📖 ***John 1:1-2,14 NKJV***
"In the beginning was the Word, and the Word was with God, and the Word was God. He was in the beginning with God....And the Word became flesh and dwelt among us, and we beheld His glory, the glory as of the only begotten of the Father, full of grace and truth."

📖 ***John 1:1-2 AMPC***
"In the beginning [before all time] was the Word (Christ), and the Word was with God, and the Word was God Himself."

> **Jesus is called the Word of God and He reveals God and manifests the will of God to us.**

Here we see that to behold the glory of God is to be looking upon Jesus and dis-covering Him as the only begotten of the Father. Jesus is He who was the Word of God with the Father before time began. Jesus is He who was the Word of God with the Father in the Genesis of creation when God was preparing to do a work on the earth. Jesus is called the Word of God and He reveals God and manifests the will of God to us. Praise God for Jesus!

IN CHRIST: The Image of God

What does God look like? How can you tell if something looks like God or looks like something that comes from God? One day God was talking to Moses, and Moses asked Him to show him His glory. God began to tell him how He would make His goodness pass before him, and how He will proclaim the name of the LORD before him accord-ing to His grace and compassion.

📖 **Exodus 33:20-23 NKJV**
"But He said, 'You cannot see My face; for no man shall see Me, and live.' And the LORD said, 'Here is a place by Me, and you shall stand on the rock. So it shall be, while My glory passes by, that I will put you <u>in the cleft of the rock</u>, and will cover you with My hand while I pass by. Then I will take away My hand, and you shall see My back; but My face shall not be seen.'"

No man can see God and live. No one has ever seen the face of God because they will die if they do. In this passage, the Lord's solution was to take Moses and put him IN a place where he could interact with the glory of God and not die. The place was in the cleft of the rock, and that Rock was Christ. Christ is the Rock that followed the children of Israel in the wilderness through whom God supplied all their needs. The apostle Paul wrote about it when he said:

📖 **1 Corinthians 10:1-4 NKJV**
"Moreover, brethren, I do not want you to be unaware that all our fathers were under the cloud, all passed through the sea, all were baptized into Moses in the cloud and in the sea, all ate the same spiritual food, and drank the same spiritual drink. For they drank of that spiritual Rock that followed them, and that Rock was Christ."

> **Christ is the interface between man and God that allows us to see God.**

Christ is the interface between man and God that allows us to see God. Christ is God's solution and means by which He provides for His people, and by whom God does all His work through. Jesus Christ is the visible manifestation of what God looks like and what God is like. He is the very image of God for man to behold.

📖 **John 1:18 NKJV**
"No one has seen God at any time. The only begotten Son, who is in the bosom of the Father, He has declared Him."
📖 **John 1:18 CEV**
"No one has ever seen God. The only Son, who is truly God and is closest to the Father, has shown us what God is like."

Not only does Jesus speak the words of God and explain what God is like, but His very life *shows* us (by example) who God is and what He is like. Jesus is the means by which God reveals Himself to mankind. He gives revelation of what it is like to see God. Jesus is the audio/visual display to hear, see, understand, and know God, because Jesus *is* the exact image of God.

  📖 **Hebrews 1:1-3 NKJV**
"God, who at various times and in various ways spoke in time past to the fathers by the prophets, has in these last days spoken to us by His Son, whom He has appointed heir of all things, through whom also He made the worlds; who being <u>the brightness of His glory and the express image of His person</u>, and upholding all things by the word of His power, when He had by Himself purged our sins, sat down at the right hand of the Majesty on high,"

Jesus is the brightness of the glory of God. Wow! He is the very expressed image of the Person of God who has appointed Jesus to be the heir of all things. That includes revelation in the knowledge of God; seeing and knowing God as He is. If you ever want to know what God looks like, you will need to come and look at Jesus. He *only* is the exact image, the exact likeness, and the exact nature of God. Jesus alone is how God reveals and unveils Himself to people. He is how God grants vision and access to Himself.

  📖 **Hebrews 1:3a AMPC**
"He is the sole expression of the glory of God [the Light-being, the outraying or radiance of the divine], and He is the perfect imprint and very image of [God's] nature, upholding and maintaining and guiding and propelling the universe by His mighty word of Power."

God has decided (in His dealings with mankind) that Jesus Christ would be the sole expression of the glory of God and the sole opportunity for a person to experience the very image of God's nature within their life. If you ever ask God, "show me Your glory," and are willing to really let Him do it, you will discover Him bringing you into a deeper revelation of Jesus, and a more intimate knowledge of Him. He is the very brightness (the Light) of His glory. Let me ask you, is your personal valuation of Jesus increasing yet? Has the Holy Spirit been opening your eyes to see that if you want to see the Father, you have to see the Son? Every child of God who will become a disciple of Jesus Christ has to learn this truth to go far in their Father's house and in His purpose for their life. Even Jesus' own disciples were learning this truth as they walked with Him. They were learning from Him and one day asked Him to show the Father to them.

> *Is your personal valuation of Jesus increasing yet? Has the Holy Spirit been opening your eyes to see that if you want to see the Father, you have to see the Son?*

📖 *John 14:8-9 NKJV*

"Philip said to Him, 'Lord, show us the Father, and it is sufficient for us.' Jesus said to him, 'Have I been with you so long, and yet you have not known Me, Philip? He who has seen Me has seen the Father; so how can you say, 'Show us the Father'?"

These men still hadn't realized the value of this Jesus they were following. They were still asking for something else because they hadn't yet discovered the treasure God has put in His Christ. They had not yet learned that seeing Jesus is how you see the Father.

📖 *Colossians 1:15 NKJV*
"He is the image of the invisible God, the firstborn over all creation."
📖 *Colossians 1:15 MSG*
"We look at this Son and see the God who cannot be seen. We look at this Son and see God's original purpose in everything created."

Jesus is the image and likeness of God. If you aim to discover and know Jesus more intimately, to make Him a lifelong pursuit, you will grow in seeing and knowing the Father who loves you. In seeing and believing on Jesus, the Father will save, deliver, and freely bestow upon you His blessings as you continue with His Son. Are you seeing Jesus more clearly? Is the Light of His life dawning upon your heart? Are you ready to change the way you interact with Him, and the way you interface with the living God who sent Him?

It is time to believe God as His Spirit is removing the veil from our eyes in order to see Jesus.

📖 *2 Corinthians 4:3-4 NKJV*

"But even if our gospel is veiled, it is veiled to those who are perishing, whose minds the god of this age has blinded, who do not believe, lest the light of the gospel of the glory of Christ, <u>who is the image of God</u>, should shine on them."

📖 *2 Corinthians 4:4 AMPC*

"For the god of this world has blinded the unbelievers' minds [that they should not discern the truth], preventing them from seeing the illuminating light of the Gospel of the glory of Christ (the Messiah), Who is the Image and Likeness of God."

> **In seeing and believing on Jesus, the Father will save, deliver, and freely bestow upon you His blessings as you continue with His Son.**

Jesus is not *an* image of God but *the* image and exact likeness of God. We will look at God's goal and purpose to conform us into the image of His Son in every area of our lives. Here, God is showing us that Jesus Christ is the Image and Likeness of God.

IN CHRIST: All Things are Created by God

📖 *Colossians 1:15-19 NKJV*

*"He is the image of the invisible God, the firstborn over all creation. For **by Him** <u>all things were created</u> that are in heaven and that are on earth, visible and invisible, whether thrones or dominions or principalities or powers. <u>All things were created</u> **through Him** and **for Him**. And He is before all things, and **in Him** all things consist. And He is the head of the body, the church, who is the beginning, the firstborn from the dead, that in all things He may have the preeminence."*

📖 *Revelation 22:13 NKJV*

"I am the Alpha and the Omega, the Beginning and the End, the First and the Last."

By the Father's design, Jesus Christ is the means by which He created all things. He did this so in all things Jesus may have the preeminence, and so God will receive all the glory through Him. Truly, God created all things BY Jesus, THROUGH Jesus, and FOR Jesus. Why? Everything God does to give mankind access to Him (and His plan for our life) has been placed in interacting with His Son. This is the value God placed in Jesus, who is the firstborn over all creation, as well as the firstborn from the dead. All things exist because of Him. All things consist of and are upheld by Him, and all things are for Him (according to God's plan). God made Jesus to be the Heir of all things, and the Person through whom He made all things, the One through whom man can know Him, have access to Him and His provisions, and obtain eternal life *in* and *through* Him.

  📖 *Hebrews 1:1-2 NKJV*
*"God, who at various times and in various ways spoke in time past to the fathers by the prophets, has in these last days spoken to us **by His Son**, whom He has appointed **heir of all things**, **through whom** also He made the worlds;"*

  📖 *Ephesians 3:8-9 NKJV*
*"To me, who am less than the least of all the saints, this grace was given, that I should preach among the Gentiles the unsearchable riches of Christ, and to make all see what is the fellowship of the mystery, which from the beginning of the ages has been hidden in God who <u>created all things **through Jesus Christ**</u>;"*

Discovering all the treasures of the mystery of God, happens in acquiring and seeing more and more of Jesus Christ. Jesus is how God does all His work; how He puts things in order, fashions things to shape, and equips them for their intended purpose. Jesus is He through whom God framed everything He made. Jesus is the substance God uses to frame everything He is yet making.

  📖 *Hebrews 11:3 NKJV*
*"By faith we understand that the worlds were framed **by the word of God**, so that the things which are seen were not made of things which are visible."*

📖 **Hebrews 11:3 AMPC**
"By faith we understand that the worlds [during successive ages] were framed (fashioned, put in order, and equipped for their intended purpose) **by the word of God**, *so that what we see was not made out of things which are visible."*

Do you see Jesus in a new light? Are you seeing Him more clearly in the Holy Scriptures? Jesus was with God in the beginning, and Jesus was the Beginning that God made all things by, through and for. Listen to Him talking in the Old Testament about these things:

> *Jesus is how God does all His work; how He puts things in order, fashions things to shape, and equips them for their intended purpose.*

📖 **Isaiah 48:12-13,16 NKJV**
"Listen to Me, O Jacob, and Israel, My called: I am He, I am the First, I am also the Last. Indeed My hand has laid the foundation of the earth, and My right hand has stretched out the heavens; when I call to them, they stand up together....Come near to Me, hear this: I have not spoken in secret **from the beginning***; from the time that it was, I* **was there***. And now the* <u>Lord GOD</u> *and* <u>His Spirit</u> *have sent* <u>Me</u>*."*

Did you see all three Persons of the Godhead in that verse? Did you see Jesus saying, "The Lord GOD and His Spirit have sent Me?" He is bearing witness He was there "from the beginning" when God made all things through Him and manifested them on the earth by His Spirit. That is how God operates in His dealings with creation and His relations with mankind. This is the reason Romans 1 says all men are without excuse because all creation bears witness that there is a God. And all creation is a witness to the features of Jesus Christ by which He made all things in the beginning.

📖 **Romans 1:20 NKJV**
"For since the creation of the world His invisible attributes are clearly seen, being understood by the things that are made, even His eternal power and Godhead, so that they are without excuse."

We need to now trace back in the Bible to examine how God did this in the beginning when He decided to create all things through Jesus Christ. We need to see Jesus in the beginning as the Light God brought forth to create all things by. I am trusting the Lord to open your eyes of understanding and grant you wisdom and revelation in the knowledge of Jesus Christ as we press on in the word of God.

IN CHRIST: The Light of God

📖 *Genesis 1:1-5 NKJV*
"In the beginning God created the heavens and the earth. The earth was without form, and void; and darkness was on the face of the deep. And the Spirit of God was hovering over the face of the waters. Then God said, 'Let there be light'; and there was light. And God saw the light, that it was good; and God divided the light from the darkness. God called the light Day, and the darkness He called Night. So the evening and the morning were the first day."

God was preparing to do His creating work on the earth in the beginning; He began to put the pieces in place for that magnificent work. His Spirit was positioned and ready (hovering) and awaiting instructtions for what to do and what to make visible (according to what God would speak). Then God said, 'Let there be light." What was this light God was bringing forth in that moment? This light was so important that it was His *first* decree on the first day of His creation plan; the light which He called *good*. Is this light the kind of light that illuminates the sky, like the sun or moon? Let's eliminate that as an option by looking at the fourth day of creation.

📖 *Genesis 1:14-19 NKJV*
"Then God said, 'Let there be lights in the firmament of the heavens to divide the day from the night; and let them be for signs and seasons, and for days and years; and let them be for lights in the firmament of the heavens to give light on the earth', and it was so. Then God made two great lights: the greater light to rule the day, and the lesser light to rule the night. He made the stars also. God set them in the firmament of the heavens to give light on the earth, and to rule over the day and over the night, and to divide the light from the

*darkness. And God saw that it was good. So the evening and the morning were **the fourth day**."*

These verses testify that on the fourth day God made the sun, moon, and stars. These are natural lights to divide the day from the night, mark days, years and seasons, and to give light on the earth. Among other things, the sun provides light and heat to the earth, it drives weather patterns and ocean currents. The moon provides light for navigation at night, causes tides, and helps to stabilize the earth with its gravitational pull. The stars provide light to see and help with orientation and direction at night. However, these cannot be the light God brought forth on the first day because these were created on a different (the fourth) day. So, let's press on to examine another place in the Bible that speaks of "In the beginning" (referring to the Genesis account), to see for sure what this light is that was the *first* thing God brought forth.

📖 *John 1:1-10 NKJV*
*"In the beginning was the Word, and the Word was with God, and the Word was God. He was in the beginning with God. All things were made **through Him**, and without Him nothing was made that was made. **In Him** was life, and the life was the light of men. And the light shines in the darkness, and the darkness did not comprehend it. There was a man sent from God, whose name was John. This man came for a witness, to bear witness of the Light, that all through him might believe. He was not **that Light**, but was sent to bear witness of **that Light**. That was the true Light which gives light to every man coming into the world. He was in the world, and the world was made through Him, and the world did not know Him."*

Jesus was the Word that was in the beginning with God. The Bible says, "without Him nothing was made that was made." Nothing! Nothing ever (by God's choice) is made by God without Jesus. All things were (and are) made through Him. God does all His work through Jesus Christ by the Spirit of God. Please remember this truth, it will be very relevant as we continue to learn the mystery of Christ, and the way of God IN Him. In Jesus is life, and the Life is the light of men. Jesus is the Life Light that God brought forth in the beginning ("Let there be light") and created everything through.

When the word of God said that John the Baptist bore witness of THAT Light, we know that John's message pointed to Jesus Christ (not some natural light), and that the writer was pointing back to the beginning we see in Genesis 1. He refers to THAT Light God brought forth in the beginning. Those were the Scriptures the Jewish people read. They understood and knew what "in the beginning" and "that Light" were referring to. The world was made through Jesus, who we have seen called the Word and the Light. This is one of the glorious dimensions and features of Jesus which God has purposed in Him. He is the Light that comes from God, and He is God. Let's hear from Jesus Himself about this.

> *God does all His work through Jesus Christ by the Spirit of God. Please remember this truth, it will be very relevant as we continue to learn the mystery of Christ, and the way of God IN Him.*

📖 *John 8:12 NKJV*
"Then Jesus spoke to them again, saying, 'I am the light of the world. He who follows Me shall not walk in darkness, but have the light of life.'"

📖 *John 8:12 AMPC*
"Once more Jesus addressed the crowd. He said, I am the Light of the world. He who follows Me will not be walking in the dark, but will have the Light which is Life."

📖 *John 9:4-5 NKJV*
"I must work the works of Him who sent Me while it is day; the night is coming when no one can work. As long as I am in the world, I am the light of the world."

Jesus is intentional in the words He speaks. He is called the Word of God and He speaks the words of God. Very deliberately He is stating

He is the Light of the world, and He is the Life that men will have if they follow Him. Jesus is the Light God makes all things through.

📖 *John 1:9-13 AMP*

"There it was- the true Light [the genuine, perfect, steadfast Light] which, coming into the world, enlightens everyone. He (Christ) was in the world, and though the world was made through Him, the world did not recognize Him. He came to that which was his own [that which belonged to Him- His world, His creation, His possession], and those who were His own [people- the Jewish nation} did not receive and welcome Him. But to as many as did receive and welcome Him, He gave the right [the authority, the privilege] to become children of God, that is, to those who believe in (adhere to, trust in, and rely on) His name- who were born, not of blood [natural conception], nor of the will of the flesh [physical impulse], nor of the will of man [that of a natural father], but of God [that is, a divine and supernatural birth- they are born of God- spiritually transformed, renewed, sanctified]."

> **When the word of God said that John the Baptist bore witness of THAT Light, we know that John's message pointed to Jesus Christ.**

📖 *Matthew 4:16 NKJV*

*"The people who sat in darkness have seen a great **light**, and upon those who sat in the region and shadow of death **Light** has dawned."*

Do you see the Light of God in the face of Jesus Christ? Are you recognizing your need to know Him better? Have you received Him and been born of God by a divine and supernatural birth? As we progress, there will be several opportunities to make that decision, but why wait? I would like to implore you now to turn to God and beg Him for this new birth in Christ if you are not completely sure.

The operation of our God and Father is to give us all things in Jesus Christ, to do all His work through Jesus Christ, and to give us life in

Jesus Christ. He is the Light of God, the illumination of the plan, purpose, and Person of the Almighty God. Praise the Lord.

IN CHRIST : The Knowledge of God

📖 *Matthew 11:25-29 NKJV*
"At that time Jesus answered and said, 'I thank You, Father, Lord of heaven and earth, that You have hidden these things from the wise and prudent and have revealed them to babes. Even so, Father, for so it seemed good in Your sight. All things have been delivered to Me by My Father, and no one knows the Son except the Father. Nor does anyone know the Father except the Son, and the one to whom the Son wills to reveal Him. Come to Me, all you who labor and are heavy laden, and I will give you rest. Take My yoke upon you and learn from Me, for I am gentle and lowly in heart, and you will find rest for your souls."

It is wonderful to *really* know it was good in the Father's sight to deliver all things into the hands of Jesus, including knowing Him. Jesus said no one knows the Father except Him, and that knowledge will only be relayed to the soul that Jesus desires to reveal it to. Then Jesus extends the invitation to "come to Me" and you will find rest (and the knowledge of God). It is in coming to Jesus you will discover and know who the Father is and will gain access into relationship with Him.

Every other religion, every other way which proposes a different avenue to know the only true God, is a false way that will lead people to hell, because no one knows the Father except they know Jesus, and no one can come to the Father except through Jesus.

> *Every other religion, every other way which proposes a different avenue to know the only true God, is a false way that will lead people to hell, because no one knows the Father except they know Jesus, and no one can come to the Father except through Jesus.*

📖 *John 14:6-7 NKJV*

"Jesus said to him, 'I am the way, the truth, and the life. No one comes to the Father except through Me. If you had known Me, you would have known My Father also; and from now on you know Him and have seen Him.'"

📖 *John 14:6-7 AMP*

"Jesus said to him, 'I am the [only] Way [to God] and the [real] Truth and the [real] Life; no one comes to the Father, but through Me. If you had [really] known Me, you would also have known My Father. From now on you know Him, and have seen Him.'"

Do you want to know Jesus in a deeper and more personal way? The reason we are laboring like this is because of how critical it is for God's children to see and know the value of Jesus Christ to their life. Not just as He who came from God to die for their sins, but to see all things in Jesus, and increase in the reality of a deep, personal, intimate knowing of God through knowing Him.

📖 *Ephesians 1:17 AMP*

"[I always pray] that the God of our Lord Jesus Christ, the Father of glory, may grant you a spirit of wisdom and of revelation [that gives you a deep and personal and intimate insight] into the true knowledge of Him [for we know the Father through the Son]."

IN CHRIST: The Foundation of God

📖 *1 Corinthians 3:10-11 NKJV*

*"According to the grace of God which was given to me, as a wise master builder I have laid the foundation, and another builds on it. But let each one take heed how he builds on it. For no other foundation can anyone lay than that which is laid, **which is Jesus Christ**."*

For a life to endure the storms that come in an earthly existence, it must be built on a solid foundation, and that foundation is Jesus Christ. He is the solid Rock that never moves and can never be carried away by created things and created beings. The foundation is the first requirement when building a new home, and without it the home being built will be carried away, unstable, and lacking integrity to withstand the pressures of a harsh environment (which is what we find in this fallen world). Jesus was tested and tried in the furnace of temptation, affliction, and enemy pressures as a Man on the earth. He was found blameless and proven faithful to God in all things. The Light that is Life, that is the foundation of God's work, must be in every child of God (Christ in you) before God's building project on that life can begin.

📖 *Isaiah 28:16 NKJV*
"Therefore thus says the Lord GOD: 'Behold, I lay in Zion a stone for a foundation, a tried stone, a precious cornerstone, a sure foundation; whoever believes will not act hastily.'"

📖 *Isaiah 28:16 AMPC*
"Therefore thus says the Lord God, Behold, I am laying in Zion for a foundation a Stone, a tested Stone, a precious Cornerstone of sure foundation; he who believes (trusts in, relies on, and adheres to that Stone) will not be ashamed or give way or hasten away [in sudden panic]"

Once you have secured from God the foundation of Christ in you (when you repented, believed on the Lord Jesus, and received Him into your heart), then you are able to learn to walk with Him and have your life built upon Him. First is the foundation, then the building process where we trust in Jesus, rely on Jesus, and adhere to Jesus in our everyday life.

> *Praise God that Jesus is the foundation that never moves and is always able to support the weight and pressures of our life.*

Praise God that Jesus is the foundation that never moves and is always able to support the weight and pressures of our life.

Let's pray.

Our Father, thank you for revealing more of Jesus Christ to us. Thank you for putting all things in Christ and beginning to show us what that actually looks like. We ask You to continue opening our eyes to see more of the treasure of Jesus, and to give us insight, understanding, and revelation in the knowledge of Him. Thank You, Father, for helping us, for we are praying to You in the name of Jesus Christ. Amen.

THE TREASURE OF JESUS CHRIST
PART 2

t was the Father's good pleasure to put all things into Jesus Christ. In Him dwells all the fullness of the Godhead bodily. What is it that God wants us all to see about Jesus? Let's continue in our study and discover more of this treasure of Christ, and what it means for our lives.

IN CHRIST: The Grace of God

📖 *2 Timothy 1:8-9; 2:1 NKJV*

"Therefore do not be ashamed of the testimony of our Lord, nor of me His prisoner, but share with me in the sufferings for the gospel according to the power of God, who has saved us and called us with a holy calling, not according to our works, but according to His own purpose and **grace** *which was given to us* **in Christ Jesus** *before time began....You therefore, my son, be strong in the grace that is* **in Christ Jesus.**"

God chose to give us access to His purpose and grace by placing them IN Christ Jesus. *Grace* is both His unmerited favor and an ability (a divine empowering) given by God which enables us to do what we otherwise would never be able to do on our own. That enabling, or strength, is only accessed in Christ Jesus and in abiding in Him, relying on Him, obeying Him, and trusting in Him in everyday life situations. God's plan for you to receive His grace (as often as you need it and which He longs to give you), comes in progressively knowing Jesus more personally and more accurately.

📖 *2 Peter 1:2-3 NKJV*

"Grace and peace be multiplied to you in the knowledge of God and of Jesus our Lord, as His divine power has given to us all things that pertain to life and godliness, through the knowledge of Him who called us by glory and virtue,"

> **Grace** *is both His unmerited favor and an ability (a divine empowering) given by God which enables us to do what we otherwise would never be able to do on our own.*

The experience of grace being multiplied to our life is conditional, as well as accessible, through the knowing of God and the Lord Jesus Christ. We have already seen that the knowledge of God comes through increasingly knowing the Lord Jesus Christ. Now we are seeing how divine power for life and godliness (grace) will be our experience as we grow in personally knowing the Lord Jesus Christ and following Him.

📖 *2 Peter 1:2 AMPC*

"May grace (God's favor) and peace (which is perfect well-being, all necessary good, all spiritual prosperity, and freedom from fears and agitating passions and moral conflicts) be multiplied to you in [the full, personal, precise, and correct] knowledge of God and of Jesus our Lord."

It is crucial to understand we *must* grow in more fully knowing Jesus. We must increase in personally knowing Him, and more precisely and correctly knowing Him. Are you desiring to *practically* experience the perfect well-being and increasing spiritual prosperity that comes from knowing Him? Ask the Lord for help even now before you keep reading. Ask Him to reveal more of the wonderful features of Jesus Christ to you, and to help you to grow in knowing Him and walking with Him. The grace that Is In Christ will bring freedom from fears and the agitating passions and moral conflicts that trouble and plague your life. As you come to Jesus and let Him teach you how to live, you will grow in grace and become strong in the grace that is in Him. He will be releasing the benefits and effects of grace into your life.

📖 *Titus 2:11-12 NKJV*
"For the grace of God that brings salvation has appeared to all men, teaching us that, denying ungodliness and worldly lusts, we should live soberly, righteously, and godly in this present age,"

Grace is not a thing but a Person, the Lord Jesus Christ. It is not some-*thing* called grace that brought salvation and teaches men, but the Lord Jesus Christ Himself who is our salvation and our Teacher. It is Jesus who says, "If anyone desires to come after Me, let him deny himself, take up His cross daily and follow Me" and "take My yoke upon you, and learn from Me". God has deliberately given us access to His divine power for living soberly, righteously, and godly in this present age, *in* and *through* the Person of Jesus Christ. It is Jesus who is full of grace, and it is in being with Him (knowing and obeying Him) that we receive grace upon grace for our life. If you cry out to God and beg Him for more grace in your life, He will point you to His Son and instruct you to know Him and follow Him for the answer. Grace and truth come through Jesus Christ alone. Jesus is the grace of God and He is the channel

> *If you cry out to God and beg Him for more grace in your life, He will point you to His Son and instruct you to know Him and follow Him for the answer. Grace and truth come through Jesus Christ alone.*

through which the Father gives us access to the grace of God. He is all in all.

📖 *John 1:14-17 NKJV*

*"And the Word became flesh and dwelt among us, and we beheld His glory, the glory as of the only begotten of the Father, full of grace and truth. John bore witness of Him and cried out, saying, 'This was He of whom I said, 'He who comes after me is preferred before me, for He was before me.' And of His fullness we have all received, and grace for grace. For the law was given through Moses, but grace and truth came **through Jesus Christ**."*

IN CHRIST: All Spiritual Blessings

📖 *Ephesians 1:3-6 NKJV*

*"Blessed be the God and Father of our Lord Jesus Christ, who has blessed us with every spiritual blessing in the heavenly places **in Christ**, just as He chose us **in Him** before the foundation of the world, that we should be holy and without blame before Him in love, having predestined us to adoption as sons **by Jesus Christ** to Himself, according to the good pleasure of His will, to the praise of the glory of His grace, by which He made us accepted in the Beloved."*

📖 *Ephesians 1:3 GNT*

*"Let us give thanks to the God and Father of our Lord Jesus Christ! For in our union **with Christ** he has blessed us by giving us every spiritual blessing in the heavenly world."*

> **It is wonderful to know how generous God has been to us who are in Christ Jesus. He has made us accepted in Him, and we have access to every spiritual blessing as we continue with Jesus.**

All spiritual blessings are placed by God in Jesus Christ. Our God and Father has already blessed us with access to them in our daily union with Christ. Did you also see that it is IN Christ we are accepted by God and chosen by God? We will discover and receive the riches of these spiritual blessings as we abide in Jesus, learn to obey Him, and grow up into Him in all things. It is wonderful to know how generous God has been to us who are in Christ Jesus. He has made us accepted in Him, and we have access to every spiritual blessing as we continue with Jesus.

IN CHRIST: The Power of God

📖 *1 Corinthians 1:23-24 NKJV*
"but we preach Christ crucified, to the Jews a stumbling block and to the Greeks foolishness, but to those who are called, both Jews and Greeks, Christ the power of God and the wisdom of God."

📖 **Matthew 28:18 KJV**
"And Jesus came and spake unto them, saying, 'All power is given unto me in heaven and in earth.'"

📖 *Matthew 28:18 AMPC*
Jesus approached and, breaking the silence, said to them, All authority (all power of rule) in heaven and on earth has been given to Me."

Christ is the Power of God, and He is the One God has given ALL power to. Everything God does is by Jesus, for Jesus, and through Jesus Christ. So, if anyone wants to personally experience the power of God, that power (Christ) has to be in them, and He must be permitted to rule from within.

> *It is the Spirit of Christ in the believer who brings forth the power of God in our daily life as we learn to yield willingly to Him.*

Every authority we ever need, and every power required for a proper walk with God, is drawn from Christ as we live in union with Him. Our daily victory depends on denying ourself and turning to Him to follow and obey Him in all things. We have no power in our own strength. Jesus said, "apart from Me you can do nothing." It is the Spirit of Christ in the believer who brings forth the power of God in our daily life as we learn to yield willingly to Him.

55

📖 **Romans 8:9-11 NKJV**

"But you are not in the flesh but in the Spirit, if indeed the Spirit of God dwells in you. Now if anyone does not have the Spirit of Christ, he is not His. And if Christ is in you, the body is dead because of sin, but the Spirit is life because of righteousness. But if the Spirit of Him who raised Jesus from the dead dwells in you, He who raised Christ from the dead will also give life to your mortal bodies through His Spirit who dwells in you."

📖 **2 Timothy 1:7 NKJV**

"For God has not given us a spirit of fear, but of power and of love and of a sound mind."

When you were born again, you received the Spirit of Christ to come and dwell in you. Christ, who is the Power of God and in Whom God has given all power to, came to live in you. This is another dimension of God's goodness toward us—to enable our lives to be victorious over sin, the devil, the world, and even our own selves.

> *The lack of power in your life for overcoming sin, fear, and the like is directly connected to the lack of your connection with and obedience to Christ in you.*

The power of God that *is* Jesus Christ, and that flows from Jesus Christ, delivers us from fear and enables us to love and have a sound mind at all times. He develops self-control and establishes peace in us as we walk with Him. The lack of power in your life for overcoming sin, fear, and the like is directly connected to the lack of your connection with and obedience to Christ in you.

📖 **2 Timothy 1:7 AMP**

"For God did not give us a spirit of timidity or cowardice or fear, but [He has given us a spirit] of power and of love and of sound judgment and personal discipline [abilities that result in a calm, well-balanced mind and self-control]."

IN CHRIST: The Wisdom of God

📖 *1 Corinthians 1:21-24 NKJV*

"For since, in the wisdom of God, the world through wisdom did not know God, it pleased God through the foolishness of the message preached to save those who believe. For Jews request a sign, and Greeks seek after wisdom; but we preach Christ crucified, to the Jews a stumbling block and to the Greeks foolishness, but to those who are called, both Jews and Greeks, Christ the power of God <u>and the wisdom of God.</u>"

📖 *1 Corinthians 1:24 AMPC*

"But to those who are called, whether Jew or Greek (Gentile), Christ [is] the Power of God and <u>the Wisdom of God.</u>"

Again, it is important to note Jesus is not only *a* wisdom that comes from God, but He is THE Wisdom of God. In the Old Testament, which bears witness of and points to Jesus, Christ can be seen to anyone who has a ready and receptive heart to see Him. Let's look at one example of seeing Jesus (as Wisdom) and hearing Him talk in the book of Proverbs. This is a lengthy section of verses, but I encourage you to read it all the way through and I ask the Holy Spirit to open your eyes to see Jesus.

📖 *Proverbs 8:12-36 NKJV*

"I, wisdom, dwell with prudence, and find out knowledge and discretion. The fear of the LORD is to hate evil; pride and arrogance and the evil way and the perverse mouth I hate. Counsel is mine, and sound wisdom; <u>I am understanding,</u> I have strength. By me kings reign, and rulers decree justice. By me princes rule, and nobles, all the judges of the earth. I love those who love me, and those who seek me diligently will find me. Riches and honor are with me, enduring riches and righteousness. My fruit is better than gold, yes, than fine gold, and my revenue than choice silver. I traverse the way of righteousness, in the midst of the paths of justice, that I may cause those who love me to inherit wealth, that I may fill their treasuries. The LORD possessed me at the beginning of His way, before His works of old. I have been established from everlasting, from the beginning, before there was ever an earth. When there were no depths I was

brought forth, when there were no fountains abounding with water. Before the mountains were settled, before the hills, I was brought forth; while as yet He had not made the earth or the fields, or the primal dust of the world. When He prepared the heavens, I was there, when He drew a circle on the face of the deep, when He established the clouds above, when He strengthened the fountains of the deep, when He assigned to the sea its limit, so that the waters would not transgress His command, when He marked out the foundations of the earth, then I was beside Him as a master craftsman; and I was daily His delight, rejoicing always before Him, rejoicing in His inhabited world, and my delight was with the sons of men. Now therefore, listen to me, my children, for blessed are those who keep my ways. Hear instruction and be wise, and do not disdain it. Blessed is the man who listens to me, watching daily at my gates, waiting at the posts of my doors. For whoever finds me finds life, and obtains favor from the LORD. But he who sins against me wrongs his own soul; all those who hate me love death."

> **Did you see Jesus saying He will cause those who love Him to inherit the wealth and riches that are in Him, and He will fill their treasuries?**

Did you see Jesus? This glorious and amazing Jesus (talking as Wisdom) who said, "I am understanding." Do you know when the Bible says "I am" it is God referring to Himself? There is not an angel, or a spirit called wisdom that makes such declarations. They are not God and cannot make such assertions; only God can.

Did you see Jesus, who has all authority and rule, declaring that (by Him) kings, rulers, princes, nobles, and judges are able to rule? He said those who seek Him diligently will find Him and riches and honor are with Him. Did you see Jesus saying He will cause those who love Him to inherit the wealth and riches that are in Him, and He will fill their treasuries? Did you see in this proverb the substance of Christ, as He announced He was there in the beginning with His Father, as He was brought forth by God to create all things through Him? It is Jesus who always rejoices before God and intercedes before Him for this inhabited world. And it is Jesus whose delight is with the sons of men. The wisdom of God is Jesus Christ, not a spirit whose only job is to impart wisdom, but Him in whom God put all things (including wisdom). It is Jesus in whom you find life and obtain favor from the Lord, and it is if you sin against Jesus that you will wrong your soul.

My friend, are you seeing Jesus? I am pleading with God to be opening your eyes in these pages to see the unsearchable riches of Christ. I am praying He will grow your hunger to pursue Him with all your heart.

📖 *James 1:5 NKJV*
"If any of you lacks wisdom, let him ask of God, who gives to all liberally and without reproach, and it will be given to him."

> **We don't need the wisdom of man but the wisdom which comes from God. Our Father has located that wisdom in Jesus Christ and gives us access to it as we rely on Him and ask Him for it.**

We need wisdom for every dimension and decision in our life. We don't need the wisdom of man but the wisdom which comes from God. Our Father has located *that* wisdom in Jesus Christ and gives us access to it as we rely on Him and ask Him for it.

📖 *1 Corinthians 1:30 NLT*
"God has united you with Christ Jesus. For our benefit God made him to be wisdom itself. Christ made us right with God; he made us pure and holy, and he freed us from sin."

IN CHRIST: The Love of God

📖 *Romans 8:38-39 NKJV*
*"For I am persuaded that neither death nor life, nor angels nor principalities nor powers, nor things present nor things to come, nor height nor depth, nor any other created thing, shall be able to separate us from the love of God **which is in Christ Jesus our Lord**."*

📖 *1 Timothy 1:14 NKJV*
*"And the grace of our Lord was exceedingly abundant, with faith and love **which are in Christ Jesus**."*
📖 *2 Timothy 1:13-14 NKJV*
*"Hold fast the pattern of sound words which you have heard from me, in faith and love **which are in Christ Jesus**. That good thing which was committed to you, keep by the Holy Spirit who dwells in us."*

The Bible says God is love, and that God demonstrated His love toward us in that while we were still sinners, Christ died for us. In fact, God loved the world so much He gave His only begotten Son to die and pay the price for our sins. But there were conditions attached to experiencing the reality of that love. A person has to hear the Gospel, believe God sent Jesus, confess, repent, turn away from their sins, and receive Jesus for a new life with God to begin. They have to be brought into His household to experience the riches and depths of His love. The experience of God's love has been located within the boundaries and circumference of Christ.

It is God who saves, but man must respond to His prescribed way in order for salvation to come to pass in his life, and for him to know His love. Christ is where access to God's love is located. For everyone who doesn't believe and respond, Jesus said they are under condemnation and will perish. They will not be able to experience God's love. The above Bible verses reveal the love of God (as wonderful and glorious as it is) is located, accessed, and experienced only in Christ Jesus. God the Father (who is love) has set things up in His dealings with mankind so that His love is found in Jesus Christ. It is experienced practically in believing *on* and walking *with* Him.

📖 *Jude 1:20-21 NKJV*
"But you, beloved, building yourselves up on your most holy faith, praying in the Holy Spirit, keep yourselves in the love of God, looking for the mercy of our Lord Jesus Christ unto eternal life."
📖 *John 14:21 NKJV*
"He who has My commandments and keeps them, it is he who loves Me. And he who loves Me will be loved by My Father, and I will love him and manifest Myself to him."

There would not be need for the apostle Paul to instruct brethren to "keep yourselves IN the love of God" unless something can happen that causes you to be *out* of knowing the love of God. Jesus was clear in saying "He who loves Me will be loved by My Father." All things from the Father, including the access and experience of the love of God, are obtained in being with Jesus and in having His commandments and keeping them. It is in walking obediently with Jesus, and growing in an intimate relationship with Him, where we will grow in the knowledge of God's love. Sin, disobedience, unfaithfulness, and independence will cause us to wander from the place of abiding in Jesus where God causes us to know His great love for us and toward us. We must depend on Jesus, rely on Him, cleave to Him, and always be with Him who is able to keep us and direct our hearts into the love of God.

> *There would not be need for the apostle Paul to instruct brethren to "keep yourselves IN the love of God" unless something can happen that causes you to be out of knowing the love of God.*

📖 *2 Thessalonians 3:3-5 NKJV*
"But the Lord is faithful, who will establish you and guard you from the evil one. And we have confidence in the Lord concerning you, both that you do and will do the things we command you. Now may the Lord direct your hearts into the love of God and into the patience of Christ."

Jesus is the One who can always keep us in the place where we can know the love of God in increasing measures. He is also the One who can direct our hearts into the love of God, if we have wandered away from following Him. The key is abiding in the Lord Jesus, like He instructed us to do in the Gospel of John.

📖 *John 15:4-5,9 NKJV*
"Abide in Me, and I in you. As the branch cannot bear fruit of itself, unless it abides in the vine, neither can you, unless you abide in Me. I am the vine, you are the branches. He who abides in Me, and I in

him, bears much fruit; for without Me you can do nothing....As the Father loved Me, I also have loved you; abide in My love."

Do you want to know the love that God has for you? Are you longing to experience that love regularly and in abundance? Jesus is the key to satisfy that longing. You can do nothing without Him, but with Him you can consistently experience and know the wonderful love of God in your life.

> *Do you want to know the love that God has for you? Are you longing to experience that love regularly and in abundance? Jesus is the key to satisfy that longing.*

📖 *1 John 4:16 NKJV*

"And we have known and believed the love that God has for us. God is love, and he who abides in love abides in God, and God in him."

IN CHRIST: The Promises of God

📖 *2 Corinthians 1:18-20 NKJV*

"But as God is faithful, our word to you was not Yes and No. For the Son of God, Jesus Christ, who was preached among you by us- by me, Silvanus, and Timothy- was not Yes and No, but in Him was Yes. For all the promises of God in Him are Yes, and in him Amen, to the glory of God through us."

📖 *2 Corinthians 1:20 AMPC*

"For as many as are the promises of God, they all find their Yes [answer] in Him [Christ]. For this reason we also utter the Amen (so be it) to God through Him [in His Person and by His agency] to the glory of God."

It is wonderful that God (who is faithful) has arranged our fellowship with Him to be fulfilled in our relationship with His Son, Jesus Christ. There are so many wonderful promises the Father has given us in His word. As we read and understand these promises, they become integrated into our prayer life with Him. The promises of God are not just yes and amen anytime we want to declare them. They are Yes

(IN Christ) and Amen (IN Christ). They are directly connected to our walking with Jesus, following Him, and living according to God's purpose for our life IN Him. And just as we have been seeing all these glorious dimensions of what God has put in Christ Jesus, so now we are seeing that all of our prayers concerning the promises of God find their answers in Him.

📖 *John 15:16 NKJV*
"You did not choose Me, but I chose you and appointed you that you should go and bear fruit, and that your fruit should remain, that whatever you ask the Father in My name He may give you."

IN CHRIST: The Peace of God

📖 *Isaiah 9:6-7 NKJV*
*"For unto us a Child is born, unto us a Son is given; and the government will be upon His shoulder. And His name will be called Wonderful, Counselor, Mighty God, Everlasting Father, **Prince of Peace**. Of the increase of His government and peace there will be no end, upon the throne of David and over His kingdom, to order it and establish it with judgment and justice from that time forward, even forever. The zeal of the LORD of hosts will perform this.""*

In Jesus, you can have peace with God, and experience the peace that comes from God, because the Father decided whoever will come under the government of Christ will have peace. The beauty of it is, as you continue under the governing rule of Christ in you, the opportunity for peace will keep increasing and there will be no end to it. Jesus gave His life for you, He shed His blood on your behalf to deal with the issue of sin which wages war in your soul. When you come to Christ, that sacrifice brings peace between you and God and enters you into

The beauty of it is, as you continue under the governing rule of Christ in you, the opportunity for peace will keep increasing and there will be no end to it.

a new dimension of being able to have peace within *by* the life of Christ.

📖 *Ephesians 2:13-15 NKJV*

*"But now **in Christ Jesus** you who once were far off have been brought near by the blood of Christ. <u>For He Himself is our peace</u>, who has made both one, and has broken down the middle wall of separation, having abolished in His flesh the enmity, that is, the law of commandments contained in ordinances, so as to create **in Himself** one new man from the two, thus making peace,"*

📖 *Ephesians 2:15b AMPC*

"that He from the two might create in Himself one new man [one new quality of humanity out of the two], so making peace."

> **Our experience of that peace comes as we learn to walk with Him in an obedient manner and let Him govern our lives from within our hearts for the glory and purpose of God.**

Jesus made peace between us and God. He gives us peace in our daily life, and He Himself IS our peace. You become a new creation when you believe on Jesus Christ and He comes to dwell in you and become your peace. Our experience of that peace comes as we learn to walk with Him in an obedient manner and let Him govern our lives from within our hearts for the glory and purpose of God.

📖 *Colossians 3:15 NKJV*

"And let the peace of God rule in your hearts, to which also you were called in one body; and be thankful."

📖 *Colossians 3:15 AMP*

"Let the peace of Christ [the inner calm of one who walks daily with Him] be the controlling factor in your hearts [deciding and settling questions that arise]. To this peace indeed you were called as members in one body [of believers]. And be thankful [to God always]."

IN CHRIST: The Righteousness of God

📖 *Jeremiah 23:5-6 NKJV*
"'Behold, the days are coming,' says the LORD, 'that I will raise to David a Branch of righteousness; a King shall reign and prosper, and execute judgment and righteousness in the earth. In His days Judah will be saved, and Israel will dwell safely; now this is His name by which He will be called: THE LORD OUR RIGHTEOUSNESS.'"

📖 *1 Corinthians 1:30-31 NKJV*
"But of Him you are in Christ Jesus, who became for us wisdom from God- and righteousness and sanctification and redemption- that, as it is written, 'He who glories, let him glory in the LORD.'"

> **Jesus is the Branch of righteousness that comes from the Father in heaven; righteousness flows through Him.**

Jesus is the Branch of righteousness that comes from the Father in heaven; righteousness flows through Him. God has located IN Christ all righteousness for mankind and called Him THE LORD OUR RIGHTEOUSNESS. He is the King who executes judgment and righteousness, by whom man can be right with God through faith in Him alone. This is so God will receive all the glory through His Son. Heaven's plan for man on earth is for the life of Christ to dwell in His children and bring forth fruits of righteousness by Jesus Christ, who is the Seed of righteousness. He is able to bring forth those fruits as we walk in vital union with Him and allow Him to shine from within us. Listen to Paul's prayer.

📖 *Philippians 1:9-11 NKJV*
*"And this I pray, that your love may abound still more and more in knowledge and all discernment, that you may approve the things that are excellent, that you may be sincere and without offense till the day of Christ, being filled with the fruits of righteousness **which are by Jesus Christ**, to the glory and praise of God."*

Jesus is the only One who can cause love to increase in us. He's also the avenue for knowledge and discernment of what is right in God's eyes to be revealed to us. As we willingly yield ourselves to Him, and walk with Him obediently, He produces the fruits of God's righteousness through us. Jesus will make us branches of His life, that bring forth the fruit which makes known Christ, who is the righteousness of God. God designed it this way. He crucified and raised Jesus so we might become the righteousness of God IN Him.

📖 *2 Corinthians 5:21 NKJV*
"For He made Him who knew no sin to be sin for us, that we might become the righteousness of God in Him."

IN CHRIST: The Upward Call of God

📖 *Philippians 3:12-14 NKJV*
"Not that I have already attained, or am already perfected; but I press on, that I may lay hold of that for which Christ Jesus has also laid hold of me. Brethren, I do not count myself to have apprehended; but one thing I do, forgetting those things which are behind and reaching forward to those things which are ahead, I press toward the goal for the prize of the upward call of God in Christ Jesus."

📖 *Philippians 3:14 KJV*
"I press toward the mark for the prize of the high calling of God in Christ Jesus."

The upward path and call of God is located in His Son and traveled upon through a lifelong commitment to Him. Jesus said, "He who endures to the end will be saved." The prize of the upward call of God, the supreme and heavenly prize to which God in Christ Jesus is calling us, is possessed and finally secured in pressing on and walking in step with Jesus and

The prize of the upward call of God, the supreme and heavenly prize to which God in Christ Jesus is calling us, is possessed and finally secured in pressing on and walking in step with Jesus and the words of God.

66

the words of God. Christ Jesus has laid ahold of you for this very purpose, to carry you all the way to heaven as you continue with Him under His yoke. This is by the Father's design. No one will ever be able to snatch you out of His hands as you walk with Jesus Christ, in whom He has located His high calling for your life.

IN CHRIST: The Salvation of God

📖 *Acts 4:12 NKJV*
"Nor is there salvation in any other, for there is no other name under heaven given among men by which we must be saved."
📖 *Acts 4:12 AMP*
"And there is salvation in no one else; for there is no other name under heaven that has been given among people by which we must be saved [for God has provided the world no alternative for salvation]."

In God's merciful plan to redeem and save fallen man, He located and gave salvation to man IN and through Christ alone. There is no other alternative or method by which anyone can be saved, *but* anyone who comes to Christ can be assured that God will save them. Jesus Christ is the salvation of God and salvation is in Him.

📖 *Luke 2:25-32 NKJV*
"And behold, there was a man in Jerusalem whose name was Simeon, and this man was just and devout, waiting for the Consolation of Israel, and the Holy Spirit was upon him. And it had been revealed to him by the Holy Spirit that he would not see death before he had seen the Lord's Christ. So he came by the Spirit into the temple. And when the parents brought in the Child Jesus, to do for Him according to the custom of the law, he took Him up in his arms and blessed God and said: 'Lord, now You are letting Your servant depart in peace, according to Your word; for <u>my eyes have seen Your salvation</u> which You have prepared before the face of all peoples, a light to bring revelation to the Gentiles, and the glory of Your people Israel.'"

📖 *Luke 2:30 AMPC*
"For with my [own] eyes I have seen Your Salvation,"

> **Salvation is not a thing but a Person to believe in, receive, abide in, and continue with—the Lord Jesus Christ.**

Simeon didn't see words on a page that defined salvation. He saw the gift of the Lord's Christ, who *is* Salvation. He held the Child Jesus who he called "Your salvation." Salvation is not a thing but a Person to believe in, receive, abide in, and continue with—the Lord Jesus Christ. He is the beginning of salvation, the process of salvation, and the final experience of salvation. Jesus is the very assurance of salvation that awaits at the end of your faith.

📖 *1 Peter 1:9 NKJV*
"receiving the end of your faith- the salvation of your souls."

IN CHRIST: Eternal Life from God

📖 *1 John 5:11-12 NKJV*
*"And this is the testimony: that God has given us eternal life, and this life is **in His Son**. He who has the Son has life; he who does not have the Son of God does not have life."*

📖 *1 John 1:1-2 NKJV*
"That which was from the beginning, which we have heard, which we have seen with our eyes, which we have looked upon, and our hands have handled, concerning the Word of life- the life was manifested, and we have seen, and bear witness, and declare to you <u>that eternal life</u> which was with the Father and was manifested to us-"

Jesus is THAT eternal life! For the benefit of all people, God has put access to eternal life in one place, IN His Son. Anyone who does not have the Son does not have life, but whoever has Christ has eternal life. We will look deeply into all Jesus has done to secure our opportunity for salvation and deliverance (both here on the earth, and for all of eternity). For now, let us just rejoice and give God praise that He has located eternal life in Jesus Christ. Jesus is the One who was with the Father, and Jesus is the One who has been manifested to man. He is *that* eternal life that comes from God.

One day Peter and some disciples of Jesus were put in a common prison. This was because of their faith and what they were doing in making known the way of God through faith in Jesus Christ.

📖 *Acts 5:19-20 NKJV*
"But at night an angel of the Lord opened the prison doors and brought them out, and said, 'Go, stand in the temple and speak to the people all the words of this life.'"

📖 *Acts 5:20 AMP*
"Go, stand and continue to tell the people in the temple [courtyards] the whole message of this Life [the eternal life revealed by Christ and found through faith in Him]."

> **Jesus alone, and the message of Jesus Christ and Him crucified and resurrected, is the only means by which eternal life is revealed to a man.**

We are seeking to see more of the whole message of this Life and of the unsearchable riches of God's Christ. Jesus alone, and the message of Jesus Christ and Him crucified and resurrected, is the only means by which eternal life is revealed to a man. It is only through faith in Him and abiding in Him that anyone will ever experience and enter into eternal life. Jesus even defined what eternal life was one day when He was praying to His Father in front of His disciples.

📖 *John 17:1-3 NKJV*
"Jesus spoke these words, lifted up His eyes to heaven, and said: 'Father, the hour has come. Glorify Your Son, that Your Son also may glorify You, as You have given Him authority over all flesh, that He should give eternal life to as many as You have given Him. And this is eternal life, that they may know You, the only true God, and Jesus Christ whom You have sent.'"

First, we see God entrusted the giving of eternal life into the hands of His Jesus. This helps us understand the importance of coming to Him, for there is no alternative the Father ordained except through faith in Jesus and the message He carries from God. Second, Jesus defines eternal life as knowing God and knowing the Christ whom He sent. What does "*know*" mean in that context?

📖 *John 17:3 AMPC*
"And this is eternal life: [it means] to know (to perceive, recognize, become acquainted with, and understand) You, the only true and real God, and [likewise] to know Him, Jesus [as the] Christ (the Anointed One, the Messiah), Whom You have sent."

The goal is an increasing relationship with God. Eternal life is not a one-time decision to believe in Jesus Christ who died for our sins, but a lifelong relationship with Jesus. It is where we grow in perceiving, recognizing, understanding, and becoming more deeply acquainted with Him and the Father who put all things in Him. In doing this we will be knowing the only true God (knowledge of Him comes through the knowledge of Jesus) and we will experience "that eternal life" that comes through this relational knowledge.

IN CHRIST: The Kingdom of God

📖 *Colossians 1:12-13 NKJV*
*"giving thanks to the Father who has qualified us to be partakers of the inheritance of the saints **in the light**. He has delivered us from the power of darkness and conveyed us **into** the kingdom of the Son of His love,"*

📖 *Colossians 1:13 TLB*
*"For he has rescued us out of the darkness and gloom of Satan's kingdom and brought us **into** the Kingdom of his dear Son,"*

We will discover greater degrees of what it means to be IN Christ and to have Christ IN us. We will examine the depths and riches of the blood, cross, and resurrection provisions of God in Jesus Christ. We will see how He delivered us from Satan's kingdom, and we will learn how to practically apply that to our lives here on earth. Already we see that God has placed the kingdom of God in Christ (the Son of His love) and made Him to be the kingdom of God in whom His children would dwell.

There was a day Jesus returned triumphantly to heaven from His mission on earth, having conquered sin, death, the world, and the devil by His work on the cross at Calvary and His resurrection from the dead. After He was raised, He spent forty days with His disciples, speaking to them of things pertaining to the kingdom of God. Then He was brought up to heaven to be presented to His Father. Daniel prophesied about it in the Old Testament.

📖 *Daniel 7:13-14 NKJV*

"I was watching in the night visions, and behold, One like the Son of Man, coming with the clouds of heaven! He came to the Ancient of Days, and they brought Him near before Him. Then to Him was given dominion and glory and a kingdom, that all peoples, nations, and languages should serve Him. His dominion is an everlasting dominion, which shall not pass away, and His kingdom the one which shall not be destroyed."

📖 *Daniel 7:14 AMPC*

"And there was given Him [the Messiah] dominion and glory and kingdom, that all peoples, nations, and languages should serve Him. His dominion is an everlasting dominion which shall not pass away, and His kingdom is one which shall not be destroyed."

This kingdom, and everything located in it, is IN Jesus Christ, according to the eternal purpose of the Ancient of Days who is the Almighty God and Father we believe in.

Jesus (the Victor) was given (by His Father) a kingdom which shall never pass away nor be destroyed. He was made the everlasting King who rules in the affairs of all peoples, nations, and languages. This kingdom, and everything located in it, is IN Jesus Christ, according to the eternal purpose of the Ancient of Days who is the Almighty God and Father we believe in.

One day, some religious leaders asked Jesus when the kingdom of God would come.

  📖 *Luke 17:20-21 NKJV*

*"Now when He was asked by the Pharisees when the kingdom of God would come, He answered them and said, 'The kingdom of God does not come with observation; nor will they say, 'See here!' or 'See there!' For indeed, the kingdom of God **is within you**.'"*

  📖 **Colossians 1:27 NKJV**

*"To them God willed to make known what are the riches of the glory of this mystery among the Gentiles: which is **Christ in you**, the hope of glory."*

The kingdom of God is not a thing (or concept) inside us, but a Person, the Lord Jesus Christ by His Spirit living in us. The kingdom is not observable outwardly with natural eyes, but dwells inside of you who are born again. As you learn to walk with Christ in you, to yield to His Spirit and obey His words, you will be seeing the kingdom of God being manifest through you. This is how God will establish His kingdom and accomplish His purpose on earth. Jesus, who has been given all dominion and authority, will be establishing the kingdom of God on earth as it is in heaven, but from within you.

IN CHRIST: The Judgment of God

  📖 *John 5:22-23 NKJV*

"For the Father judges no one, but has committed all judgment to the Son, that all should honor the Son just as they honor the Father. He who does not honor the Son does not honor the Father who sent Him."

  📖 *John 5:22 AMP*

"For the Father judges no one, but has given all judgment [that is, the prerogative of judging] to the Son [placing it entirely into His hands],"

In the Bible God says, "it is appointed for men to die once, but after this the judgment." That judgment will be performed by Jesus Christ, His Son. It is because God committed all judgment to Him, placing it entirely into His faithful hands. Do you see how critical it is for you to be with Jesus (and know Jesus) to be prepared for the Day of the Lord's return and God's judgment? It is a serious matter in the eyes of God. He has ordered things in such a way that not honoring His Son (believing on Him and following Him) is not honoring the Father. God now expects everyone to come back to Him through faith in Jesus Christ and the message He carried to mankind from His Father. Listen to Jesus:

📖 *Luke 9:26 NKJV*
"For whoever is ashamed of Me and My words, of him the Son of Man will be ashamed when He comes in His own glory, and in His Father's, and of the holy angels."

Judgment is the place where your life will be sorted out by God; how you lived on earth and what your eternal fate will be. When you die, you will be brought to judgment and the One who will be seated at the judgment seat is Jesus Christ. Jesus said:

> **When you die, you will be brought to judgment and the One who will be seated at the judgment seat is Jesus Christ.**

📖 *John 5:26-29 NKJV*
"for as the Father has life in Himself, so He has granted the Son to have life in Himself, and has given Him authority to execute judgment also, because He is the Son of Man. Do not marvel at this; for the hour is coming in which all who are in the graves will hear His voice and come forth-those who have done good, to the resurrection of life, and those who have done evil, to the resurrection of condemnation."

My friend, as we are looking upon the goodness and glory of God in the face of Jesus Christ, are you persuaded yet of your complete need of Jesus in every dimension of your life? When God raises you from the dead, and brings you to judgment, do you know (without any doubt) which resurrection will be yours? Jesus Christ is the One you will be brought to, and He is the One who will decide where you go. He is the One the Father gave the words of eternal life to, the One whom we must believe and obey. Jesus said:

📖 *John 12:48-50 NKJV*

"He who rejects Me, and does not receive My words, has that which judges him- the words that I have spoken will judge him in the last day. For I have not spoken on My own authority; but the Father who sent Me gave Me a command, what I should say and what I should speak. And I know that His command is everlasting life. Therefore, whatever I speak, just as the Father has told Me, so I speak."

And the apostle Paul said:

📖 *Romans 2:16 NKJV*

*"in the day when God will judge the secrets of men **by Jesus Christ,** according to my gospel."*

Your life and your eternity will be determined by what you do with Jesus Christ. If you casually confess Him and live life according to the dictates of your own heart (and not according to Christ) you may find yourself (on that Day) hearing Jesus, say, 'I never knew you; depart from Me, you who work iniquity." That is not the Father's desire, but He gives each soul the opportunity to repent and turn back to Him through faith in His Son, Jesus. God will judge the world in righteousness. He will do it through and by Jesus Christ as His standard. He will not look away but make all things right.

> **Your life and your eternity will be determined by what you do with Jesus Christ.**

📖 *Acts 17:30-31 NKJV*

*"Truly, these times of ignorance God overlooked, but now commands all men everywhere to repent, because He has appointed a day which He will judge the world in righteousness **by the Man** whom He has ordained. He has given assurance of this to all by raising Him from the dead."*

📖 *Acts 17:30-31 AMP*

"Therefore God overlooked and disregarded the former ages of ignorance; but now He commands all people everywhere to repent

*[that is, to change their old way of thinking, to regret their past sins, and to seek God's purpose for their lives], because He has set a day when He will judge the inhabited world in righteousness **by a Man whom He has appointed** and destined for that task, and He has provided credible proof to everyone by raising Him from the dead."*

God sent Jesus to die on the cross and pay the penalty for your sins and unrighteousness. He raised Him from the dead and offers you a new life in Him if you will repent, believe on Jesus, and receive Him into your heart. Are you ready to do that? It involves regretting your past sins, confessing them and repenting, putting them away and asking Him to forgive you. It involves you opening your heart to Jesus and asking Him to come in and give you a new life. Before reading any further, can you please talk to God and ask Him to do this for you? God put all judgment into the hands of Jesus, and your assurance on that Day will be by believing on and being with Him.

📖 *Romans 1:20 TLB*
"Since earliest times men have seen the earth and sky and all God made, and have known of his existence and great eternal power. So they will have no excuse when they stand before God at Judgment Day."

IN CHRIST: The Name Above All Names

📖 **Philippians 2:8-11 NKJV**
"And being found in appearance as a man, He humbled Himself and became obedient to the point of death, even the death of the cross. Therefore God also has highly exalted Him and given Him the name which is above every name, that at the name of Jesus every knee should bow, of those in heaven, and of those on earth, and of those under the earth, and that every tongue should confess that Jesus Christ is Lord, to the glory of God the Father."

Jesus is the One in whom God the Father has put all things. Jesus has been given the Name that is above all names. All the names of God in the Bible find their fulfillment and personal experience for a man's life in Christ. God ordained it to be that way in His interaction with

His created ones. In the Old Testament the Scriptures reveal many names of God, which show different dimensions and characteristics of the nature of God. Names like Yahweh Nissi (The Lord is my Banner); Yahweh Shalom (The Lord is Peace); Yahweh Rohi (The Lord my Shepherd); Yahweh Tsidkenu (The Lord our Righteousness); Elohim (Strong One); and many other such wonderful names of God. All of those names are fulfilled and realized in the name of Jesus Christ, which God made to be the Name above all names. All of those names point to Jesus as the means by which to experience God, according to the provision described in each name. This in no way diminishes the greatness and glory of our God and Father who is in heaven. It is actually *His* plan (and His idea) to put all things in His Son, and in the name of Jesus Christ, for the glory of God forever and ever. Amen.

We have attempted to look at the unsearchable riches God has placed in Christ. We did this to increase our own personal valuation of the treasure that Christ is for our life. As a result of valuing Jesus more highly, we will in turn value other things lower. The purpose is to help us be more willing to forsake all to follow Jesus. We have been blessed to see many things, but I want to tell you that we have barely scratched the surface of who Jesus is, and all the Father located in Him (for us) through our daily union with Him.

> *It is actually His plan (and His idea) to put all things in His Son, and in the name of Jesus Christ, for the glory of God forever and ever.*

In each of these dimensions, because of space, I had to leave out many Scripture references to further elaborate on each point. It has been more of an introductory look at the riches of Jesus, hoping you will decide to search for yourself (in the word of God) for more of Him. It is impossible to write down everything Jesus is, Jesus has done, and Jesus is doing. Listen to the apostle John describe it.

📖 *John 21:24-25 NKJV*
"This is the disciple who testifies of these things, and wrote these things; and we know that his testimony is true. And there are many

other things that Jesus did, which if they were written one by one, I suppose that even the world itself could not contain the books that would be written. Amen."

📖 ***John 20:30-31 NKJV***

"And truly Jesus did many other signs in the presence of His disciples, which are not written in this book; but these are written that you may believe that Jesus is the Christ, the Son of God, and that believing you may have life in His name."

I am hoping and trusting the Lord helps you to see this Wonderful Jesus more clearly than you ever have. The rest of the book is dedicated to continuing to develop more insight and revelation knowledge into the Person of Jesus Christ and the message of Him and Him crucified. May God aid you to grow in seeing and knowing Jesus as the gift of God, in whom He has located everything for your life. May He help you long for Christ and ask for more of Him.

📖 ***John 4:10 NKJV***

"Jesus answered and said to her, 'if you knew the gift of God, and who it is who says to you, 'Give Me a drink,' you would have asked Him, and He would have given you living water.'"

Let us stop to pray and ask the Lord God for further illumination and practical, relational experience with Jesus Christ.

Our God and Father in heaven, we want to praise You and give You all the glory for what You have done in Jesus Christ. Thank you for the revelation You have given us, and we want to ask You to continue to enlarge our capacity to receive even more. Please prepare our hearts to receive Your word, and let it be mixed with understanding and faith in us. Let it result in Your will and purpose for our lives being fulfilled completely. Please help us to see and know Jesus even more in the name of Jesus Christ. Amen.

THE GOODNESS OF GOD

I n earlier chapters, we looked at the mystery of Christ and the vast treasure God put in Him for our lives. Now, we will spend some time looking at the nature and key characteristics of the God and Father who sent Jesus. The God who decided to put all things in Christ. We need to examine the goodness of this God of our salvation, the Creator and only true God.

📖 *Romans 11:19-22 NKJV*
"You will say then, 'Branches were broken off that I might be grafted in.' Well said. Because of unbelief they were broken off, and you stand by faith. Do not be haughty, but fear. For if God did not spare the natural branches, He may not spare you either. Therefore consider the goodness and severity of God: on those who fell, severity; but toward you, goodness, if you continue in His goodness. Otherwise you also will be cut off."

To understand God is to know He is both good and severe; He saves, and He judges; He's merciful, yet just. We will come to consider His severity and that which separates us from God, but our first focus will be to examine the goodness of God, because the Bible tells us to *consider His goodness*. The word "consider" implies examining, staring into, and taking note of His goodness as we look into the Scriptures.

📖 ***Psalm 106:1 NKJV***
"Praise the LORD! Oh, give thanks to the LORD, for He is good! For His mercy endures forever."
📖 ***Psalm 119:67-68 NKJV***
"Before I was afflicted I went astray, but now I keep Your word. You are good, and do good; teach me Your statutes."
📖 ***Psalm 25:8 NKJV***
"Good and upright is the LORD; therefore He teaches sinners in the way."

God is good and He does good! He is not good because He tries to be but because His very nature is entirely good. He, by His being, is morally perfect, upright, and pure in every way. All His motives and actions proceed from His goodness and His love. And because He is good, God teaches sinners about Himself and about His way, so they can experience

> *To understand God is to know He is both good and severe; He saves, and He judges; He's merciful, yet just.*

His goodness, and continue in His goodness in order to have everlasting life. Listen to Jesus describe God.

📖 ***Matthew 19:16-17 NKJV***
"Now behold, one came and said to Him, 'Good Teacher, what good thing shall I do that I may have eternal life?' So He said to him, 'Why do you call Me good? No one is good but One, that is, God. But if you want to enter into life, keep the commandments.'"
📖 ***Matthew 19:17 AMP***
"Jesus answered, 'Why are you asking Me about what is [essentially] good? There is only One who is [essentially] good; but if you wish to enter into eternal life, keep the commandments.'"

God is essentially good! It is His very essence. The word *essentially* is used to emphasize the basic, fundamental, intrinsic nature of God. He is good because He is good throughout His being. He has never been anything else but good. And out of His goodness and love, He designed the way for you to enter into eternal life through the sacrifice of His Son, Jesus Christ; through the knowledge of HIm who is true and good. Jesus said it like this:

📖 *John 17:3 NKJV*
"And this is eternal life, that they may know You, the only true God, and Jesus Christ whom You have sent."

We have looked at the treasure of Jesus Christ, and we're beginning to see and know Him more clearly. Now, we are looking at the God who sent Him, so that we may see and know *Him* as well. This will better prepare us to travel through the remaining chapters and content of this book. It is critical for us to understand and know Him; and to know what drives Him in exercising all of His decisions and actions toward us.

📖 *Jeremiah 9:24 NKJV*
"'But let him who glories glory in this, that he understands and knows Me, that I am the LORD, exercising lovingkindness, judgment, and righteousness in the earth. For in these I delight,' says the LORD."
📖 *Jeremiah 9:24 AMPC*
"But let him who glories glory in this: that he understands and knows Me [personally and practically, directly discerning and recognizing My character], that I am the Lord, Who practices lovingkindness, judgment, and righteousness in the earth, for in these things I delight, says the Lord."

> **God is good and He does good! He is not good because He tries to be, but because His very nature is entirely good.**

Please take note of the order God established for His righteousness to be done in the earth: lovingkindness, judgment, and righteousness. The truth is, God is righteous, and He will always establish His righteousness in the actions He takes. He can establish His righteousness through His judgment, and He can establish His righteousness through His lovingkindness. But He always prefers to practice His lovingkindness before He would need to execute judgment. That is because of His goodness. At this point, we need to trust the Holy Spirit to open our eyes to see the goodness of this great and glorious God. We need Him to help us personally and practically know God, discerning His goodness and recognizing His character in a way we have never known. Holy Spirit, please help us to really know (by experience) the goodness of God in our lives.

> *It is critical for us to understand and know Him; and to know what drives Him in exercising all of His decisions and actions toward us.*

In the Old Testament, after the LORD delivered the children of Israel from their slavery in Egypt, God was talking to Moses on the top of Mt Sinai. While talking, the people below got tired of waiting for Moses to return with instructions from the LORD for their life. They said to Moses' brother Aaron (who was left in charge) "Come, make us gods that shall go before us; for as for this Moses, the man who brought us up out of the land of Egypt, we do not know what has become of him." Then Aaron proceeded to make a golden calf and an altar for the people to worship it. Then they declared, "This is your god, O Israel, that brought you out of the land of Egypt!" As this was happening, God told Moses about it while they were meeting on the mountain top.

📖 *Exodus 32:7-10 NKJV*

"And the LORD said to Moses, 'Go, get down! For your people whom you brought out of the land of Egypt have corrupted themselves. They have turned aside quickly out of the way which I commanded them. They have made themselves a molded calf, and worshiped it and sacrificed to it, and said, 'This is your god, O Israel, that brought

you out of the land of Egypt!' And the LORD said to Moses, 'I have seen this people, and indeed it is a stiff-necked people! Now therefore, <u>let Me alone</u>, that My wrath may burn hot against them and I may consume them. And I will make of you a great nation.'"

Here we are getting a glimpse of the severity of God towards sin and disobedience. God hates sin and the wages of sin is death. His judgment demands swift action towards sin to make things right, and He delights in practicing righteousness on the earth.

> **But He always prefers to practice His lovingkindness before He would need to execute judgment. That is because of His goodness.**

But I want you to take note of something God said to Moses, 'let Me alone.' Did you see that? Why would God say it that way to Moses? If He wanted to, because He is God, He could just execute His wrath right there and right then, whether Moses was present or not. But in saying, 'let Me alone,' we are getting an insight into the essence of the goodness of God and what He really wants to happen. It would be different if God only said, "Go, get down!", or something like "Depart from Me," or "Get out of here now." Those would be orders telling Moses to leave with no space or option for further conversation. But God said, 'let Me alone,' which has a different implication if we are willing to look. In God's heart, He was desiring Moses (His mediator) to talk to Him about the situation and plead with Him for mercy and forgiveness on behalf of Aaron and the people. God was wanting to express His mercy rather than His judgment. He was desiring to practice His lovingkindness rather than His severity.

📖 ***James 2:13b NKJV***
"...Mercy triumphs over judgment."
📖 ***Hosea 6:6 NKJV***
"For I desire mercy and not sacrifice, and the knowledge of God more than burnt offerings."

📖 **Matthew 9:13 NKJV**
"But go and learn what this means: 'I desire mercy and not sacrifice.' For I did not come to call the righteous, but sinners, to repentance."

It is the essence of God's goodness and love that drives His mercy to triumph over His judgment, though both are good. Judgment is always final and leaves no room for hope of change. Love and mercy allow space for hope to flourish and for God's will to be done in the lives of people.

📖 **Proverbs 17a NKJV**
"He who covers a transgression seeks love,"
📖 **1 Corinthians 13:4a NKJV**
"Love suffers long and is kind;"

> *Judgment is always final and leaves no room for hope of change. Love and mercy allow space for hope to flourish and for God's will to be done in the lives of people.*

Though His judgment is righteous, good and perfectly just, He prefers (even longs for) people to experience His love and His mercy through the goodness of His longsuffering with them. Out of His goodness, He is even willing to cover transgressions in the hope the sinner will turn to Him. He desires all to turn away from sin, repent, and turn to Him before judgment has to come. He does that by His goodness.

📖 **Romans 2:2-4 NKJV**
"But we know that the judgment of God is according to truth against those who practice such things. And do you think this, O man, you who judge those practicing such things, and doing the same, that you will escape the judgment of God? Or do you despise the riches of His goodness, forbearance, and longsuffering, not knowing that the goodness of God leads you to repentance?"

It is out of God's abundant goodness that He bears patiently and holds back His judgment, creating space for the sinner to repent and turn to Him. Longsuffering is God willing to suffer, for a long time, the delay of His righteous judgment, which is good and which He delights in, in order for a soul to experience His mercy, lovingkindness, and the knowledge of Him through repentance. *That* proceeds from the goodness of God; He would rather save than judge. This goodness is on display throughout the Bible in God's dealings with the children of Israel, who constantly sinned against Him. We also see it in the days of the flood, and in the days of Sodom and Gomorrah. God raised Noah to be a preacher of righteousness before the flood came, but the people rejected God and had no regard for His goodness. As a result, they experienced wrath and judgment instead. At Sodom and Gomorrah, the Lord came and visited Abraham, giving him space to intercede so the Lord would have mercy on those cities rather than execute His judgment. It is His goodness and love that makes Him willing to hear the prayers of a man begging Him to withhold His wrath from sinful people, and to grant repentance leading to life with God.

📖 **Romans 2:4 AMP**

"Or do you have no regard for the wealth of His kindness and tolerance and patience [in withholding His wrath]? Are you [actually] unaware or ignorant [of the fact] that God's kindness leads you to repentance [that is, to change your inner self, your old way of thinking-seek His purpose for your life]?"

It is out of God's abundant goodness that He bears patiently and holds back His judgment, creating space for the sinner to repent and turn to Him.

Back on Mt. Sinai, God was angry at Aaron and the people of Israel because of the sins they committed and because they so quickly turned aside, out of the way which He commanded them. He was frustrated with them, and His wrath was kindled against them. He was ready to consume them and start over with Moses. But instead of making Moses leave His Presence and then pouring out His judgment on them, He left a space for Moses to plead with Him for a different outcome. The Bible says Moses began to plead with the LORD, asking Him to turn from His fierce wrath and relent from harming the people. Moses was even reminding God of promises He previously made. Then out of His goodness, God chose mercy and relented.

📖 *Exodus 32:14 NKJV*
"So the LORD relented from the harm which He said He would do to His people."

📖   *Exodus 32:14 TLB*
"So the Lord changed his mind and spared them."

> *He will always judge sin, but He allows His mercy (which flows from His goodness) to give souls an opportunity to change their way of thinking and to seek His purpose for their life.*

That is who God is at His core. He is good, and He does good. He chose to spare the people rather than give them the death they deserved. He will always judge sin, but He allows His mercy (which flows from His goodness) to give souls an opportunity to change their way of thinking and to seek His purpose for their life. Because of space, we will not go into all the details of this story, but fast forward to when God was now starting to instruct Moses to get the people moving toward the land which He promised their fathers.

📖 *Exodus 33:1 NKJV*
"Then the LORD said to Moses, 'Depart and go up from here, you and the people whom you have brought out of the land of Egypt, to the land of which I swore to Abraham, Isaac, and Jacob, saying, 'To your descendants I will give it.'"

If you continued to read this story, you would discover the LORD is still upset with them because they are still a stiff-necked people. However, His mercy was triumphing over His judgment, and He was making a way for them to yet turn to Him. One day Moses was meeting with the LORD and made a request.

📖 *Exodus 33:12-14 NKJV*

"Then Moses said to the LORD, 'See, You say to me, 'Bring up this people.' But You have not let me know whom You will send with me. Yet You have said, 'I know you by name, and you have also found grace in My sight.' Now therefore, I pray, if I have found grace in Your sight, show me now Your way, that I may know You and that I may find grace in Your sight. And consider that this nation is Your people.' And He said, 'My Presence will go with you, and I will give you rest.'"

Moses is feeling the weight of leading the people. He is having a conversation with God, longing to know Him and His way, wanting to find grace in His sight; and even asking God to send someone with him to help. God's solution was to say His Presence will go with him, and He Himself (being with Him) will be how Moses will find rest. *This is also His solution for your life in Christ Jesus now.* So, Moses and the LORD continued to talk.

📖 *Exodus 33:18-19 NKJV*

"And he said, 'Please, show me Your glory.' Then He said, 'I will make all My goodness pass before you, and I will proclaim the name of the LORD before you. I will be gracious to whom I will be gracious, and I will have compassion on whom I will have compassion.'"

> **The glory of God is located in His goodness. It wasn't in bright lights and loud noises and in miracles and all such things, but in the very goodness of who He is; His very essence which is good.**

Isn't that extraordinary? God's answer to the request "show me Your glory" was to make all His *goodness* pass before Moses. The glory of God is located in His goodness. It wasn't in bright lights and loud noises and in miracles and all such things, but in the very goodness of who He is; His very essence which is good. Look what happened when this experience came for Moses.

📖 *Exodus 34:5-9 NKJV*

"Now the LORD descended in the cloud and stood with him there, and proclaimed the name of the LORD. And the LORD passed before him and proclaimed, 'The LORD, the LORD God, merciful and gracious, longsuffering, and abounding in goodness and truth, keeping mercy for thousands, forgiving iniquity and transgression and sin, by no means clearing the guilty, visiting the iniquity of the fathers upon the children and the children's children to the third and the fourth generation.' So Moses made haste and bowed his head toward the earth, and worshiped. Then he said, 'If now I have found grace in Your sight, O Lord, let my Lord, I pray, go among us, even though we are a stiff-necked people; and pardon our iniquity and our sin, and take us as Your inheritance.'"

From this point on, the Bible says God made a covenant with the people to do an awesome thing with them and marvels such as have not been done in the earth. Out of His goodness, He decided to walk with sinful, stiff-necked people, delaying His judgment, and creating a space for them to be able to choose to walk with Him, before it would be too late. Do you see the goodness of God? Yes, He judges sin and iniquity, and His judgment is always righteous and good. But when God came to make all His goodness pass before Moses, and to proclaim His name (make known who He is) His judgment was the last thing He made known. The first declaration from the mouth of God, in declaring His goodness, was that He is merciful and gracious, He is longsuffering, and He is abounding in goodness and truth. *Abounding* means overflowing, surging, and very plentiful. His mercy and love are always surging forth from His goodness, and He greatly desires for you to obtain mercy from Him rather than judgment. His glory towards man is in the abundance of His goodness. He desires to forgive iniquity, transgression, and sin, and He keeps mercy stored

> **Even though He will always judge sin and iniquity, no one has to experience the wrath of His judgment against unrighteousness, if they will abide in His goodness.**

up for those who cry out to Him in humility and repentance, walking with Him according to His way. Even though He will always judge sin and iniquity, no one *has* to experience the wrath of His judgment against unrighteousness, if they will abide in His goodness.

Let me ask you, have you come to know the goodness of God in your life? Is it practical and personal for you or merely intellectual and without daily experience? As a Christian, has there been many times in your journey where God would have had every right to judge you and condemn you to death? When you have sinned and offended God, aren't you glad His judgment is not the first thing He brought forth, but rather His mercy? Please take a moment, before reading any further, and give God the glory for exercising lovingkindness towards you, rather than the just punishment for your sins. Please thank Him, that from His goodness, He has been very merciful and gracious to you, granting you repentance out of His kindness, and preserving you from His righteous judgment which you have deserved. Hallelujah!

God wants to help you consider and know His goodness, and to walk in that reality for the rest of your life. Let's continue to examine the riches of His goodness, so we may better know Him and the great depths of His character.

He sent His own Son to come and bear His righteous judgment and make a way for us to obtain His mercy and find grace to help our lives.

📖 *1 John 4:8-10 NKJV*

"He who does not love does not know God, for God is love. In this the love of God was manifested toward us, that God has sent His only begotten Son into the world, that we might live through Him. In this is love, not that we loved God, but that He loved us and sent His Son to be the propitiation for our sins."

God is love! It is not only that He loves, but He *is* love. His very nature is love, which emanates from His goodness, and goodness which emanates from His love. The desire in God's heart is that we (who have sinned against Him) might experience life through faith in His Son, Jesus Christ. He loved us so much that He sent His own Son to come and die for us. He sent His own Son to come and bear His right-eous judgment and make a way for us to obtain His mercy and find grace to help our lives. He manifested His love toward us by the sac-rifice of Jesus and made a way for us to be brought into His family; to discover His good plans for our new life in Christ.

📖 *Jeremiah 29:11 NKJV*
"'For I know the thoughts that I think toward you,' says the LORD, 'thoughts of peace and not of evil, to give you a future and a hope.'"

📖 *Jeremiah 29:11 NLT*
"'For I know the plans I have for you,' says the LORD. 'They are plans for good and not for disaster, to give you a future and a hope.'"

📖 *Jeremiah 31:14 NKJV*
"I will satiate the soul of the priests with abundance, and My people shall be satisfied with My good-ness,' says the LORD."

> **The heart of God is to satisfy His people with His goodness. He doesn't have to work hard to try and be good to His people, it is the very essence of His character to love them and do good to them.**

The heart of God is to satisfy His people with His goodness. He doesn't have to work hard to try and be good to His people, it is the very essence of His character to love them and do good to them. His plans for His people are good and they bring outcomes of peace and futures filled with hope. Even His thoughts that He thinks toward us (who belong to Christ) are con-tinually directed for our good, according to His will and by His goodness. He longs for His people to understand and know Him and His goodness more truly.

📖 *Jeremiah 9:24 MSG*
"If you brag, brag of this and this only: that you understand and know me. I'm God, and I act in loyal love. I do what's right and set things

right and fair, and delight in those who do the same things. These are my trademarks.' GOD's Decree."

📖 *2 Timothy 2:13 NKJV*
"If we are faithless, He remains faithful; He cannot deny Himself."

📖 *2 Timothy 2:13 AMPC*
"If we are faithless [do not believe and are untrue to Him], He remains true (faithful to His Word and His righteous character), for He cannot deny Himself."

> **Faithfulness is a trademark of who God is. He doesn't change who He is because of circumstances, but His righteous character comes forth in everything He does.**

Faithfulness is a trademark of who God is. He doesn't change who He is because of circumstances, but His righteous character comes forth in everything He does. God is loyal in His love for souls. That proceeds from His goodness. Even when we are untrue to Him, out of His mercy and love for our soul, He looks for ways to bring us back to Himself before it is too late; before He must execute His judgment. Do you remember the prophet, Jonah? The great city of Nineveh was going to face God's judgment because of their sins. Instead of bringing forth His judgment to destroy them, God sent His servant, Jonah, to preach to them, saying, "Yet forty days, and Nineveh shall be overthrown!" A mighty revival occurred in that city as all 120,000 of its citizens believed God and repented of their sins. God saw "that they turned from their evil way, and God relented from the disaster that He had said He would bring upon them." For whatever reason, Jonah's heart was wrong, and he was angry God granted repentance to Nineveh and saved them. But at this point, I am not wanting to look at Jonah's behavior as much as what Jonah knew about the goodness of God.

📖 *Jonah 4:1-2 NKJV*
"But it displeased Jonah exceedingly, and he became angry. So he prayed to the LORD, and said, 'Ah, LORD, was not this what I said when I was still in my country? Therefore I fled previously to Tarshish;

for I know that You are a gracious and merciful God, slow to anger and abundant in lovingkindness, One who relents from doing harm.'"

CEV "You always show love, and you don't like to punish anyone"
GNT "always ready to change your mind and not punish"
NLT "You are eager to turn back from destroying people"

Though Jonah greatly disliked Nineveh, and would rather see them judged than delivered, God is not a man to think in such a way. By the goodness of His character, He is not easily angered, and He delays the finality of His judgment so He can be merciful and gracious, hoping His goodness will lead a man to repentance and restoration. Jonah, despite his hard heart, still knew about the goodness of God. Are you starting to see it too?

   📖 *Psalm 103:8 NKJV*
"The LORD is merciful and gracious, slow to anger, and abounding in mercy."
   📖 *Isaiah 55:6-7 NKJV*
"Seek the LORD while He may be found, call upon Him while He is near. Let the wicked forsake his way, and the unrighteous man his thoughts; let him return to the LORD, and He will have mercy on him; and to our God, for He will abundantly pardon."
   📖 *Psalm 86:15-16 NKJV*
"But You, O Lord, are a God full of compassion, and gracious, long-suffering and abundant in mercy and truth. Oh, turn to me, and have mercy on me! Give Your strength to Your servant, and save the son of Your maidservant."

In chapter 6, we will examine the problems between man and God which require repentance and faith toward God. But first, we are seeing that God, by nature of His goodness, is full of compassion and is longsuffering toward the unrighteous and the wicked. His heart doesn't first turn to anger and the expression of His wrath, but to compassion and the desire to practice mercy. It is important to see that if ANYONE returns to the LORD, HE WILL have mercy on them, and HE WILL abundantly pardon. That flows from His goodness, His love, and the faithfulness of His character. He is not partial. There is no one God will not pardon and save if they humble themselves, repent, and ask Him to save them. God does not desire for anyone to experience His judgment and eternal separation from Him. He takes no pleasure in the death of anyone.

📖 *Ezekiel 33:11 NKJV*
"Say to them: 'As I live,' says the Lord God, 'I have no pleasure in the death of the wicked, but that the wicked turn from his way and live. Turn, turn from your evil ways! For why should you die, O house of Israel?'"

Do you hear God crying out to the house of Israel, imploring them to turn from their wickedness, which will bring death and judgment to them? God takes no pleasure in watching people perish in sin, but His will is for them to repent and live.

> *God, out of His love and His goodness, is extending mercy to every human being, delaying His righteous judgment, and creating space for ANY to repent and believe on His Son. He suffers long with sinners because He passionately longs for the soul's safety.*

📖 **2 Peter 3:9 NKJV**
"The Lord is not slack concerning His promise, as some count slackness, but is longsuffering toward us, not willing that any should perish but that all should come to repentance."

📖 **1 Timothy 2:3-6 NKJV**
"For this is good and acceptable in the sight of God our Savior, who desires all men to be saved and to come to the knowledge of the truth. For there is one God and one Mediator between God and men, the Man Christ Jesus, who gave Himself a ransom for all, to be testified in due time,"

Do you see the goodness of God in these passages? He is willing to suffer wrong and suffer long with sinners who are out of His way. Though His judgment demands that the wages of sin is death, He does not desire ANY to perish, but for ALL to be saved. God the Father, out of His love and His goodness, is extending mercy to every human being, delaying His righteous judgment, and creating space for ANY to repent and believe on His Son, Jesus Christ. He suffers long with sinners because He passionately longs for the soul's safety and not its destruction.

📖 **2 Peter 3:15 AMPC**
"And consider that the long-suffering of our Lord [His slowness in avenging wrongs and judging the world] is salvation (that which is conducive to the soul's safety), even as our beloved brother Paul also wrote to you according to the spiritual insight given him,"

CEV *"Don't forget that the Lord is patient because he wants people to be saved."*
NLT *"And remember, our Lord's patience gives people time to be saved."*

Jesus spoke of His Father's goodness like this:

📖 **Matthew 18:14 NKJV**
"Even so it is not the will of your Father who is in heaven that one of these little ones should perish."
📖 **Luke 12:31-32 NKJV**
"But seek the kingdom of God, and all these things shall be added to you. Do not fear, little flock, for it your Father's good pleasure to give you the kingdom."
📖 **John 6:40 NKJV**
"And this is the will of Him who sent Me, that everyone who sees the Son and believes in Him may have everlasting life; and I will raise him up at the last day."

God is good! He desires everyone to have everlasting life in Jesus Christ. It brings rejoicing and happiness to the Father when a soul turns away from sin and turns to Him so He can, out of His goodness, bring them into His kingdom. This is true for the unrepentant sinner who hears the gospel, and for the Christian who has strayed from the Lord and is currently living in sin. This is the good pleasure of the Father who is in heaven.

📖 *Luke 15:7 NLT*
"In the same way, there is more joy in heaven over one lost sinner who repents and returns to God than over ninety-nine others who are righteous and haven't strayed away!"

📖 *Luke 15:10 AMP*
"In the same way, I tell you, there is joy in the presence of the angels of God over one sinner who repents [that is, changes his inner self- his old way of thinking, regrets past sins, lives his life in a way that proves repentance; and seeks God's purpose for his life]."

Do you want to seek God's purpose for your life? The will of God is always to express His goodness and goodwill toward men through faith in Jesus Christ. Jesus is the expression of His goodwill toward us and the manifestation of His love. Even the angels declared it when He left heaven and came to earth to save mankind.

> **The will of God is always to express His goodness and goodwill toward men through faith in Jesus Christ. Jesus is the expression of His goodwill toward us and the manifestation of His love.**

📖 *Luke 2:14 NKJV*
"Glory to God in the highest, and on earth peace, goodwill toward men!"

Are you ready to praise God for His goodness toward you in Jesus Christ? Are you ready to completely surrender your life to Jesus and follow Him? Have you put your trust in the God who sent Him, and tasted and seen that He is good? Do you want to know His goodness and His Presence more and more in this present life?

📖 *Psalm 34:8 NKJV*
"Oh, taste and see that the LORD is good; blessed is the man who trusts in Him!"

📖 *Psalm 27:13 NKJV*
"I would have lost heart, unless I had believed that I would see the goodness of the LORD in the land of the living."

Can you deliberately and with your whole heart ask God to help you see and know His goodness and His love? I believe He wants to reveal Himself more fully to you, wherever you are in life, and show You how good He is as you put your trust fully in Him. He has good intentions towards you in Christ and by Christ living in you.

📖 *Ephesians 3:19 AMPC*
"[That you may really come] to know [practically, through experience for yourselves] the love of Christ, which far surpasses mere knowledge [without experience]; that you may be filled [through all your being] unto all the fullness of God [may have the richest measure of the divine Presence, and become a body wholly filled and flooded with God Himself]!"

Let's pray.

God, we have seen in the word of God that You are good, and You do good. We have seen that You prefer to exercise Your mercy and lovingkindness rather than Your judgment. And You have shown us how You have extended mercy to us when we didn't deserve it. We want to thank You for Your faithfulness and great goodness. We thank You for suffering long with our disobedience and our hard hearts. We are grateful that You don't execute judgment upon us every time we ever sin, but You delay Your judgment in the hopes that we will repent and turn back to You. Now Lord, we ask You to show us more of Your goodness and Your love. We ask You to take us down the path where we will become filled with the richest measure of Your divine Presence. We offer ourselves to You as willing and ready to see all You want to show us, and we ask You to help us to respond and put our trust in You. Thank You, Father God, for You are good, and we are praying to you in the name of Jesus Christ. Amen!

WHAT'S THE PROBLEM?

A *problem* is a matter or situation regarded as unwelcome or harmful and needing to be dealt with and overcome. Not understanding a problem correctly can lead to great error and possible damage to a person's life. So, what are the problems that exist between mankind and God? If there are things separating people from being right with God, we need to search the Scriptures to discover those problems and receive the solution God has devised. This is to bring us help through faith in the finished work and Person of Jesus Christ. Let's begin.

THE PROBLEM OF NOT KNOWING THE TRUTH

Ignorance - lack of knowledge or information; not knowing.

One of the greatest problems for people is a lack of understanding the true knowledge of God, which comes from the word of God. When a child of God doesn't know the basic concepts, conditions, and principles (the realities) of who God is, what He has done to save and preserve them from sin, and His offer of new life in Christ, that child will struggle and miss out on many of the blessings, power, and intimate life with God which He has purposed through faith in Jesus Christ.

📖 *Isaiah 5:12-13 NKJV*
"The harp and the strings, the tambourine and flute, and wine are in their feasts; but they do not regard the work of the Lord, nor consider the operation of His hands. Therefore My people have gone into captivity, because they have no knowledge; their honorable men are famished, and their multitude dried up with thirst."

It is in failing to regard (in the Scriptures) what God says and what He has done to help us, that His people's lives go into captivity. The lack of consideration and diligence to discover *for yourself* the operation of His hands for your salvation and daily victory, will deprive you of the knowledge of Him and His Son, Jesus Christ; maybe even eternal life. Ignorance of the truth produces a dried-up soul; a life that is famished, weary, unfruitful, and captive to sin. Are you a captive? Do you present to the world a life that is free, but in truth you know you are experiencing destruction and deterioration in your inner life? Even if in small degrees? Is it in your marriage, in your family, in your heart? God is calling for you and inviting you to come to Him and learn more accurately His way so that you will know Him, and understand Him, and learn to live by the words that proceed from His mouth.

> **It is in failing to regard (in the Scriptures) what God says and what He has done to help us, that His people's lives go into captivity.**

One day, a group of religious leaders came to test Jesus; to test His knowledge of the truth in the Scriptures concerning the resurrection from the dead relating to marriage. Unfortunately, they were not teachable enough to learn of God from Him but rather rejected it and were determined to believe there is no resurrection from the dead. They even brought out a passage of Scripture, trying to prove their point according to their own understanding. But Jesus, who *is* the Truth, corrected them.

📖 ***Mark 12:24-27 NKJV***

"Jesus answered and said to them, 'Are you not therefore mistaken, because you do not know the Scriptures nor the power of God? For when they rise from the dead, they neither marry nor are given in marriage, but are like angels in heaven. But concerning the dead, that they rise, have you not read in the book of Moses, in the burning bush passage, how God spoke to him, saying, 'I am the God of Abraham, the God of Isaac, and the God of Jacob?' He is not the God of the dead, but the God of the living. You are therefore greatly mistaken.'"

Jesus boldly told men who read the Scriptures, memorized the Scriptures, and proudly declared Scriptures, that they were greatly mistaken because they did not KNOW the Scriptures. As a result, they did not know the power of God in their life.

📖 ***Mark 12:24 AMPC***

"Jesus said to them, is not this where you wander out of the way and go wrong, because you know neither the Scriptures nor the power of God?"

Ignorance of what God says and what He has done causes the heart to wander out of His way and go in a direction that is counter to the will of God. Good intentions and right desires can still bring error and misdirection to a life if there is not correct understanding, which leads to an accurate knowledge of God and His way in Christ Jesus. It is not a light matter to deal treacherously with the fate of your own soul by wandering from the way of God through misunderstanding.

📖 ***Proverbs 21:16 NKJV***

"A man who wanders from the way of understanding will rest in the assembly of the dead."

Are you one of those wanderers who rehearses the word of God well, but your life bears little evidence that you understand and live according to it? Do you really want to learn from Jesus the truth that

He has heard from God; the message and teaching that delivers you from destruction? God said:

📖 **Hosea 4:6 NKJV**
"_My people_ are destroyed for lack of knowledge. Because you have rejected knowledge, I also will reject you from being priest for Me; because you have forgotten the law of your God, I also will forget your children."

> *It is not a light matter to deal treacherously with the fate of your own soul by wandering from the way of God through misunderstanding.*

The Lord God is not inviting you to destruction, but (in love) to an experience of knowing Him personally and intimately. Can you imagine how much His heart breaks to see those He created and gave His life for not knowing Him, rejecting Him, and experiencing destruction and captivity in their lives? All because they have little understanding and knowledge of who He is and what He has done through Jesus Christ. Where are you? Do you want to scoff at His invitation and reject the knowledge of Him, or are you ready to commit yourself to Him and ask the Lord for a teachable heart? Can you acknowledge that maybe you don't know Jesus as well as you thought you did; your life being the very proof?

📖 **Proverbs 14:6 NKJV**
"A scoffer seeks wisdom and does not find it, but knowledge is easy to him who understands."

📖 **Proverbs 14:6 AMPC**
"A scoffer seeks Wisdom in vain [for his very attitude blinds and deafens him to it], but knowledge is easy to him who [being teachable] understands."

Jesus is standing ready to help you if you will humble yourself and cry out to Him for help. He is willing to pray to the Father, on your behalf, for your freedom. Hear what He said to people who believed Him.

📖 *John 8:30-32 NKJV*

"As He spoke these words, many believed in Him. Then Jesus said to those Jews who believed Him, 'If you abide in My word, you are My disciples indeed. And you shall know the truth, and the truth shall make you free.'"

Will you please talk to God and ask Him to help you?

God, I want to understand and know You more correctly and personally. I have had a complacent attitude towards Your word, which has blinded and hindered me from knowing You and walking in Your truth. Even my own misunderstanding of the word of God has produced a lack of experiencing Your power in my life. Please forgive me and help me; begin to teach me from the Scriptures and open my eyes to see the truth. Please give me a fresh hunger for the truth and develop understanding in me which leads to an increasing and progressive personal knowing of You and Your Son, Jesus. Thank you for hearing me, for I am praying to You in the name of Jesus Christ. Amen.

THE PROBLEM OF SINS

Let us now look into the problem of sins, how they affect the fate of our souls, and our standing with God. First, we will define sin. Second, we shall observe examples of what it is and what it brings into our lives. Lastly, we will look at what our response is to be and what God is offering us for help.

📖 *Romans 6:23 NKJV*

"For the wages of sin is death, but the gift of God is eternal life in Christ Jesus our Lord."

Sin is an offense against God, committed by man, which leaves the sinner guilty before Him and requires the just sentence of death and eternal separation from God. Sin is a *disobedience* considered to be a transgression against the divine will and law of God. Sins are thoughts, behaviors, attitudes, and actions proceeding from the nature of man, contrary to God, displeasing to God, and make man to miss the mark of God's requirements for righteousness.

📖 *Romans 3:10-12 NKJV*

"As it is written: 'There is none right-eous, no, not one; there is none who understands; there is none who seeks after God. They have all turned aside; they have together become unprofit-able; there is none who does good, no, not one.'"

> **Sin is a disobedience considered to be a transgression against the divine will and law of God.**

📖 *Romans 8:7-8 GNT*

"And so people become enemies of God when they are controlled by their human nature; for they do not obey God's law, and in fact they cannot obey it. Those who obey their human nature cannot please God."

Below are examples of sins that are manifested and visible in a person's life.

📖 *Galatians 5:19a GNT*

"What human nature does is quite plain. It shows itself..."

📖 *Galatians 5:19-21 NKJV*

"Now the works of the flesh are evident, which are: adultery, forni-cation, uncleanness, lewdness, idolatry, sorcery, hatred, contentions, jealousies, outbursts of wrath, selfish ambitions, dissensions, here-sies, envy, murders, drunkenness, revelries, and the like; of which I tell you beforehand, just as I also told you in time past, that those who practice such things will not inherit the kingdom of God."

📖 *2 Timothy 3:1-5 NKJV*

"But know this, that in the last days perilous times will come: For men will be lovers of themselves, lovers of money, boasters, proud, blas-phemers, disobedient to parents, unthankful, unholy, unloving, un-forgiving, slanderers, without self-control, brutal, despisers of good, traitors, headstrong, haughty, lovers of pleasure rather than lovers *of God, having a form of godliness but denying its power. And from such people turn away!"*

These are only SOME examples of what the human nature does from within a man; the sins (or activities) the sinful, human nature produces. The Bible says they are quite plain. They are evidence of a wrong life inside that is sinning, which loves self and pleasure more than loving God. My friend, it is quite plain! Do you love money? Are you headstrong, refusing to forgive anyone? Are you a self-confident, proud person who boasts of yourself and lacks self-control? Is sexual sin a part of your life? Are you envious of the success of others and jealous when good comes their way? Do you speak poorly about people behind their backs? Do fits of anger stir up in you, and become outbursts of wrath when you don't get your way? Is this you? In these lists of sins, is your name attached to any of them? Are you practicing sin and treating it as a light matter? Those who practice such things will *not* inherit the kingdom of God. Please look again at the list, make sure you are right with God. Or is there something you need to cry out to Him for help with?

📖 **Galatians 5:19-21 AMP**

"Now the practices of the sinful nature are clearly evident: they are sexual immorality, impurity, sensuality (total irresponsibility, lack of self-control), idolatry, sorcery, hostility, strife, jealousy, fits of anger, disputes, dissensions, factions [that promote heresies], envy, drunkenness, riotous behavior, and other things like these. I warn you beforehand, just as I did previously, that those who practice such things will not inherit the kingdom of God."

Weak conversions are the result of weak convictions. His salvation will only be meaningful to us if we understand what He is offering to deliver us from, through faith in Jesus.

Are you feeling convicted of sin? Is your conscience aroused from the word of God? Normally I would call you to repent at this stage. But I want to beg you to wait and keep reading so you have a greater grasp of what the problem is between you and God concerning sins. Weak conversions are the result of weak convictions. His salvation will only be meaningful to us if we understand what He is offering to deliver us from, through faith in Jesus. Therefore, let's continue to examine the effects and consequences of the sins we commit. We need to do this so we can come to a proper place of repentance, an authentic place of repentance, in order to fully receive God's offer of forgiveness and new life.

📖 *Ezekiel 18:4 NKJV*
"Behold, all souls are Mine; the soul of the Father as well as the soul of the son is Mine; <u>the soul who sins shall die</u>."

In Romans 6:23 we saw, "the wages of sin is death." Now we see that the soul who sins shall die. It is God who owns all souls; we belong to Him. He created us, and He is the rightful owner of each particular soul. I will not die because my earthly father sins, or because of someone else's sins. I will only die because I am the one who sins against God. And the Bible says:

📖 *Romans 3:23 NKJV*
"for all have sinned and fall short of the glory of God,"

I pray God will open our eyes to see clearly the gravity and weight of sins and the problem they present to the eternal well-being of all men and women on the earth. I pray He will give us revelation to see what causes Him to hide His face from us.

📖 *Isaiah 59:1-3 NKJV*
"Behold, the LORD's hand is not shortened, that it cannot save; nor His ear heavy, that it cannot hear. But your iniquities have separated you from your God; and <u>your sins have hidden His face from you, so that He will not hear</u>. For your hands are defiled with blood, and your fingers with iniquity; your lips have spoken lies, your tongue has muttered perversity."

📖 *Proverbs 5:21-23 NKJV*
"For the ways of man are before the eyes of the LORD, and He ponders all his paths. His own iniquities entrap the wicked man, <u>and he</u>

is caught in the cords of his sin. He shall die for lack of instruction, and in the greatness of his folly he shall go astray."

Did you see the word of God? It is YOUR iniquities; YOUR sins; YOUR hands; YOUR fingers; YOUR lips; YOUR tongue that causes His face to be hidden from you and makes it so God will not hear you. It is personal to YOU and YOU ALONE in God's eyes. Sins entrap you in an earthly cage that is anchored to hell. They wrap around you like strong cords that you cannot break. They strangle you in the clutches of darkness, waiting for the day of your death and eternal separation from God.

> *Sins entrap you in an earthly cage that is anchored to hell. They wrap around you like strong cords that you cannot break.*

Without proper instruction for how to be delivered, man will die in that state. It is not that God's hand is too short to reach down and save you, or that His ears are not capable of hearing you. It is because your iniquities have separated you from Him, and He will only hear the cry of a truly sorrowful heart (for sinning against Him) and the wailing of a desperate soul that desires forgiveness of sins. And let us not deceive ourselves into thinking that God is not aware of every sin we ever commit. He is aware of even the most secretive sins that no one else knows about; the hidden sins you would not want people to know you do in secret. It will be a great folly to pretend and act in such a way.

  📖 *Galatians 6:7 NKJV*
"Do not be deceived, God is not mocked; for whatever a man sows, that he will also reap."
  📖 *Psalm 69:5 NKJV*
"O God, You know my foolishness; and my sins are not hidden from You."
  📖 *Isaiah 59:12 NKJV*
"For our transgressions are multiplied before You, and our sins testify against us; for our transgressions are with us, and as for our iniquities, we know them:"

📖 *Psalm 90:8 NKJV*

"You have set our iniquities before You, our secret sins in the light of Your countenance."

📖 *Psalms 90:8 TLB*

"You spread out our sins before you- our secret sins- and you see them all."

God sees everything! Not only the sins we outwardly do, but also the sins that are in the heart. He sees the intentions and motives behind even the *supposed* good things we do. Every sin will be brought into judgment, and the just penalty for sin will be executed upon us if we do not repent and obey God.

📖 *Ecclesiastes 12:13-14 KJV*

"Let us hear the conclusion of the whole matter: fear God, and keep his commandments: For this is the whole duty of man. For God shall bring every work into judgment, with every secret thing, whether it be good, or whether it be evil."

Are you still in your sins? Will you please get on your knees and beg God for mercy? Do not hide from God anymore, but bring out all your sins before Him, agree with Him and cry out to Him so you may prosper in His will and receive mercy.

📖 *Proverbs 28:13 NKJV*

"He who covers his sins will not prosper, but whoever confesses and forsakes them will have mercy."

📖 *Proverbs 28:13 GNT*

"You will never succeed in life if you try to hide your sins. Confess them and give them up; then God will show mercy to you."

Do you want to experience the goodness of God today? Are you ready to obey Him, to confess and repent of your sins, and to give them up so God will show mercy to you and forgive you of it all? It is His great love and kindness that is stretching forth His hand to you. He will rescue you from the penalty of your sins if you love Him and obey Him today. It is time to repent if you value His goodness.

📖 **Romans 2:4 NKJV**

"Or do you despise the riches of His goodness, forbearance, and long-suffering, not knowing that the goodness of God leads you to repentance?"

God loves you! His solution for your sins is the Gospel. He sent His Son, Jesus, to shed His blood and die on the cross for your sins, and He raised Him up from the dead on the third day, so that if you will believe on Him, and receive Him, you will receive everlasting life.

📖 **John 3:16-18 NKJV**

"For God so loved the world that He gave His only begotten Son, that whoever believes in Him should not perish but have everlasting life. For God did not send His Son into the world to condemn the world, but that the world through Him might be saved. He who believes in Him is not condemned; but he who does not believe is condemned already, because he has not believed in the name of the only begotten Son of God."

Do not hide from God anymore, but bring out all your sins before Him, agree with Him and cry out to Him so you may prosper in His will and receive mercy.

God did not send Jesus to condemn you, but to make a way to save you through faith in Him. He was born of a virgin by the Holy Spirit of God, and He came to save you from your sins.

📖 **Matthew 1:21 NKJV**

"And she will bring forth a Son, and you shall call His name JESUS, for He will save His people from their sins."

📖 **1 Corinthians 15:1-4 NKJV**

"Moreover, brethren, I declare to you the gospel which I preached to you, which also you received and in which you stand, by which also you are saved, if you hold fast that which I preached to you- unless you believed in vain. For I delivered to you first of all that which I also received: that Christ died for our sins according to the Scriptures, and

*that He was buried, and that He rose again the third day according
to the Scriptures,"*

Not only did Jesus die on the cross for our sins, but when He died
and was buried, God raised Him on the third day so that if we would
believe on Him, God would deliver us from darkness and give us a
new life (in the light) through our faith in Him.

📖 *1 John 1:5-9 NKJV*
*"This is the message which we have heard from Him and declare to
you, that God is light and in Him is no darkness at all. If we say that
we have fellowship with him, and walk in darkness, we lie and do not
practice the truth. But if we walk in the light as He is in the light, we
have fellowship with one another, and the blood of Jesus Christ His
Son cleanses us from all sin. If we say that we have no sin, we deceive
ourselves, and the truth is not in us. If we confess our sins, He is faithful and just to forgive us our sins and to cleanse us from all unrighteousness."*

Are you ready to surrender your life to God and believe in Jesus? Do
you want God to apply the blood of Christ to the stain of your sins
and cleanse you from all unrighteousness? Please pray.

**Father God, I see from the word of God that I am a sinner in need
of saving. I confess and acknowledge my sins and agree with You
that they will condemn me to death if I don't turn to You for
forgiveness and salvation. I am sorry for offending You by my sins.
I repent of them, and I ask You to forgive and cleanse me from all
unrighteousness. I believe that Jesus came from You, and that He
died on the cross for my sins. I believe that He was buried, and
You raised Him from the dead, and I am asking You to save me
through my faith in Jesus Christ. Lord Jesus, I receive You as Lord
and Savior, and I ask You to come into my heart. Thank You for
hearing me Father, for I am asking You to do this in the name of
Jesus Christ. Amen.**

THE PROBLEM OF THE HEART OF MAN

To this point, we see that not knowing the truth and the sins of man bring great problems to the life of a man or woman. But the actual activity of outward sins is not the only issue. The greater issue is the heart within a man that desires to do such things; to plot and scheme to have its own way, to determine what is good and evil, and to live apart from the reign of its Creator. The heart of the matter between man and God is the heart within a man. Therefore, what does God have to say about the human heart?

📖 *Jeremiah 17:9-10 NKJV*
"The heart is deceitful above all things, and desperately wicked; who can know it? I, the LORD, search the heart, I test the mind, even to give to every man according to his ways, according to the fruit of his doings."
📖 *Jeremiah 17:9 GNT*
"Who can understand the human heart? There is nothing else so deceitful; it is too sick to be healed."

God's evaluation is that the heart is desperately wicked and too sick to be healed. It is so deeply entrenched and corrupted by sin that it has become deceitful above all other things. Can you imagine? There is no other thing of God's creation on earth which is corrupted by sin, more deceitful than the human heart. The depth of that deceit runs deeper than human understanding can descend. Even at the Genesis of human life on earth, listen to how God describes the human heart, when He was evaluating the condition of mankind who were living according to the dictates of their hearts. This was the reason He was going to send judgment by way of the great flood upon the earth.

📖 *Genesis 6:5-8 NKJV*
"Then the LORD saw that the wickedness of man was great in the earth, and that every intent of the thoughts of his heart was only evil continually. And the LORD was sorry that He had made man on the earth, and He was grieved in His heart. So the LORD said, 'I will destroy man whom I have created from the face of the earth, both

109

man and beast, creeping thing and birds of the air, for I am sorry that I have made them.' But Noah found grace in the eyes of the LORD."

The Divine assessment was man's heart was so evil that death was the only reasonable solution. It is because the heart of man (through sin) is too sick to be healed, and God was not interested in multiplying that kind of man on His earth. It became so bad He became sorry He made man.

> **This corrupted heart is not only a problem to those who are adults on the face of the earth, but to all men; all women; and all children, for all have sinned and fall short of the glory of God, even from their youth.**

This corrupted heart is not only a problem to those who are adults on the face of the earth, but to all men; all women; and all children, for all have sinned and fall short of the glory of God, even from their youth. Did you notice that children, pregnant women, aunts, uncles, moms, dads, grandparents and siblings all died? And according to the Lord, every man born of a woman; born of the flesh and born into sin has a heart that is deceitful and selfish above all things; a heart set on evil.

📖 *Ecclesiastes 8:11 NKJV*
"Because the sentence against an evil work is not executed speedily, therefore the heart of the sons of men is fully set in them to do evil."

The heart deceives a man who is secretly sinning to think there is not a problem between he and God, giving himself an excuse to keep on sinning. Though God *will* judge him according to his works, that judgment will not happen until the Lord Jesus returns as the Judge of the living and the dead.

📖 *Romans 2:16 NKJV*
"in the day when God shall judge the secrets of men by Jesus Christ according to my gospel."

And because of the delay in sentencing, man is fooled by his own heart to think that his soul is well with God. What about you? Do you see this kind of heart at work within you? Are you prepared for that day of the Lord Jesus? What is God's assessment?

📖 *Ecclesiastes 9:3 NKJV*

"This is an evil in all that is done under the sun: that one thing happens to all. Truly the hearts of the sons of men are full of evil; madness is in their hearts while they live, and after that they go to the dead."

Even after the flood, when God purged the earth of such wickedness, and spared eight persons in His ark, He still acknowledged the problem of man's heart.

📖 *Genesis 8:21 NKJV*

"And the LORD smelled a soothing aroma. Then the LORD said in His heart, 'I will never again curse the ground for man's sake, although the imagination of man's heart is evil from his youth; nor will I again destroy every living thing as I have done.'"

God was going to provide a solution to the problem of man's heart, which made God sorry He created them. His solution would be His Son, Jesus Christ, and Him crucified and resurrected. Jesus would come from God at the set time to bring salvation to mankind and the opportunity to receive a new heart from God. In His time on earth as a Man, Jesus also made an evaluation of the heart of man.

> *Jesus would come from God at the set time to bring salvation to mankind and the opportunity to receive a new heart from God.*

📖 *Mark 7:17-23 NKJV*

"When He had entered a house away from the crowd, His disciples asked Him concerning the parable. So He said to them, 'Are you thus without understanding also? Do you not perceive that whatever enters a man from outside cannot defile him,

because it does not enter his heart but his stomach, and is elim-
inated, thus purifying all foods?' And He said, 'What comes out of a
man, that defiles a man. For from within, <u>out of the heart</u> of men,
proceed evil thoughts, adulteries, fornications, murders, thefts,
covetousness, wickedness, deceit, lewdness, an evil eye, blasphemy,
pride, foolishness. All these evil things come from within and defile a
man.'"

The heart in every person born of a woman is inherently sick,
deceitful, filled with pride and wicked. We were born with it, and it
is impossible to discard it just because you don't like it. This heart is
hypocritical and has no real desire to be with God and to live
according to His word. It is a heart that pretends to be righteous but
inwardly is full of lies, deception, and hypocrisy. Listen to Jesus:

📖 *Matthew 15:7-9 NKJV*
"Hypocrites! Well did Isaish prophesy about you, saying: "These people draw near to Me with their mouth, and honor Me with their lips, but their heart is far from Me. And in vain do they worship Me, teaching as doctrines the commandments of men.'"

> **Man needs a heart transplant; the cutting away of his old heart so that a new heart from God can be given to Him.**

The heart produces a vain, hypocrit-
ical kind of worship toward God. Man needs a heart transplant; the
cutting away of his old heart so that a new heart from God can be
given to Him. This is part of the Gospel message and offer God makes
to deal with the problem of the heart, which He judges wicked and
worthy of death.

📖 *Ezekiel 18:30-32 NKJV*
*"'Therefore, I will judge you, O house of Israel, every one according
to his ways,' says the Lord God. 'Repent, and turn from all your transgressions, so that iniquity will not be your ruin. Cast away from you
all the transgressions which you have committed, and <u>get yourselves
a new heart and a new spirit</u>. For why should you die, O house of*

Israel? For I have no pleasure in the death of the one who dies,' says the Lord God. 'Therefore turn and live!'"

When you believed on Jesus, did you receive a new heart or did you believe in vain? Did you cast away all your transgressions so iniquity will not be your ruin? God wants to give you a new heart that pumps the blood of His new life and not the life of the old. This is a spiritual operation only He can perform when you humble yourself and obey His word. You cannot have two hearts within you. When someone has a bad heart, that is too sick to be healed, they go to the hospital for a heart transplant. The surgeon doesn't cut the chest open and put the new heart next to the old one and sew it up. He cuts away the first, removes and discards it, and puts in the new one to take its place.

That is what God is offering you. Has your heart been hardened by sin and the consequences of bad decisions in your life? Are you weighed down with heavy burdens and wrong desires, tired of that old heart, and ready to receive a new one from God? Turn to Him and live! He is faithful to save you and do what He says He will do.

📖 *Ezekiel 36:26 NKJV*
"I will give you a new heart and put a new spirit within you; I will take the heart of stone out of your flesh and give you a heart of flesh."

📖 *Ezekiel 36:26-27 TLB*
"And I will give you a new heart- I will give you new and right desires- and put a new spirit within you. I will take out your stony hearts of sin and give you new hearts of love. And I will put my Spirit within you so that you will obey my laws and do whatever I command."

God sent Jesus to die on the cross as a means to deal with your sinful, stubborn, and rebellious heart. He made a way, through His resurrection, to offer you a brand-new heart. He says come "and get yourselves a new heart." Will you please pray to Him and ask Him to perform this surgery on you? He is ready, willing, and able to do it as you humble yourself before Him.

✟

Oh Lord God, I see that my heart is bad and too sick to be healed. Your word is showing me the truth, and I want to agree with you and ask You for this spiritual heart transplant to be performed on me. Please take this old, stony heart of sin out of me and give me the new heart that You promise, the new spirit that You promise, and Your Spirit that You promise to come and live in me, which gives me a new life in Christ. I turn to You and plead with You for mercy and ask You to do this in the name of Jesus Christ. Amen.
Thank You Father.

CHAPTER 7

THE SINFUL NATURE

Having discovered the problems of not knowing the truth, the sins we commit, and the stony heart that keeps us from God—and having prayed through them—we now need to look at the greatest obstacle between a soul and God.

THE PROBLEM OF THE SIN NATURE

First, the sin nature is a problem *within* man.

📖 *John 2:23-25 NKJV*
"Now when He was in Jerusalem at the Passover, during the feast, many believed in His name when they saw the signs which He did. But Jesus did not commit Himself to them, because He knew all men, and had no need that anyone should testify of man, for He knew what was in man."

The issue was not "what man DOES" (the sins) but "what was IN man" (the nature), which Jesus knew about, and which did not allow Him to commit Himself to them. We have already seen how Jesus' death dealt with the sins we committed, but the word of God is raising another issue here; a serious problem between God and man which must be reconciled. There is a difference between the activities of a person (the sins) and the person (the sinner) who does the activities. So, what exactly is Jesus referring to here? What keeps Him from committing Himself to a man?

📖 *John 2:24-25 AMP*

"But Jesus, for His part, did not entrust Himself to them, because He knew all people [and understood the superficiality and fickleness of human nature], and He did not need anyone to testify concerning man [and human nature], for He Himself knew what was in man [in their hearts-in the very core of their being]."'

> **There is a difference between the activities of a person (the sins) and the person (the sinner) who does the activities.**

Not only did sins separate us from God—and those sins so thoroughly stained and defiled our hearts to the extent that they became too sick to be healed and desperately wicked—but we are starting to see that it is a nature inside the very core of our being that is the underlying problem. That corrupt, sinful nature we were all born with, has lusts, appetites, and desires which are contrary to God. It generates behaviors and thoughts that are disobedient to God, making us children of wrath. Only God can deliver us from this problem.

📖 *Ephesians 2:1-3 NKJV*

"And you He made alive, who were dead in trespasses and sins, in which you once walked according to the course of this world, according to the prince of the power of the air, the spirit who now works in the sons of disobedience, among whom also <u>we all</u> once conducted ourselves in the lusts of our flesh, fulfilling the desires of the flesh and of the mind, <u>and were by nature</u> children of wrath, just as the others."

It is not by sins (activities) we are born children of wrath, but by nature. Paul is talking to believers who have received a new life in

Christ through faith. He is reminding them that, before they came to Christ, they were dead in trespasses and sins, and they had a nature working in them which produced disobedience and put them under the wrath of God. It wasn't just *some* people, but he said "we ALL" had such a life. And he said it was by nature we were that way.

📖 **Ephesians 2:3 NLT**
"All of us used to live that way, following the passionate desires and inclinations of our sinful nature. By our very nature we were subject to God's anger, just like everyone else."

A person is not a sinner because they sin, but because they are born with a sinful nature that produces sins from within. For example, if a factory produces soap as its product, the whole inside of that factory is configured and set up to produce soap; soap is its product, and it cannot produce anything else. The soap doesn't come out of the factory by itself but only because of that which is inside the factory that produced it and sent it into the world. In the same way, the reason sins come out of a person is because the factory inside the person (the sin nature) is at work producing what it knows to produce —sins.

Not only did sins separate us from God, and those sins so thoroughly stained and defiled our hearts to the extent that they became too sick to be healed and desperately wicked, but we are starting to see that it is a nature inside the very core of our being that is the underlying problem.

A lion is a lion by nature. You can raise it from its birth in your home and cut its hair to make it look like a dog. You can feed it dog food and try to make it your pet, but eventually it will do things a lion does because *the nature inside* is that of a lion. Likewise, all mankind has been born with a sinful, evil nature inside, ever since the fall of Adam at the beginning.

📖 *Ephesians 2:3 TLB*
"All of us used to be just as they are, our lives expressing the evil within us, doing every wicked thing that our passions or our evil thoughts might lead us into. We started out bad, being born with evil natures, and were under God's anger just like everyone else."

Do you see how serious this problem is? Do you still have this nature in you that easily produces sins from within you? Does it still control you? This is a nature that you cannot externally discipline into obedience to God. Nor can you fast it into submission to the will of God and holy living. It is not pleasing to God in any way.

> **This is a nature that you cannot externally discipline into obedience to God. Nor can you fast it into submission to the will of God and holy living.**

📖 **Romans 8:8 NKJV**
"So then, those who are in the flesh cannot please God."
📖 **Romans 8:8 NLT**
"That's why those who are still under the control of their sinful nature can never please God."

It is a nature within that we were all born with and inherited from the first man, Adam. A nature that leads to death, judgment, and eternal separation from God. Just as we saw how "the wages of sin is death", we also need to see that we were dead because of this sinful nature; the flesh we were joined to which wasn't yet removed.

📖 *Colossians 2:13 NKJV*
"And you, being dead in your trespasses <u>and</u> the uncircumcision of your flesh, He has made alive together with Him, having forgiven you all trespasses,"
📖 *Colossians 2:13 NLT*
"You were dead because of your sins <u>and because your sinful nature was not yet cut away.</u> Then God made you alive with Christ, for he forgave all our sins."

There are dual reasons for your death. The sinful nature you were born with AND the sins it produces which lead to death; both are problems that need to be reconciled by God. The definition of *nature* is the basic, inherent features, character, or qualities of something; inborn characteristics that influence or determine personality. The origin of the word comes from words like *born* and *birth*. It's a problem we inherited by birth that automatically produces sins; sin produces sins. The human body is the factory building that houses the sin nature (inside), which then produces and brings out sins into the world through each person.

> *The definition of nature is the basic, inherent features, character, or qualities of something; inborn characteristics that influence or determine personality.*

Second, the sin nature is a *birth* problem.

📖 *Psalm 51:5 NKJV*
"Behold, I was brought forth in iniquity, and in sin my mother conceived me."
📖 *Psalm 51:5 AMP*
"I was brought forth in [a state of] wickedness; in sin my mother conceived me [and from my beginning I, too, was sinful]."
📖 *Psalm 51:5 NLT*
"For I was born a sinner- yes, from the moment my mother conceived me."
📖 *Psalm 58:3 NKJV*
"The wicked are estranged from the womb; they go astray as soon as they are born, speaking lies."

The psalmist did not say he was brought forth "by sin" but "in sin." It is not that the parents sinned in having intimate marital relations which brought forth a child. But the reality of the sinful, human nature, which passes through natural conception into the child, and causes that child to be born sinful, even before it has committed a sin. Listen to Jesus.

119

  📖 **John 3:5-6 NKJV**

"Jesus answered, 'Most assuredly, I say to you, unless one is born of water and the Spirit, he cannot enter the kingdom of God. That which is born of the flesh is flesh, and that which is born of the Spirit is spirit.'"

  📖 **John 3:6 TLB**

"Men can only reproduce human life, but the Holy Spirit gives new life from heaven."

All humans, born through a woman as the product of a man and a woman having intercourse, are conceived and born in sin. The life they are born with is natural and sinful by nature. The only solution is a *brand-new* life that comes from heaven and is born of the Spirit of God. That which is born of the flesh is only flesh and can only reproduce flesh. The flesh (sinful nature) is unclean, impure, and unrighteous. It makes every person a child of the flesh and not a child of God.

  📖 **Job 14:4 NKJV**

"Who can bring a clean thing out of an unclean? No one!"

  📖 **Job 15:14 NKJV**

"What is man, that he could be pure? And he who is born of a woman, that he could be righteous?"

  📖 **Job 25:4 NKJV**

"How then can man be righteous before God? Or how can he be pure who is born of a woman?"

  📖 **Romans 9:8 NKJV**

"That is, those who are the children of the flesh, these are not the children of God; but the children of the promise are counted as the seed."

How did this happen to mankind? What caused even newborn children from the womb, born of the flesh, who have never committed a sin in this world, to be sinful, disobedient, and by nature children of wrath in need of deliverance from condemnation and eternal judgment and of salvation from sin?

Third, the sin nature is an inherited problem.

📖 *Romans 5:12 NKJV*
"Therefore, just as through one man sin entered the world, and death through sin, and thus death spread to all men, because all sinned-"
📖 *Romans 5:19 NKJV*
"For as by one man's disobedience many were made sinners, so also by one Man's obedience many will be made righteous."

Man was originally created by God in His image and after His likeness. That image and life (nature) came *into* man when God breathed His life into the first man, Adam. And God instructed Adam how to continue in life.

📖 *Genesis 2:15-17 NKJV*
"Then the LORD God took the man and put him in the garden of Eden to tend and keep it. And the LORD God commanded the man, saying, 'Of every tree of the garden you may freely eat; but of the tree of the knowledge of good and evil you shall not eat, <u>for in the day that you eat of it you shall surely die</u>.'"

> *When Adam disobeyed God's simple instructions and offended his Creator, something happened to the man and the woman; the death that God promised came.*

When Adam disobeyed God's simple instructions and offended his Creator, something happened to the man and the woman; the death that God promised came. God said "in the day" you eat of it you shall surely die, not later on or some other day. It's easy to see, when they ate, they did not fall down and physically die, but something happened to them which produced death. The Bible says that sin entered into the world, and death through sin (because the wages of sin is death), and thus death spread to all men, *internally* by a new nature that entered into them. This sin nature is naturally transferred and passed on from one generation to another; to all men and women.

121

📖 *1 Corinthians 15:21-22 NKJV*

"For since by man came death, by Man also came the resurrection of the dead. For as in Adam all die, even so in Christ all shall be made alive."

📖 *1 Corinthians 15:22 TLB*

"Everyone dies because all of us are related to Adam, being members of his sinful race, and <u>wherever there is sin</u>, death results. But all who are related to Christ will rise again."

Wherever there is sin, death results! This is the declaration God makes. This is not talking about sins that a person commits, but wherever there is *sin*. This is the problem IN man that has to be resolved. Sin changed man into something other than what God intended, according to the word of God.

📖 *Genesis 5:1-3 NKJV*

"This is the book of the genealogy of Adam. <u>In the day</u> that God created man, He made him in the likeness of God. He created them male and female, and blessed them and called them Mankind <u>in the day they were created</u>. And Adam lived one hundred and thirty years, and begot a son in his own likeness, after his image, and named him Seth."

We need to read our Bibles carefully now. Did you see that "in the day" God created man, He made them in the likeness of God? In "the day" (singular) is referring to the moment He made them in the beginning on that particular day.

📖 *Genesis 1:27; 2:7 NKJV*

"So God created man in His own image; in the image of God He created him; male and female He created them....And the LORD God formed man of the dust of the ground, and breathed into his nostrils the breath of life; and man became a living being."

This all happened in the day that God made them. But the word says that by the time Adam began to have children they were born in his *own* likeness and after *his* image; not God's. Mankind was no longer in the image of God but in the image and likeness of Adam. Man was now under the power of sin (within them)—which does not do good and holds man down under its power and control.

📖 **Romans 3:9-12 NKJV**

"What then? Are we better than they? Not at all. For we have previously charged both Jews and Greeks that they are all under sin. As it is written: 'There is none righteous, no, not one; there is none who understands; there is none who seeks after God. They have all turned aside; they have together become unprofitable; there is none who does good, no, not one.'"

📖 **Romans 3:9 AMPC**

"Well then, are we [Jews] superior and better off than they? No, not at all. We have already charged that all men, both, Jews and Greeks (Gentiles), are under sin [held down by and subject to its power and control]."

For a deeper understanding of the problem and reality of sin (as a life and nature) within us, let us hear from the apostle Paul as he told his story relating to the sin nature.

📖 **Romans 7:15-20 NKJV**

"For what I am doing, I do not understand. For what I will to do, that I do not practice; but what I hate, that I do. If, then, I do what I will not to do, I agree with the law that it is good. But now, it is no longer I who do it, but sin that dwells in me. For I know that in me (that is, in my flesh) nothing good dwells; for to will is present with me, but how to perform what is good I do not find. For the good that I will to do, I do not do; but the evil I will not to do, that I practice. Now if I do what I will not to do, it is no longer I who do it, but sin that dwells in me."

📖 **Romans 7:18 NIV**

"For I know that good itself does not dwell in me, that is, in my sinful nature. For I have the desire to do what is good, but I cannot carry it out."

Paul was describing what his old life was like, the one he was born with before he came to Christ and experienced the death of the cross and the new life in Christ. We can know he was talking about his old life, and not his current one in Christ, because of verse 5.

📖 *Romans 7:5 NKJV*
"For <u>when we were in the flesh</u>, the sinful passions which <u>were aroused</u> by the law <u>were at work</u> in our members to bear fruit to death."
📖   *Romans 7:5 TLB*
"<u>When your old nature was still active</u>, sinful desires were at work within you, making you want to do whatever God said not to and producing sinful deeds, the rotting fruit of death."

> **Paul was describing what his old life was like, the one he was born with before he came to Christ and experienced the death of the cross and the new life in Christ.**

He is using words in the past tense like "when we *were*" in the flesh, "which *were* aroused" and "*were* at work in our members." We see that the sinful nature in man is hostile to God and it doesn't allow a man to do good, even when he wants to. Six times Paul said he *willed* (or desired) to do or not to do something, but he found something in him overriding his will and making him do the opposite of what he desired. That was *sin* (the sinful nature at work in him). This was not activities that were in him, but a life that dwelled in him called sin (according to verses 17 and 20).

📖 *Romans 7:17 AMP*
"So now [if that is the case, then] it is no longer I who do it [the disobedient thing which I despise], but the sin [nature] which lives in me."
📖 *Romans 7:17 TLB*
"But I can't help myself because I'm no longer doing it. It is sin inside me that is stronger than I am that makes me do these evil things."

The nature man is born with is an internal life that man is bound to and overpowered by. Sins are not a life that can live or dwell, but merely activities and actions that proceed from a life. Man will be led by whatever life (nature) is inside of him, and he will bring forth the fruits of his union with that life. If sin still lives in a man, sins will be the product no matter how hard he tries to fight it.

📖 ***Romans 7:20 NIV***
"Now if I do what I do not want to do, it is no longer I who do it, but <u>it is sin living in me</u> that does it."
📖 ***Romans 7:20 TLB***
"Now if I am doing what I don't want to, it is plain where the trouble is: sin still has me in its evil grasp."

My friend, does sin still have you in its evil grasp? Are you still captive to sin? Is this nature still inside of you? The Good News of Jesus Christ is that you can be born again and receive a new life from God; a life that will dwell *in* you and enable you to follow and obey Him. But you cannot have sin still living in you. You cannot have sin as a master *and* Jesus as a Master both living in you; you cannot serve *two* masters. Just like we saw with a heart transplant—the surgeon does not leave both hearts in the chest, but he removes the old one in order for the new one to be put in its place. This new life and nature from Christ will bring forth what *He* produces and not what sin produces. The nature that comes from Christ will produce the fruits of Christ's life. The nature of sin will produce the fruits of sin's life. You cannot have two natures at the same time.

📖 ***James 3:11-12 NKJV***
"Does a spring send forth fresh water and bitter from the same opening? Can a fig tree, my brethren, bear olives, or a grapevine bear figs? Thus no spring yields both salt water and fresh."

What water is coming out of the spring of your inner life; fresh or bitter? The Lord Jesus Christ says you will know a person by the fruits that they bear.

📖 ***Matthew 7:17-20 NKJV***
"Even so, every good tree bears good fruit, but a bad tree bears bad fruit. A good tree cannot bear bad fruit, nor can a bad tree bear good

fruit. Every tree that does not bear good fruit is cut down and thrown into the fire. Therefore by their fruits you will know them."

📖 **Matthew 15:13-14 NKJV**

"But He answered and said, 'Every plant which My heavenly Father has not planted will be uprooted. Let them alone, they are blind leaders of the blind. And if the blind leads the blind, both will fall into a ditch.'"

Have you been planted by the heavenly Father into Christ Jesus? Has He uprooted the sinful nature you were born with and given you a new nature in Christ? Do you see how serious the issue of the sin nature is and why it has to be dealt with before Jesus can entrust Himself to you? Let's ask God to open our eyes further. We need to see the full scope of this problem, so as we continue, we can be better prepared to study, understand, and fully receive God's solution through His wonderful provision of the blood, the cross, and the resurrection of Jesus Christ.

> *Have you been planted by the heavenly Father into Christ Jesus? Has He uprooted the sinful nature you were born with and given you a new nature in Christ?*

Fourth, the sin nature presents a locational problem.

📖 **Luke 13:22-27 NKJV**

"And He went through the cities and villages, teaching, and journeying toward Jerusalem. Then one said to Him, 'Lord, are there few who are saved?' And He said to them, 'Strive to enter through the narrow gate, for many, I say to you, will seek to enter and will not be able. When once the Master of the house has risen up and shut the door, and you begin to stand outside and knock at the door, saying, 'Lord, Lord, open for us,' and He will answer and say to you, 'I do not know you, where you are from,' then you will begin to say, 'We ate and drank in Your presence, and You taught in our streets.' But He will say, 'I tell you I do not know you, where you are from. Depart from Me, all you workers of iniquity.'"

📖 *Matthew 7:21-23 NKJV*

"Not everyone who says to Me, 'Lord, Lord,' shall enter the kingdom of heaven, but he who does the will of My Father in heaven. Many will say to Me in that day, 'Lord, Lord, have we not prophesied in Your name, cast out demons in Your name, and done many wonders in Your name?' And then I will declare to them, 'I never knew you; depart from Me, you who practice lawlessness!'"

The question asked to Jesus was "Lord, are there few who are saved?" This question arose from a challenge in the heart of the people because of what Jesus was teaching them concerning the kingdom of God and who will be allowed to enter, and who will not be. Jesus answered by telling them the problem that will keep them from heaven on the Day the Lord arises to shut the door. The problem is *location*. It's because of the nature *in* them which works lawlessness; sin that produces sins, iniquity that works iniquities; the old man, the flesh. He said, "I do not know you, where you are from. Depart from Me, all you workers of iniquity." It is not workers of *iniquities* (immoral activities, actions), but *iniquity* (the unjust *life* of sin). Just like in Romans 6:23, it is not the wages of SINS that is death, but "the wages of SIN is death." Anyone who still has the sin nature dwelling in them is working for sin (producing sins by nature), and those wages (that payday) is death.

> *Sin, living in man, locates him in a place that keeps Jesus from knowing and entrusting Himself to him, and keeps that man from being in the household of God.*

According to Jesus, on that Day, many people who call Jesus Lord will plead and present their case, saying, "we ate and drank in Your presence, You taught in our streets, we cast out devils, did many wonders, and prophesied in Your name," but Jesus will say, "I do not know you, where you are from." Sin, living in man, locates him in a place that keeps Jesus from knowing and entrusting Himself to him, and keeps that man from being in the household of God.

📖 *Luke 13:25-27 AMPC*

"When once the Master of the house gets up and closes the door, and you begin to stand outside and to knock at the door [again and again], saying, Lord, open to us! He will answer you, I do not know where [what household- certainly not Mine] you come from. Then you will begin to say, We ate and drank in your presence, and You taught in our streets. But He will say, I tell you, I do not know where [what household- certainly not Mine} you come from; depart from Me, all you wrongdoers!"

This is amazing! Jesus says there will be men and women, who call Jesus their Lord, who have been serving God in the name of Jesus, and who have even experienced ministerial success in His name, that will be restrained by Jesus from entering into heaven. Sin (by nature) tethers, confines, and restricts man to an earthly existence, ultimately bound to be located in hell for eternity.

> **Sin (by nature) tethers, confines, and restricts man to an earthly existence, ultimately bound to be located in hell for eternity.**

📖 *Proverbs 5:21-22 NKJV*

"For the ways of man are before the eyes of the LORD, and He ponders all his paths. His own iniquities entrap the wicked man, and he is caught in the cords of his sin."

If you do not do the will of the Father, you will not be permitted, by Jesus, to enter the kingdom of heaven. If you are still carrying about, inside of you, the life of sin that produces iniquities and entraps you and binds you to a lower existence, a worldly life, you will never make it to be with Jesus in heaven, no matter how hard you seek Him.

📖 *John 8:21-24 NKJV*

"Then Jesus said to them again, 'I am going away, and you will seek Me, <u>and will die in your sin</u>. Where I go you cannot come.' So the Jews said, 'Will He kill Himself, because He says, 'Where I go you cannot come?' And He said to them, 'You are from beneath; I am from above. You are of this world; I am not of this world. Therefore I said

to you that you will die in your sins; for if you do not believe that I am
He, you will die in your sins.'"

Everyone born of the flesh is of this world. You must be born of the
Spirit to avoid this disaster; you must be born-again into the household of God with the life that comes from above. You must experience the death of the cross so the resurrection life of Christ can
come live in you. Friend, which life
is in you? We are learning there is a
difference between sin and sins.
One is the producer within, and the
other is the product. Both are a
problem for every soul, and both
lead to death and eternal separation from God. Did you see Jesus
uses both in the Scripture above?
He said, 'you will seek Me, and will
die in your SIN,' and "if you do not
believe that I am He, you will die in

> *Seeking Jesus alone*
> *will not get you to*
> *heaven; the sin nature*
> *makes it impossible to*
> *come where He is.*
> *Even His disciples were*
> *subject to this truth.*

your SINS." Because of sin living in a man, and the sins he commits,
the place where Jesus abides in heaven is a place where he cannot
go unless both are addressed and dealt with—unless the proper life
from heaven dwells *in* him. Seeking Jesus alone will not get you to
heaven; the sin nature makes it impossible to come where He is.
Even His disciples were subject to this truth. In Luke 13:32-37 we saw
Jesus address the crowd to make known this problem which faces
them. But Jesus also addressed His disciples personally one night, after they ate dinner together. He was speaking to them of His return
to heaven.

📖 *John 13:33-36 NKJV*

"'Little children, I shall be with you a little while longer. You will seek
Me; and as I said to the Jews, 'Where I am going, you cannot come,'
so now I say to you. A new commandment I give to you, that you love
one another; as I have loved you, that you also love one another. By
this all will know that you are My disciples, if you have love for one
another.' Simon Peter said to Him, 'Lord, where are You going?' Jesus

answered him, 'Where I am going <u>you cannot follow Me now</u>, but you shall follow Me <u>afterward.'"</u>

These men already left all to follow Jesus. They repented of and acknowledged they were sinners, and they believed, by their own confessions, that Jesus was the Christ, the Son of the living God. They were traveling up and down with Him, witnessing miracles and the power of God on display through Jesus. They were even sent out by Him, by the Spirit of God He sent with them, to do mighty works in His name. Yet, after all that, Jesus still said, "where I am going, you cannot follow me NOW." Why not *now*? It seems like they have met all the criteria to be right with God and be permitted to enter heaven where Jesus was going. But! There was still one major problem that dwelled in them by birth; sin was living *in* them. That problem was not yet dealt with because Jesus had not yet gone to the cross. Jesus said the Holy Spirit was not yet in them, but only *with* them.

📖 *John 14:15-17 NKJV*
"If you love Me, keep My commandments. And I will pray the Father, and He will give you another Helper, that He may abide with you forever- the Spirit of truth, whom the world cannot receive, because it neither sees Him nor knows Him; but you know Him, <u>for He dwells with you and will be in you.</u>"

> **Though they knew the Holy Spirit to be "with" them by experiences they were having, the Holy Spirit was not yet "in" them because Jesus had not yet gone to the cross to deal with the problem of their sin, and to be raised from the dead.**

They could not follow Jesus to heaven yet because of the life that was still in them; they were not born of the Spirit until the night of the resurrection when Jesus breathed His life into them and said, 'receive the Holy Spirit'. Though they knew the Holy Spirit to be "with" them by experiences they were having, the Holy Spirit was not yet "in" them because Jesus had not yet gone to the cross to deal with the problem of their sin, and to be raised from the dead.

📖 *John 7:37-39 NKJV*

"On the last day, that great day of the feast, Jesus stood and cried out, saying, 'If anyone thirsts, let him come to Me and drink. He who believes in Me, as the Scripture has said, out of his heart <u>will</u> flow rivers of living water.' But this He spoke concerning the Spirit, whom those believing in Him <u>would receive</u>; for the Holy Spirit was not yet given, because Jesus was not yet glorified."

Before the cross, the Holy Spirit was not yet given to dwell in man, because Jesus was not yet glorified. He came to earth as the Lamb of God to take away the *sin* of the world, and He was going to do that. He was going to offer His life as a sacrifice for sins *and* die on the cross to deal with sin. And ultimately (and gloriously) be raised from the dead to be the firstborn from the dead (and come to dwell in man by the Holy Spirit). Until then, all men were still under the power of sin which dwelled in their mortal bodies. The apostle Paul knew this earthly prison and said:

📖 *Romans 7:24-25 NLT*

"Oh, what a miserable person I am! Who will free me from this life that is dominated by sin and death? Thank God! The answer is in Jesus Christ our Lord. So you see how it is: In my mind I really want to obey God's law, but because of my sinful nature I am a slave to sin."

My friend, are you a slave to sin? Do you see how grave a situation this sinful nature is? Let's keep looking at the problems this nature produces in a man's life.

Fifth, the sin nature creates a problem for man with the devil.

📖 *1 John 5:19 NKJV*

"We know that we are of God, and the whole world lies under the sway of the wicked one."

📖 *1 John 5:19 TLB*

"We know that we are the children of God and that all the rest of the world around us is under Satan's power and control."

In Christ, we are now able to declare that Jesus, who is in us, is greater than he who is in the world (the devil). But before coming to Christ, we (along with everyone else in the world) were subject to and under the power and control of the wicked one. This was because of the sinful nature we were born with. We were children of the world and not yet children of God. Remember Paul in Romans 7 talking about how he was under the sway of sin living in him; and the power and control it had over his life? That sin-life brings *all* to be under the sway and influence of the wicked one, from within. And until you come to Jesus Christ, it will be that same spirit working in you to produce sin and eternal separation from God.

📖 *Ephesians 2:1-2 NKJV*
"And you He made alive, who were dead in trespasses and sins, <u>in which you once walked</u> according to the course of this world, according to the prince of the power of the air, the spirit who now works in the sons of disobedience,"

📖 *Ephesians 2:2 NLT*
"You used to live in sin, just like the rest of the world, obeying the devil- the commander of the powers in the unseen world. He is the spirit at work in the hearts of those who refuse to obey God."

Everyone born of the flesh, not yet born of the Spirit, is vulnerable to the powers of darkness being able to work in them; producing selfishness, disobedience, carelessness, and rebellion against God. The person who carries the sin nature is bound to habitually follow the patterns of this world and be under the directions, suggestions, and compelling of the enemies of God in the spiritual realm—the devil and all those demon spirits who serve and follow him.

📖 *Ephesians 2:2 AMPC*
"In which at one time you walked [habitually]. You were following the course and fashion of this world [were under the sway of the tendency of this present age], following the prince of the power of the air. [You were obedient to and under the control of] the [demon] spirit that still constantly works in the sons of disobedience [the

careless, the rebellious, and the unbelieving, who go against the purposes of God]."

Are you easily persuadable by unseen voices which you obey, proceeding to take action that is against the purposes and will of God? It may be that you have not yet known or received the fullness of the promise of the Gospel to take away the first (old life) and establish the second (new creation life) from God. Is it possible that you still have the spirit of the world dwelling in you and not the Spirit who is from God?

📖 *1 Corinthians 2:11-12 NKJV*

"For what man knows the things of the man except the spirit of the man which is in him? Even so no one knows the things of God except the Spirit of God. Now we have received, not the spirit of the world, but the Spirit who is from God, that we might know the things that have been freely given to us by God."

> **It may be that you have not yet known or received the fullness of the promise of the Gospel to take away the first (old life) and establish the second (new creation life) from God.**

Do you need further proof that what we are saying is true? Let us hear what Jesus has to say about the matter. In John 8, Jesus is talking to Jewish people who were Pharisees; men who were religious, believed in the God of Israel, and took the Scriptures and the law of Moses very seriously.

📖 *John 8:23-24 NKJV*

"And He said to them, 'You are from beneath; I am from above. You are of this world; I am not of this world. Therefore I said to you that you will die in your sins; for if you do not believe that I am He, you will die in your sins.'"

They continued in a discussion and Jesus kept preaching to them the words His Father told Him to say, which bring forgiveness, deliverance, and salvation to mankind. Then in verse 30 the Bible says, "As He spoke these words, many believed in Him." But Jesus didn't just take them at their word, that they had believed from their heart. Instead, He continued the conversation, telling them the next instruction they would need to follow after believing. He said to those Jews who believed Him, "*If you abide in My word, you are My disciples indeed. And you shall know the truth, and the truth shall make you free.*" From then on, they began to argue with Him and the words that were proceeding from His mouth. That is where we will enter this passage.

📖 *John 8:33-47 NKJV*

"They answered Him, 'We are Abraham's descendants, and have never been in bondage to anyone. How can You say, 'You will be made free?'' Jesus answered them, 'Most assuredly, I say to you, whoever commits sin is a slave of sin. <u>And a slave does not abide in the house forever, but a son abides forever</u>. Therefore if the Son makes you free, you shall be free indeed. I know that you are Abraham's descendants, but you seek to kill Me, because My word has no place in you. I speak what I have seen with My Father, and you do what you have seen with your father.

> **Jesus said... "If you abide in My word, you are My disciples indeed. And you shall know the truth, and the truth shall make you free."**

They answered and said to Him, 'Abraham is our father.' Jesus said to them, 'If you were Abraham's children, you would do the works of Abraham. But now you seek to kill Me, a Man who has told you the truth which I heard from God. Abraham did not do this. You do the deeds of your father.' Then they said to Him, 'We were not born of fornication; we have one Father-God.' Jesus said to them, <u>'If God were your Father, you would love Me</u>, for I proceeded forth and came from God; nor have I come of Myself, but He sent Me. Why do you not understand My speech? Because you are not able to listen to My word. <u>You are of your father the devil</u>, and the desires of your father you want to do. He was a murderer from the beginning, and does not stand in the truth, be-

cause there is no truth in him. When he speaks a lie, he speaks from his own resources, for he is a liar and the father of it. But because I tell the truth, you do not believe Me. Which of you convicts Me of sin? And if I tell the truth, why do you not believe Me? He who is of God hears God's words; therefore you do not hear, because you are not of God.'"

Jesus said that when the devil speaks a lie, he speaks from his own resources. That is to say, He draws from the nature inside of him that produces such things like lying and murder and self-seeking. He who is filled with the spirit of the world, who has the sinful nature and is under the sway of the wicked one, does the same by the resources (nature) in him. He does not accept what Jesus has to say or understand the things He is communicating. Jesus said, "he who commits sin is a slave of sin, and slaves do not abide in the house forever," only sons. These men proudly declared to Jesus that God was their Father, but He told them they were of their father the devil. He said the desires of their father was what they wanted to do. He told them to their faces the reason they couldn't hear what God was saying through Him was because they were not of God. The truth is, the sin nature abiding in them will habitually bear the fruits of the same nature that is in all the children of the devil.

  📖 ***1 John 3:9-10 AMPC***
"No one born (begotten) of God [deliberately, knowingly, and habitually] practices sin, for God's nature abides in him [His principle of life, the divine sperm, remains permanently within him]; and he cannot practice sinning because he is born (begotten) of God. By this it is made clear who take their nature from God and are His children and who take their nature from the devil and are his children: no one who does not practice righteousness [who does not conform to God's will in purpose, thought, and action] is of God; neither is anyone who does not love his brother (his fellow believer in Christ)."

Sin from within sins and brings forth a life hostile to God and His way of righteousness in Christ Jesus. The sin nature, inherited from Adam, makes us children of the devil, in need of deliverance from the bondage of sin and the blindness the god of this world produces in those who do not believe in Jesus Christ. The sin nature makes people slaves and will not allow them to have eternal life and be in the Father's house forever. It is a lower nature that does not (and cannot) conform to God's will in purpose, thought, or action. And it is a nature under the power of the devil and full of error, dragging a man under the condemnation and wrath of God.

> *The Good News is that the Son of God, Jesus Christ, can set you free from this bondage, evict the spirit of the world from within you, and make you a child of God by His Spirit coming to dwell in you.*

The Good News is that the Son of God, Jesus Christ, can set you free from this bondage, evict the spirit of the world from within you, and make you a child of God by His Spirit coming to dwell in you.

Has the Son of God made you free indeed from this nature? There will be evidence of this reality if so. I am asking the Holy Spirit to help you understand the truth and gravity of where you really are, and not to be led by the spirit of error. Have you been calling yourself a Christian but realizing you still have this sinful nature living inside of you? We must acknowledge the problem before the solution will be valuable to us. Are you actually a child of God? What nature is in you?

📖 *1 John 3:9-10 GNT*
"Those who are children of God do not continue to sin, for God's very nature is in them; and because God is their Father, they cannot continue to sin. Here is the clear difference between God's children and the Devil's children: those who do not do what is right or do not love others are not God's children."

📖 *1 John 3:9-10 MSG*
"People conceived and brought into life by God don't make a practice of sin. How could they? God's seed is deep within them, making them who they are. It's not in the nature of the God-born to practice and parade sin. Here's how you tell the difference between God's children

and the Devil's children: The one who won't practice righteous ways isn't from God, nor is the one who won't love brother or sister. A simple test."

My friend, do you pass the test? Before we move on to discover God's provisions for our deliverance from this nature and its actIvities, can I beg you to humble yourself, pray to God, and ask Him for help?

Oh God, I see the problem of the sinful nature in me. Your word is very clear to me, and I don't know what to do. I want to know the way out from this problem that lives inside of me and compels me to sin and not do what is right in Your eyes. I see this nature in me still ruling my life, keeping me from loving others, deliberately hiding my sins, and making me to selfishly do what is right in my own eyes. Please have mercy on me, Oh Lord, and show me the way out. Please forgive me and open my eyes of understanding to see what You have done to deliver me from the sinful nature and give me a new life and a new nature in Christ Jesus. Please help me, God, I don't want to live this way anymore. In the name of Jesus Christ I pray. Amen.

CHAPTER 8

THE BLOOD OF JESUS CHRIST

We have seen the problems between us and God. We saw how God sent Jesus to die on the cross for our sins and how He raised Him from the dead. We repented of our sins, put our faith in Jesus, and have received Him into our hearts. Now what? A great struggle exists in the lives of many sincere Christians; vagueness in knowing and understanding *all* God did for us in Christ, particularly in the message of the cross. When we don't fully understand the will of God and the provisions He has given us in Christ, our Christian lives will be lacking direction, lacking victory, and lacking precision and focus in the will of God.

 📖 *Ephesians 5:17 NKJV*
"Therefore do not be unwise, but understand what the will of the Lord is."
 📖 *Ephesians 5:17 AMPC*
"Therefore do not be vague and thoughtless and foolish, but understanding and firmly grasping what the will of the Lord is."

Let us now begin to give thought to and examine closely all that God has done for our deliverance from sins (and the sin that produced them) and for the new life we have received in Christ Jesus. We will begin with the blood of Christ.

  📖 *Psalm 130:1-4,7-8 NKJV*
"Out of the depths I have cried to You, O LORD; Lord, hear my voice! Let Your ears be attentive to the voice of my supplications. If You, LORD, should mark iniquities, O Lord, who could stand? But there is forgiveness with You, that You may be feared...O Israel, hope in the LORD; for with the LORD there is mercy, and with Him is abundant redemption. And He shall redeem Israel from all his iniquities."

  📖 *Ephesians 1:7 NKJV*
"In Him we have redemption through His blood, the forgiveness of sins, according to the riches of His grace"

What is the blood of Jesus? What role does this great provision play in the plan and purpose of God for my new life in Christ? These are important questions we as children of God need to have answered. Unfortunately, many Christians have not learned the whole truth concerning the blood, from the Scriptures, and as a result their lives are in confusion and lack the full experience and blessing of this provision of God.

  📖 *Proverbs 16:22a NKJV*
"Understanding is a wellspring of life to him who has it."

  📖 *Hebrews 12:24 NKJV*
"to Jesus the Mediator of the new covenant, and to the blood of sprinkling that speaks better things than that of Abel."

  📖 *Hebrews 12:24 GNT*
"You have come to Jesus, who arranged the new covenant, and to the sprinkled blood that promises much better things than does the blood of Abel."

There is a sprinkling of the blood upon our lives that is necessary for maximum benefit of what God has supplied us to be realized. And while forgiveness of sins is something many have understood and known as a wonderful aspect of the blood of Christ, that insight alone will be lacking effectiveness without knowing the many other benefits God provided through the shed blood of Jesus Christ.

📖 *Psalm 103:1-2 NKJV*
"Bless the LORD, O my soul; and all that is within me, bless His holy name! Bless the LORD, O my soul, and forget not all His benefits:"

We will now dig into the word of God and let Him sprinkle us with understanding and knowledge of what Christ Jesus accomplished by shedding His blood for us. With the help of the Holy Spirit, we will see the benefits and applications that proceed from that sacrifice. There are many teachings about "the blood" that come from the ideas and doctrines of men, so we need to look directly into the Scriptures to gain insight, understanding, and knowledge of the truth. Then we can begin applying it for practical, victorious, every-day life which brings rest to the soul. Let's commence to draw water from the well of life.

But first, let's pray.

Our Father in heaven, we ask that by Your Spirit, You will teach us and cause us to understand more clearly what You say in Your word concerning the blood of Christ. Please give us eyes to see, ears to hear, and understanding in our hearts. Grant us wisdom and full revelation in the knowledge of the truth of the Gospel, and the role the blood plays in it. Thank You for hearing us Father, for we are praying to You in the name of Jesus Christ. Amen.

The Sprinkling Benefits of the Blood of Christ

THE BLOOD OF CHRIST: For Redemption and Forgiveness

📖 *Ephesians 1:7 NKJV*
"In Him we have redemption through His blood, the forgiveness of sins, according to the riches of His grace"

📖 *Ephesians 1:7 GNT*

"For by the blood of Christ we are set free, that is, our sins are forgiven. How great is the grace of God,"

📖 *Ephesians 1:7 AMP*

"In Him we have redemption [that is, our deliverance and salvation] through His blood, [which paid the penalty for our sin and resulted in] the forgiveness and complete pardon of our sin, in accordance with the riches of His grace"

Redemption is the payment of a ransom in full. A ransom is the price paid to release a captive. The blood of Christ was the price to purchase our freedom and forgiveness of sin. We were born in sin, under the power of darkness, and by nature enslaved to sin and its evil. We were held in bondage by the cords of our sins and unable to deliver ourselves or pay the price for our freedom. We had nothing to offer the just and righteous God for the penalty and debt our sins accrued. Jesus came to set us free from those sins and the bondage they brought to our lives. He sacrificed His life to deliver us from their *just* penalty. His shed blood was the redemption-price paid for our release from captivity. That payment resulted in the forgiveness and complete pardon of our sins.

> **We were held in bondage by the cords of our sins and unable to deliver ourselves or pay the price for our freedom.**

📖 *Colossians 1:13-14 NKJV*

"He has delivered us from the power of darkness and conveyed us into the kingdom of the Son of His love, in whom we have redemption through His blood, the forgiveness of sin."

📖 *Colossians 1:13-14 AMPC*

"[The Father] has delivered and drawn us to Himself out of the control and the dominion of darkness and has transferred us into the kingdom of the Son of His love, in Whom we have our redemption through His blood, [which means] the forgiveness of our sins."

Forgiveness is the pardon of an offender by which he is considered and treated as *not guilty*. It brings freedom, liberty and pardon from sins. The Father is who initiated our deliverance by sending His only begotten Son to offer His perfect life on earth for our sinful life on earth. It is important to recognize that God did not have to do it, but He chose to do it out of His love. He had every right to wipe man off the face of the earth, but instead, He decided to provide a way for man to come back to Him by the shed blood of Jesus Christ. Forgiveness is found through faith in Jesus Christ, who offered His precious, unblemished life on behalf of sinful men. God purposed this and set a requirement for mankind to repent (turn from their old lives and turn to God) as His condition. Repentance is required for forgiveness and release from sins; it is required in order to be redeemed from the conduct of your old life.

📖 *1 Peter 1:18-20 NKJV*

"knowing that you were not redeemed with corruptible things, like silver or gold, from your aimless conduct received by tradition from your fathers, but with the precious blood of Christ, as of a lamb without blemish and without spot."

📖 *1 Peter 1:18-19 NLT*

"For you know that God paid a ransom to save you from the empty life you inherited from your ancestors. And it was not paid with mere gold or silver, which lose their value. It was the precious blood of Christ, the sinless, spotless Lamb of God."

> **Forgiveness is the pardon of an offender by which he is considered and treated as not guilty. It brings freedom, liberty and pardon from sins.**

The life of a man who has not come to Christ to be redeemed and forgiven of his sins, is an empty life inherited from his ancestors. It is independent of God and utterly unable to please Him. The sinless, spotless Lamb of God suffered an agonizing death for us offenders. He offered His life as the payment to redeem us to God, to grant us forgiveness of sins, and to make a way for us to enter into the kingdom of God through the life He offers in Christ. Do you want to thank God for this sacrifice? Can you take a moment to appreciate the Lord Jesus for what He did for you? Thank You, Jesus, for suffering such a horrific death and shedding Your blood so I could be redeemed and forgiven by God.

THE BLOOD OF CHRIST: For Remission of Sins

   📖 *Matthew 26:26-28 NKJV*
"And as they were eating, Jesus took bread, blessed and broke it, and gave it to the disciples and said, 'Take, eat; this is My body.' Then He took the cup, and gave thanks, and gave it to them, saying, 'Drink from it, all of you. For this is My blood of the new covenant, which is shed for many for the remission of sins.'"

Remission is the discharge or relinquishment of a claim or right, the cancellation of a debt. It also has meanings of deliverance, liberty, forgiveness, and pardon. Jesus shed His blood so the debt we acquired from committing sins could be discharged, along with the accompanying punishment and claim the devil had over our lives in sin. As long as our sins were unpaid for, we could never be right with God and receive salvation from Him.

   📖 *Luke 24:46-47 NKJV*
"Then He said to them, 'Thus it is written, and thus it was necessary for the Christ to suffer and to rise from the dead the third day, and that repentance and remission of sins should be preached in His name to all nations, beginning at Jerusalem.'"

The Gospel requires repentance in order for sins to be remitted. A man must agree with God that he is a sinner and that Jesus shed His blood and died for his sins. This must happen before he can ever have his sins forgiven and receive the new life by the gift of the Holy Spirit.

   📖 *Acts 2:37-38 NKJV*
"Now when they heard this, they were cut to the heart, and said to Peter and the rest of the apostles, 'Men and brethren, what shall we do?' Then Peter said to them, 'Repent, and let every one of you be

baptized in the name of Jesus Christ for the remission of sins; and you shall receive the gift of the Holy Spirit.'"

Repentance and believing in Jesus are mandatory prerequisites for God to remit the sins of a man. The cancellation of the sin-debt hinges on repentance and faith toward God. There is no other way.

> 📖 **Hebrews 9:22 AMPC**
> *"[In fact] under the Law almost everything is purified by means of the blood, and without the shedding of blood there is neither release from sin and its guilt nor the remission of the due and merited punishment for sins."*

> *Repentance and believing in Jesus are mandatory prerequisites for God to remit the sins of a man. The cancellation of the sin-debt hinges on repentance and faith toward God. There is no other way.*

The sins we committed brought so many problems to our lives. The blood of Christ is God's provision to deal with them. Already we see that this glorious sacrifice of Jesus Christ (the blood He shed in His life offering) was for our redemption, for forgiveness of our sins, and for our sin-debt to be discharged and completely wiped out. No one can experience this freedom unless they come under the blood of Christ for God to apply these benefits to their life. When we came to Christ through repentance and faith toward God, then and only then, did God apply the blood of Christ on our behalf.

THE BLOOD OF CHRIST: A Life Sacrifice for Atonement

> 📖 **Leviticus 17:11 NKJV**
> *"For the life of the flesh is in the blood, and I have given it to you upon the altar to make atonement for your souls; for it is the blood that makes atonement for the soul."*

It is important to note the blood offering of Jesus was not just drops of blood that came from His body. The blood was the offering of His sinless, humble, and obedient life to God on our behalf. The life He lived on earth as a *Man* to save *man*kind. In the Old Testament, priests offered daily sacrifices of the blood of bulls and goats for the sins of the people. Each bull and goat lost its life for its blood to be applied to the sins of the people. But the problem is the blood of bulls and goats cannot take away sins permanently. It cannot deliver from the continual reminder of sins.

📖 ***Hebrews 10:3-4 NKJV***
"But in those sacrifices there is a reminder of sins every year. For it is not possible that the blood of bulls and goats could take away sins."
📖 ***Hebrews 10:11-12 GNT***
"Every Jewish priest performs his services every day and offers the same sacrifices many times; but these sacrifices can never take away sins. Christ, however, offered one sacrifice for sins, an offering that is effective forever, and then he sat down at the right side of God."

Before coming to Christ, we deserved to die because of our sins and because of our sinful nature which produced them. The wages of sin is death, and God would be perfectly just to make us pay the price for our sinful lives. However, in His great mercy and love, He decided to accept the life sacrifice of Jesus as the means to make atonement for our souls. It is not the blood of animals that takes away sins from a man's life, but the precious blood of Jesus Christ (a Man for man). His life was offered on our behalf; the just for the unjust, the righteous for the unrighteous, the holy for the unholy.

📖 ***Romans 5:8-11 NKJV***
"But God demonstrates His own love toward us, in that while we were still sinners, Christ died for us. Much more then, having now been justified by His blood, we shall be saved from wrath through Him. For if when we were enemies we were reconciled to God through the death of His Son, much more, having been reconciled, we shall be saved by His life. And not only that, but we also rejoice in God through our Lord Jesus Christ, through whom we have now received the reconciliation."

KJV *"by whom we have now received the atonement"*

> *It is not the blood of animals that takes away sins from a man's life, but the precious blood of Jesus Christ (a Man for man).*

We will see various words used in the Bible that mean similar things. Here we have King James using "atonement" and New King James using "reconciliation." *Atonement* is a purification and cleansing from sins that purifies us in order to enter the Lord's presence. It is a restoration to divine favor and access to God. Christ's atoning sacrifice purified my soul from sins and permitted me access to enter into the holiest place. Access to the presence of God is restricted to the sinful man because he is unholy—by virtue of the sin nature in him and the stain of the sins he has committed. His soul has been defiled by a life-time of sins, and he needs to be cleansed and purified in order to draw near to God. Jesus offered His pure life for our souls to be purified from our sins and to restore us to divine favor and access to God.

THE BLOOD OF CHRIST: That Brings Us Near And Gives Us Access To God

📖 *Ephesians 2:11-13 NKJV*
"Therefore remember that you, once Gentiles in the flesh- who are called Uncircumcision by what is called the Circumcision made in the flesh by hands- that at that time you were without Christ, being aliens from the commonwealth of Israel and strangers from the covenants of promise, having no hope and without God in the world. But now in Christ Jesus you who once were far off have been brought near by the blood of Christ."
📖 *Ephesians 2:13 TLB*
"But now you belong to Christ Jesus, and though you once were far away from God, now you have been brought very near to him because of what Jesus Christ has done for you with his blood."

If there is no blood to forgive and cleanse us from sin, we cannot approach God for help in our lives. He won't even hear what we have to say until our sins are dealt with and covered by the blood.

📖 **Psalm 66:18 NKJV**

"If I regard iniquity in my heart, the Lord will not hear."

📖 **Psalm 66:18 AMP**

"If I regard sin and baseness in my heart [that is, if I know it is there and do nothing about it], the Lord will not hear [me];"

📖 **John 9:31 NKJV**

"Now we know that God does not hear sinners; but if anyone is a worshiper of God and does His will, He hears him."

Sin always causes God to look away. Sin is a barrier between a person and God that can only be removed by repentance, confession, and the application of the blood. God is too holy to look upon sin, but the pure lifeblood of Christ is God's provision to deal with this problem that blocks our access. This is what Jesus Christ has done for you in shedding His blood. Without the blood we were far from God, but with the blood we have been brought very near to Him and have a new access to Him.

> *Sin is a barrier between a person and God that can only be removed by repentance, confession, and the application of the blood.*

📖 **Ephesians 2:17-19 AMPC**

"And He came and preached the glad tidings of peace to you who were afar off and [peace] to those who were near. For it is through Him that we both [whether far off or near] now have an introduction (access) by one [Holy] Spirit to the Father [so that we are able to approach Him]. Therefore you are no longer outsiders (exiles, migrants, and aliens, excluded from the rights of citizens), but you now share citizenship with the saints (God's own people, consecrated and set apart for Himself); and you belong to God's [own] household."

The blood of Jesus gives us an introduction to the Father. It makes the way for a true relationship with God possible. A man must pass through the blood of Christ before he can ever be right with and know God. He must pass through the blood, through the cross, and into the resurrection where he becomes born again of the Spirit of

God in him. Then he gains *ongoing* access to God by the blood and by the Spirit. This is the new and living way God has made for us.

📖 *Hebrews 10:16-22 NKJV*
"'This is the covenant that I will make with them after those days, says the LORD: I will put My laws into their hearts, and in their minds I will write them,' then He adds, 'Their sins and their lawless deeds I will remember no more.' Now where there is remission of these, there is no longer an offering for sin. Therefore, brethren, having boldness to enter the Holiest <u>by the blood of Jesus</u>, by a new and living way which He consecrated for us, through the veil, that is, His flesh, and having a High Priest over the house of God, let us draw near with a true heart in full assurance of faith, having our hearts sprinkled from an evil conscience and our bodies washed with pure water."

📖 *Hebrews 10:19-20 CEV*
"My friends, the blood of Jesus gives us courage to enter the most holy place by a new way that leads to life! And this way takes us through the curtain that is Christ himself."

> **Praise God that in His eternal purpose He provided us with the blood of Christ so we could have daily access to God through our faith in Him who gave His life for us.**

Jesus voluntarily left heaven to make a way for us to be redeemed and saved by God. The provision of His blood (His perfect life sacrifice) was the first part of that salvation in order to deal with the problem concerning our sins. Without the blood, we could never have access to God, and our knowledge of our sins would prohibit us from having any confidence to approach Him for any need in our life. Praise God that in His eternal purpose He provided us with the blood of Christ so we could have daily access to God through our faith in Him who gave His life for us.

📖 *Ephesians 3:11-12 AMP*
"This is in accordance with [the terms of] the eternal purpose which He carried out in Christ Jesus our Lord, in whom we have boldness and confident access through faith in Him [that is, our faith gives us

sufficient courage to freely and openly approach God through Christ]."

THE BLOOD OF CHRIST: For Being Reconciled To God

📖 *Romans 5:9-10 NKJV*
"*Much more then, having now been justified by His blood, we shall be saved from wrath through Him. For if when we were enemies we were reconciled to God through the death of his Son, much more, having been reconciled, we shall be saved by His life.*"

Reconciled is to be brought into friendship from a state of disagreement or enmity; to call back an enemy into union and friendship. Reconciliation is the restoring of friendly relations and right relationship with God.

📖 *Romans 5:9-10 AMPC*
"*Therefore, since we are now justified (acquitted, made righteous, and brought into right relationship with God) by Christ's blood, how much more [certain is it that] we shall be saved by Him from the indignation and wrath of God. For if while we were enemies we were reconciled to God through the death of His Son, it is much more [certain], now that we are reconciled, that we shall be saved (daily delivered from sin's dominion) through His [resurrection} life.*"

TLB "*what blessings he must have for us now that we are his friends and he is living within us*"
GNT "*Now that we are God's friends, how much more will we be saved by Christ's life*"

By the blood, God reconciles us back to Himself, delivers us from the disagreement (of sins) between us, and makes a way for us (who were His enemies) to become His friends through faith in Jesus Christ. The blood acquitted us (freed us from guilt), it made us righteous and restored us to a right relationship with God. This is the blood's assignment, and the power God has attributed to it. However, the blood itself was not His means to deliver us from the dominion of sin living in us (as a nature). The blood was applied to cleanse us from sins and pay the price for them, but what saves us from God's wrath and delivers us from being God's enemy is the cross, which puts to death the life in us that was hostile to God. The blood and the cross work hand-in-hand to bring us to the resurrection life of Christ, which saves us from within. Part of the blood's job was to restore us to friendly relations with God so we could receive the new life to come and live in us, by which we are saved ("having been reconciled, <u>we shall be saved by His life</u>"). We will study that in upcoming chapters, but now, let's note that the blood deals with the problem of *sins*, the cross with the problem of *sin*, and the resurrection is the solution of a *new life* coming to live in us, which God gives to those who repent and believe.

The blood acquitted us (freed us from guilt), it made us righteous and restored us to a right relationship with God. This is the blood's assignment, and the power God has attributed to it.

📖 **2 Corinthians 5:18 NKJV**
"Now all things are of God, who has reconciled us to Himself through Jesus Christ, and has given us the ministry of reconciliation,"

📖 **2 Corinthians 5:18 AMPC**
"But all things are from God, Who through Jesus Christ reconciled us to Himself [received us into favor, brought us into harmony with Himself] and gave to us the ministry of reconciliation [that by word and deed we might aim to bring others into harmony with Him]."

The wonderful gift of Christ we've received through faith in His death, burial, and resurrection, is completely by the grace of God. He is the One who sent Jesus. He is the One who devised the means by which we are reconciled back to Him to find favor with Him. He is the One who loved us so much He was willing to send His only begotten Son to die and pay the price for our sins. He did this so that we could become His eternal friends in Christ Jesus. The blood provision, and all its wonderful benefits, originates from the heart of God and reconciles us back to Him.

📖 *2 Chronicles 29:23-24 KJV*

"And they brought forth the he goats for the sin offering before the king and the congregation; and they laid their hands upon them: And the priests killed them, and they made reconciliation with their blood upon the altar, to make an atonement for all Israel: for the king commanded that the burnt offering and the sin offering should be made for all Israel."

> *Let's note that the blood deals with the problem of sins, the cross with the problem of sin, and the resurrection is the solution of a new life coming to live in us, which God gives to those who repent and believe.*

In the Old Testament, the blood of animals was shed as a sign showing God's solution for dealing with sins was through blood. Blood was shed to cleanse and restore (or maintain) the Israelites to friendly relations with God. Sins regularly disrupted that relationship, and the blood served to restore it. However, the life sacrifice of animals is insufficient to deal with sins permanently. Man sinned against God, and it requires a Man to make things right with God; to restore friendly relations. The blood of Christ's life offering was *without* blemish, holy, and perfect before God. It was the acceptable sacrifice for all who were *with* blemish, unholy, and imperfect. The Lamb of God offered His life, the life He lived on earth in humble submission and perfect obedience to His Father, as a sacrifice to reconcile all who would believe on Him back to God. Praise the Lord!

THE BLOOD OF CHRIST: For Peace With and From God

📖 *Colossians 1:19-22 NKJV*

"For it pleased the Father that in Him all the fullness should dwell, and by Him to reconcile all things to Himself, by Him, whether things on earth or things in heaven, having made peace through the blood of His cross. And you, who once were alienated and enemies in your mind by wicked works, yet now He has reconciled in the body of His flesh through death, to present you holy, and blameless, and above reproach in His sight-"

152

📖 *Colossians 1:20 AMPC*

"And God purposed that through (by the service, the intervention of) Him [the Son] all things should be completely reconciled back to Himself, whether on earth or in heaven, as through Him, [the Father] made peace <u>by means of the blood of His cross</u>."

We were children of wrath (enemies of God) by the nature we were born with and the sins we committed. By the intervention of Jesus Christ, the Father made a way for peace between mankind and Himself possible through the blood. God has purposed the blood component of the cross to be the means by which He offers peace to any and all who will believe on the work of Jesus Christ. Through faith the Father draws us to Himself, applies the blood to our wicked works, and grants us peace with Him, presenting us as holy, blameless, and above reproach in His sight.

> *By the intervention of Jesus Christ, the Father made a way for peace between mankind and Himself possible through the blood.*

📖 *Romans 5:1-2 NKJV*

"Therefore, having been justified by faith, we have peace with God through our Lord Jesus Christ, through whom also we have access by faith into this grace in which we stand, and rejoice in hope of the glory of God."

📖 *Romans 5:1-2 NLT*

"Therefore, since we have been made right in God's sight by faith, we have peace with God because of what Jesus Christ our Lord has done for us. Because of our faith, Christ has brought us into this place of undeserved privilege where we now stand, and we confidently and joyfully look forward to sharing God's glory."

God's approval comes by faith in Jesus Christ and what He has done. He located our peace in knowing Jesus and in being with Jesus. We must abide in Him and always remember it is by His finished work alone we are able to stand in the grace of God.

THE BLOOD OF CHRIST: Where Every Accusation Written Against Us Was Blotted Out

📖 *Revelation 12:10-11 NKJV*

"Then I heard a loud voice saying in heaven, 'Now salvation, and strength, and the kingdom of our God, and the power of His Christ have come, for the accuser of our brethren, who accused them before our God day and night, has been cast down. And they overcame him by the blood of the Lamb and by the word of their testimony, and they did not love their lives to the death."

Before coming to Christ, Satan always accused us day and night and we were continually guilty before God. There was nothing we could say, no excuse or defense we could present, because the life of sin we had was always producing sins, which were defiling us. The blood of Jesus came to blot out and wipe away those accusations so the devil would have no legal right to accuse us before God. The life sacrifice of Jesus on the cross at Calvary was the place where God nailed every accusation ever written against us and wiped it out.

📖 *Colossians 2:13-14 NKJV*

"And you, being dead in your trespasses and the uncircumcision of your flesh, He has made alive together with Him, having forgiven you all trespasses, having wiped out the handwriting of requirements that was against us, which was contrary to us. And He has taken it out of the way, having nailed it to the cross."

KJV "Blotting out the handwriting of ordinances that was against us"

Our old life in sin produced an extensive record of offenses toward God. These were compiled, written down, and meticulously noted as violations of the ordinances and law of God, contrary to His right-eous requirements. When God saw us, He saw this certificate of debt and the accusations binding us to judgment, the legal decrees against us constantly hanging over our heads. This was ammunition for the devil to accuse us before God. By means of the blood of Christ, when we believed, God blotted those violations out for our deliverance. *Blotted* means to render unreadable and make unrecoverable to identify. God, in His mercy and love, took the handwriting of ordinances that was against us and nailed it to the cross. When we came to Christ, He took the blood, which has power to completely blot out our record of sins, and He made those accusations unreadable, impossible to identify, and forever unrecoverable. He blotted out forever every ordinance against us and did away with it completely, never to be seen again.

> *Our old life in sin produced an extensive record of offenses toward God. These were compiled, written down, and meticulously noted as violations of the ordinances and law of God, contrary to His righteous requirements.*

📖 **Revelation 12:11a GNT**

"They won the victory over him by the blood of the Lamb and by the truth which they proclaimed;"

Our victory over the devil's accusations against us does not come by shouting or mustering up strength to try and fight him. Our victory is completely in the life offering of the Lamb of God on the cross. For we who have believed, every record of our sins, whether in heaven or hell, has been blotted out by the mighty power of the blood of Jesus Christ. Praise the Lord!

THE BLOOD OF CHRIST: For the Cleansing of Our Conscience

📖 *Hebrews 9:11-14 NKJV*

"But Christ came as High Priest of the good things to come, with the greater and more perfect tabernacle not made with hands, that is, not of this creation. Not with the blood of goats and calves, but with His own blood He entered the Most Holy Place once for all, having obtained eternal redemption. For if the blood of bulls and goats and the ashes of a heifer, sprinkling the unclean, sanctifies for the purifying of the flesh, how much more shall the blood of Christ, who through the eternal Spirit offered Himself without spot to God, cleanse your conscience from dead works to serve the living God?"

Conscience is a person's moral sense of right and wrong, acting as a guide for behavior. When we sin, our conscience is meant to alert us that what we are doing is wrong. The conscience is a gift from God to help serve as a warning of impending danger if we proceed in the direction we are headed. The more a person sins, the greater their conscience is seared, damaged, and defiled from its designed intention.

> *The conscience is a gift from God to help serve as a warning of impending danger if we proceed in the direction we are headed. The more a person sins, the greater their conscience is seared, damaged, and defiled from its designed intention.*

All unconfessed sins (dead works) come with memories, along with shame, guilt, and a heavy weight. If you try to serve God without repenting of sin, your conscience will always remind you of those things and it will hinder your ability to do so. The blood of Christ has power to cleanse your conscience from those dead works which releases you to serve God with a clean conscience.

📖 *Hebrews 9:14 NIV*
"How much more, then, will the blood of Christ, who through the eternal Spirit offered himself unblemished to God, cleanse our consciences from acts that lead to death, so that we may serve the living God!"

Cleanse means to purge or purify; the taking away of guilt that weighs heavily on the mind and burdens the sinner.

When you come to Christ, God applies the blood to your conscience and purifies you from the constant memory of things you did. The blood frees you to begin serving the living God in a new, lighter way. By the sacrifice of Christ, God purged and purified our conscience from the sinful deeds of the past, and through Christ, made a new way for us to worship and serve the living God.

156

THE BLOOD OF CHRIST: For Healing and Wholeness

📖 *1 Peter 2:24 NKJV*

"who Himself bore our sins in His own body on the tree, that we, having died to sins, might live for righteousness- by whose stripes you were healed."

📖 *1 Peter 2:24 AMP*

"He personally carried our sins in His body on the cross [willingly offering Himself on it, as on an altar of sacrifice], so that we might die to sin [becoming immune from the penalty and power of sin] and live for righteousness; for by His wounds you [who believe] have been healed."

You who believe have been healed because Jesus was wounded and shed His blood for you when He carried our sins in His body on the cross. *Healing* means to become sound or healthy again, to be made whole. What used to burden our hearts has been taken away, and the Bible says, "you were healed," not that you will be healed, but "you *were* healed." Listen to Jesus confirm that He came to heal.

📖 *Isaiah 61:1 NKJV*

"The Spirit of the Lord GOD is upon Me, because the LORD has anointed Me to preach good tidings to the poor; He has sent Me to heal the brokenhearted, to proclaim liberty to the captives, and the opening of the prison to those who are bound."

Jesus came to heal you, even of a broken heart. Mentally, emotionally, physically, and spiritually, you can be healed (made whole) right now if you will mix this word with faith in your heart; if you will agree with God that the shed blood of Jesus Christ brings you healing in the plan and purpose of God. Listen to Isaiah prophesy of Jesus, and what He went through for our healing.

📖 *Isaiah 53:5 NKJV*

"But He was wounded for our transgressions, He was bruised for our iniquities; the chastisement for our peace was upon Him, and by His stripes we are healed."

📖 *Isaiah 53:5 AMPC*

"But He was wounded for our transgressions, He was bruised for our guilt and iniquities; the chastisement [needful to obtain] peace and well-being for us was upon Him, and with the stripes [that wounded] Him we are healed and made whole."

When Jesus was wounded, He shed His blood. When He was bruised, He shed His blood. When Jesus was chastised, He shed His blood. When Jesus bore the stripes of whips with broken glass and sharp rocks, He shed His blood *for you*. By

Mentally, emotionally, physically, and spiritually, you can be healed (made whole) right now if you will mix this word with faith in your heart.

His blood you are healed and made whole. This is the work of God— His good means that is activated when you repent and believe on Jesus Christ.

📖 *Psalm 103:2-3 NKJV*

"Bless the LORD, O my soul, and forget not all His benefits: who forgives all your iniquities, who heals all your diseases,"

📖 *Psalm 103:3 AMPC*

"Who forgives [every one of] all your iniquities, Who heals [each one of] all your diseases."

Jesus bore all your sicknesses and all your diseases. Healing is one of the benefits God releases to us as we believe on Jesus and follow Him. The Bible says the word does not profit us unless it is mixed with faith in our hearts. I encourage you to believe God and take Him at His word. You will see Him be faithful to what He has promised through Jesus Christ as you cry out to Him.

📖 *Psalm 107:19-20 NKJV*

"Then they cried out to the LORD in their trouble, and He saved them out of their distresses. He sent His word and healed them, and delivered them from their destructions."

THE BLOOD OF CHRIST: That Washes Us From Our Sins

📖 *Revelation 1:4-5 NKJV*

"John, to the seven churches which are in Asia: Grace to you and peace from Him who is and who was and who is to come, and from the seven Spirits who are before His throne, and from Jesus Christ, the faithful witness, the firstborn from the dead, and the ruler over the kings of the earth. To Him who loved us and washed us from our sins in His own blood,"

The blood of Christ is powerful. Whenever applied, it completely cleanses every stain of sin. The way to receive this cleansing is to come to God, who is able and willing to wash us through faith in Jesus. Look at the invitation He gave to the children of Israel in the Old Testament. It is the same invitation He makes to you.

📖 *Isaiah 1:18 NKJV*

"'Come now, and let us reason together,' says the LORD, 'though your sins are like scarlet, they shall be as white as snow; though they are red like crimson, they shall be as wool.'"

📖 *Isaiah 1:16-18 GNT*

"'Wash yourselves clean. Stop all this evil that I see you doing. Yes, stop doing evil and learn to do right. See that justice is done- help those who are oppressed, give orphans their rights, and defend widows.' The Lord says, 'Now, let's settle the matter. You are stained red with sin, but I will wash you as clean as snow. Although your stains are deep red, you will be as white as wool.'"

That is what sin does; it leaves stains on the human soul that no amount of strength from a man can remove. Jesus says come to Him and His Father will apply the blood to every stain of sin on your life and completely remove it, as if it was never there.

The stain that sin produces can never be removed from the efforts of a man or woman. It is like doing laundry and dealing with a deep red stain on a white shirt. No matter what you do, there is evidence something happened to that shirt, and it left a stain that cannot be hidden. You may even throw the shirt away because the stain is so apparent and has ruined the shirt. That is what sin does; it leaves stains on the human soul that no amount of strength from a man can remove. Jesus says come to Him and His Father will apply the blood to every stain of sin on your life and completely remove it, as if it was never there. This is the power of the blood to wash us from all our sins, and there is no stain of sin that the blood of Christ cannot wash completely away.

THE BLOOD OF CHRIST: That Sanctifies Us and Continues to Sanctify Us

📖 *1 Corinthians 6:9-11 NKJV*
"Do you not know that the unrighteous will not inherit the kingdom of God? Do not be deceived. Neither fornicators, nor idolaters, nor adulterers, nor homosexuals, nor sodomites, nor thieves, nor covetous, nor drunkards, nor revilers, nor extortioners will inherit the kingdom of God. And such were some of you. But you were washed, but you were sanctified, but you were justified in the name of the Lord Jesus and by the Spirit of our God."

We were so filthy from the conduct of our old life and the sinful nature we were born with, which caused it to be so. Both would result in us *not* inheriting the kingdom of God. But by the blood of Jesus Christ and the Spirit of our God, we were sanctified.

📖 *Hebrews 13:12 NKJV*
"Therefore Jesus also, that he might sanctify the people with His own blood, suffered outside the gate."
📖 *Hebrews 13:12 AMPC*
"Therefore Jesus also suffered and died outside the [city's] gate in order that He might purify and consecrate the people through [the shedding of] His own blood and set them apart as holy [for God]."

Sanctify means to make holy and to purify from sin. It is to consecrate and set apart men as holy unto God. A man cannot offer himself as holy, nor can an animal be an acceptable sacrifice for the un-holiness of men. Only by the shed blood of Jesus Christ (and the holiness of His life offering) can one be made holy before God and receive the inheritance God is offering.

📖 **Acts 20:32 NKJV**
"So now, brethren, I commend you to God and to the word of His grace, which is able to build you up and give you an inheritance among all those who are sanctified."

AMPC *"to give you [your rightful] inheritance among all God's set apart ones (those consecrated, purified, and transformed of soul)."*

Our inheritance with God cannot be obtained until we are first forgiven and sanctified by the blood through faith in Jesus Christ.

Jesus bore the disgrace of the cross to sanctify us and set us apart as holy to God. Through His blood we have been made holy, purified, and conse-crated unto God. When we believed, God completely cleansed us and set us apart in order to know Him. Our inheritance with God cannot be obtained until we are first forgiven and sanctified by the blood through faith in Jesus Christ.

📖 **Acts 26:18 NKJV**
"to open their eyes, in order to turn them from darkness to light, and from the power of Satan to God, that they may receive forgiveness of sins and an inheritance among those who are sanctified by faith in Me."

THE BLOOD OF CHRIST: For Our Justification

📖 **Job 25:4-6 NKJV**
"How then can man be righteous before God? Or how can he be pure who is born of a woman? If even the moon does not shine, and the stars are not pure in His sight, how much less man, who is a maggot, and the son of man, who is a worm?"

Justification is where God accepts us as righteous on account of the merits of the Savior. He regards us as *just* and pardons and clears us from all guilt. The blood justifies us and makes us innocent.

📖 *Job 25:4-6 CEV*
"How can anyone be innocent in the sight of God? To him, not even the light of the moon and stars can ever be pure. So how can we humans, when we are merely worms?"

No one can justify themselves or declare themselves innocent before God. In this passage, God relates people who are still in their sin to maggots and worms. Man has no strength or power to clear himself from the guilt of his sin. The sin nature produces sins which make a man guilty, impure, and unclean. There is no righteousness in anyone who is born of a woman. There must be another way by which we can be justified and considered righteous before God. The blood of Christ was God's devised means to make us right with Him, declare us innocent from the guilt of our sins, and make a way for the provisions of the cross and resurrection to be applied to our lives; for us to be saved.

> *Justification is where God accepts us as righteous on account of the merits of the Savior. He regards us as just and pardons and clears us from all guilt.*

📖 *Romans 5:8-10 NKJV*
"But God demonstrates His own love toward us, in that while we were still sinners, Christ died for us. Much more then, having now been justified by His blood, we shall be saved from wrath through Him. For if when we were enemies we were reconciled to God through the death of His Son, much more, having been reconciled, we shall be saved by His life."

📖 *Romans 5:9 TLB*
"And since by his blood he did all this for us as sinners, how much more will he do for us now that he has declared us not guilty? Now he will save us from all of God's wrath to come."

It is God's love that compelled Him to leave heaven and endure the gruesome death of the cross. From that love, Christ sacrificed His life's blood for us to be accepted by God. God's love was greater than the truth that we were His enemies, by nature, and guilty before Him. The blood of Christ justifies us and absolves us from every violation of God's law. Praise God for the blood!

📖 *Acts 13:38-39 AMPC*

"So let it be clearly known and understood by you, brethren, that through this Man forgiveness and removal of sins is now proclaimed to you; and that through Him everyone who believes [who acknowledges Jesus as his Savior and devotes himself to Him] is absolved (cleared and freed) from every charge from which he could not be justified and freed by the Law of Moses and given right standing with God."

By the offering and sacrifice of the life of Christ we are justified in all things before God. God cleared us and freed us from every charge by the blood of Jesus. Now He expects us to devote ourselves to Jesus—who redeemed, cleansed, sanctified, and justified us—and walk with Him according to our Father's will.

THE BLOOD OF CHRIST: For Purchasing the Church of God

📖 *Acts 20:28 NKJV*

"Therefore take heed to yourselves and to all the flock, among which the Holy Spirit has made you overseers, to shepherd the church of God which He purchased with His own blood."

AMPC *"which He obtained for Himself [buying it and saving it for Himself] with His own blood"*
GNT *"which he made his own through the blood of his Son"*

You are now a member of the church of God which He purchased with the blood of His Son. You were bought and saved for Him, for His good pleasure, and for His will to be done in and through Christ in you. Will you agree with God that you belong to Him? Can you ask

Him to help you learn to walk with Jesus and devote yourself to Him fully? If you ask Him, He will help you because He is heavily invested in you now. His Son shed His blood in order to acquire you and bring you back to Himself, for His glory and for your good. Praise Him who bought us with the price of the precious blood of Christ Jesus! Praise God who has given so many wonderful benefits to our lives through the provision of the sacrifice of His Son.

THE BLOOD OF CHRIST: As An Ongoing Provision for Cleansing From Sin

📖 *1 John 1:5-10 NKJV*

"This is the message which we have heard from Him and declare to you, that God is light and in Him is no darkness at all. If we say that we have fellowship with Him, and walk in darkness, we lie and do not practice the truth. But if we walk in the light as He is in the light, we have fellowship with one another, and <u>the blood of Jesus Christ His Son cleanses us from all sin</u>. If we say that we have no sin, we deceive ourselves, and the truth is not in us. If we confess our sins, He is faithful and just to forgive us our sins and to cleanse us from all unrighteousness. If we say that we have not sinned, we make Him a liar, and His word is not in us."

While the blood of Christ initially cleansed us from all our sins when we first believed, it also serves as an ongoing provision for cleansing to those who walk with the Lord Jesus according to God's truth. The blood functions as an ever-present cleansing agent as we walk with Jesus and are being progressively conformed to His image. The context of these verses is in light of an ongoing relationship with Jesus, looking unto Him, handling Him, listening to and obeying Him, and living and moving with Him in the light. As we are now in a process of growing up into Him and learning how to walk with Him apart from sin, The goal is

> **The blood functions as an ever-present cleansing agent as we walk with Jesus and are being progressively conformed to His image.**

unbroken fellowship and continued obedience. It is never God's desire for us to sin.

📖 **1 John 2:1-2 NKJV**
"My little children, these things I write to you, <u>so that you may not sin</u>. And if anyone sins, we have an Advocate with the Father, Jesus Christ the righteous. And He Himself is the propitiation for our sins, and not for ours only but also for the whole world."

As we learn Christ and grow, we make mistakes along the way which will require immediate attention before God. Jesus is our Advocate with the Father, and the blood of Christ is God's ongoing provision to cleanse us, heal us, and make us right with Him. If our heart departs and we disobey Him, we separate ourselves from Him and wound ourselves by committing sin. Sin always wages war against the soul and brings damage to our progress with God.

> *As we are now in a process of growing up into Him and learning how to walk with Him apart from sin, The goal is unbroken fellowship and continued obedience. It is never God's desire for us to sin.*

📖 **1 Peter 2:11 NIV**
"Dear friends, I urge you, as foreigners and exiles, to abstain from sinful desires, which wage war against your soul."

📖 **1 Peter 2:11 AMP**
"Beloved, I urge you as aliens and strangers [in this world] to abstain from the sensual urges [those dishonorable desires] that wage war against the soul."

Sin is dishonorable; it tears apart and cuts the heart. Sin wounds, infects, and attacks the soul, leaving damage in need of repair. I heard a dear Christian brother put it this way, the blood (as an ongoing provision for cleansing from sin) is like a hospital. You have a hospital in your city that is always open, is always available and has the best physician for you to go to if you get hurt or sick. You are grateful for access to the hospital and for its help to restore you when needed. You appreciate the presence of the hospital, and it gives you a sense of security knowing it is there. But I don't know anyone who says, "I really like going to the hospital," or "I would really like to spend most of my life in the hospital." The sane person wants to avoid having to make trips to the hospital on a regular basis. While grateful for the provision, their best-case scenario would be to remain hospital free. They don't want to spend their life in and out of the hospital.

In God's provision of the blood of Christ, we have a hospital always available to run into if we need it; our bills are prepaid by the blood. In that hospital, we can be cleansed and healed from the wounding, defilement, and infection of sin, and restored to fellowship with God. Our soul can be repaired from the damage it incurs when we depart from the Lord and engage in unrighteousness. The hospital aspect (of the blood) repairs us and our fellowship with the Lord, but only *if* we need it, come to it, and confess to the Physician what we have done to warrant another visit.

📖 *1 John 1:6-7 AMPC*

"[So] if we say we are partakers together and enjoy fellowship with Him when we live and move and are walking about in darkness, we are [both] speaking falsely and do not live and practice the Truth [which the Gospel presents]. But if we [really] are living and walking in the Light, as He [Himself] is in the Light, we have [true, unbroken] fellowship with one another, and the blood of Jesus Christ His Son cleanses (removes) us from all sin and guilt [keeps us cleansed from sin in all its forms and manifestations]."

> **Our soul can be repaired from the damage it incurs when we depart from the Lord and engage in unrighteousness.**

As we walk with God the Father and the Lord Jesus Christ, we must confess our sins to Him immediately, bringing them under the blood (i.e. entering the hospital). If we do, He will cleanse us, forgive our sins, heal us, and purify us from all unrighteousness with Christ's blood. He will remove from us all sin and all its forms and manifestations and restore true, unbroken fellowship with Him. It is not God's desire for us to always be in and out of the hospital. The next chapters will reveal God's provision of the cross and resurrection of Christ as His means to deliver us from the power of sin, and to help us not make the hospital our regular dwelling place. For now, we will rejoice and give God praise for the blood of Christ, which is always available to us for cleansing as we learn to walk with Jesus and continue in His word obediently.

THE BLOOD OF CHRIST: As An Ongoing Covering for Fellowship with God While He Works Out Our Salvation

📖 *Philippians 2:12-13 NKJV*
"Therefore, my beloved, as you have always obeyed, not as in my presence only, but now much more in my absence, work out your own salvation with fear and trembling; <u>for it is God who works in you</u> both to will and to do for His good pleasure."

The blood is God's covering provision for us to maintain fellowship with Him while He works out our salvation from within. The blood covers us as we abide in Jesus, and it allows a holy God to work on unholy people. As newborn babes in Christ, we have many old appetites, desires, impulses, urges, and ways of thinking that are displeasing to Him. The blood acts as a covering for God to look at those things through the sacrifice of Christ.

For example, some newborn babies are put in incubators that have hand holes in the side to handle the baby. An incubator, in part, is an enclosure in which conditions can be regulated for optimal growth, and through which human hands can reach to interact with the baby. In a sense, that is what the blood of Jesus does for us in allowing us to interact with God, and God to interact with us. Christ's blood covers us and encloses us in God's covering mercy so He can stretch forth His hands to fashion, feed, and grow us according to His good purpose and for His glory. The offering of the sinless life of Jesus (our great High Priest) gives us access to ongoing fellowship with God, in His presence, so we can find help for our lives.

📖 *Hebrews 4:14-16 NKJV*

"Seeing then that we have a great High Priest who has passed through the heavens, Jesus the Son of God, let us hold fast our confession. For we do not have a High Priest who cannot sympathize with our weaknesses, but was in all points tempted as we are, yet without sin. Let us therefore come boldly to the throne of grace, that we may obtain mercy and find grace to help in time of need."

📖 *Hebrews 10:19-20 NKJV*

"Therefore, brethren, having boldness to enter the Holiest by the blood of Jesus, by a new and living way which He consecrated for us, through the veil, that is, His flesh,"

The blood Christ shed allows intimate fellowship with God and makes way for Him to do His will in our life. Our everyday access to Him and entrance into His presence, is only by the blood of Jesus our High Priest. It is not because we have amassed many days, weeks, months, or years of continued obedience that gives us access into the Holiest, but by the blood of Christ alone. The blood of Jesus acts as a continual covering over us (as we abide in Him) and keeps us right with God, giving us intimate access to Him for the working out of our salvation. If a Christian chooses to sin and allow his heart to depart from Christ, he will be dwelling in the place where sin abounds and find himself defiled by the life he is choosing to live. He left the covering of the blood and made himself vulnerable. The blood then serves as a provision available for cleansing him from the stain of his sins, granting forgiveness and reconciliation toward God, and bringing him back into the possibility of continued fellowship with the Lord. However, that is only true if he humbles himself before the Lord, confesses and forsakes his sin, repents, and turns back to God.

> **It is not because we have amassed many days, weeks, months, or years of continued obedience that gives us access into the Holiest, but by the blood of Christ alone.**

The in and out life is not God's design for us. He wants us to learn to abide in Christ regularly. The blood is in place to help us when we go astray while He is working out our salvation. However, there is a limit to the God-given assignment of the blood. While there is no stain or guilt of sin that cannot be forgiven, blotted out, and covered by the blood, there is one thing the blood provision is not designed to deal with—the sinful nature of man.

📖 *Hebrews 9:22 NKJV*
"And according to the law <u>almost all things</u> are purified with blood, and without shedding of blood there is no remission."

📖 *Hebrews 9:22 AMP*
"In fact under the Law <u>almost everything</u> is cleansed with blood, and without the shedding of blood there is no forgiveness [neither release from sin and its guilt, nor cancellation of the merited punishment]."

In this chapter, the Holy Spirit helped us see (in the word of God) many benefits of the blood of Christ. But, by God's design, as wonderful as the blood of Christ is in dealing with sins, it is not His ultimate solution for dealing with the problem of sin living within us that produces those sins. The life and nature we were born with is beyond cleansing, it's too sick to be healed, and requires

> *The in and out life is not God's design for us. He wants us to learn to abide in Christ regularly.*

death, removal, and replacement. That provision is given to us in the means of the cross and resurrection of Christ. The Good News of the Gospel of God is what He has done through the *blood*, *cross*, and *resurrection* of Jesus Christ. One aspect cannot exist without the other and each has a particular purpose for our deliverance and salvation. The blood of Christ's life offering deals with sins and their effects. It prepares the way for the ministry of the cross to deal with the nature of sin that caused those sins. The cross opens the door and makes space for the resurrection provision of Christ to come and dwell in us. So, before we proceed to look at the cross of Christ more intently, let us give thanks to God for devising and revealing to us the glory of the blood of Jesus, which He shed for us.

Father God, we thank You for Your great faithfulness and what You have done in sending Your Son to shed His blood for us. We want to appreciate You for Your mercy and kindness toward us in Christ, and for all the benefits of the blood of Christ. And Lord Jesus, we praise You and give God all the glory for what You have done for us by Your selfless sacrifice to rescue us from sin. Thank You, Lord. Now Father, as we proceed, please keep opening our eyes of understanding to see Jesus Christ and Him crucified, and to understand what that means for our new life in Him. Thank You for hearing our prayer, for we are making our requests known to You in the name of Jesus Christ. Amen.

THE CROSS OF JESUS CHRIST

W e ended the last chapter hearing the word of God say, "according to the law <u>almost</u> all things are purified with blood." The law, as good as it is, cannot deal with the issue of sin living *within* a person, which commits sins that violate God's law. The sin nature refuses to comply with God's law and renders all law weak in its ability to stop sin. Neither has the blood of Christ alone been assigned the God-given task to deal with the sin nature (but the products it produces). As we begin to look at God's provision of the cross of Christ, let's briefly reinforce this truth with a Scripture from the book of Romans.

📖 ***Romans 8:3 NKJV***
"For what the law could not do in that it was weak through the flesh, God did by sending His own Son in the likeness of sinful flesh, on account of sin: he condemned sin in the flesh,"
📖 ***Romans 8:3 AMP***
"For what the Law could not do [that is, overcome sin and remove its penalty, its power] being weakened by the flesh [man's nature with-

out the Holy Spirit}, God did: He sent His own Son in the likeness of sinful man as an offering for sin. And He condemned sin in the flesh [subdued it and overcame it in the person of His own Son],"

The Law was not able to restrain the sinful nature of man. Sin does not submit to the Law because he is an enemy of God. Sin only wants to protect himself and do what is right in his own eyes. For example, imagine two men (who carry the sinful nature) are plotting to rob a bank. One morning they grab their weapons, put on dark clothes and masks to hide their faces, and approach the bank in their car. As they get within eyesight of their target, they notice two police cars parked in front of the bank, so they quickly decide not to rob it. Let me ask you, did they decide not to rob the bank because that was God's will for their life and the right thing to do? Of course not! They didn't want to get caught or go to jail, so they only suspended their desire to rob the bank and delayed it until a more opportune time. The presence of the law merely dissuaded them from carrying out their sinful desires, but it did *not* deliver them from sin inside that greedily compelled them to do it. The cross is God's devised means to deal with that sin nature. It is the instrument He uses to release His power to fully deliver us from sin.

The cross is that which connects the blood and the resurrection. One flows into it, the other flows out of it.

📖 *1 Corinthians 1:18 NKJV*

"For the message of the cross is foolishness to those who are perishing, but to us who are being saved it is the power of God."

The cross is that which connects the blood and the resurrection. One flows into it, the other flows out of it. The cross is the place where everything changes in a person's life because it is what God uses to deal with the sin nature in man. For us, the only solution for that corrupted life is to condemn it to death and take it away so a new one can come. The blood is God's means to deal with all the transgressions and consequences of violating His law, but it does not deal with the life inside that readily disobeys it. At the cross, Jesus did what the

Law could not do by condemning that nature to death in His body. He subdued and condemned sin in His body in order to free us from bondage to sin. He crucified our old man.

📖 *Romans 6:6-7 NKJV*
"knowing this, that <u>our old man was crucified</u> with Him, that the body of sin might be done away with, <u>that we should no longer be slaves of sin. For he who has died has been freed from sin.</u>"

When Jesus died on the cross, our old man was crucified with Him. He did this so we would no longer be slaves of sin. And for us who have believed, He has indeed freed us from sin. The Bible doesn't say we are in the process of being freed from sin, but that we HAVE BEEN freed from sin. We will now explore the glory of the cross of Christ to better understand the depths of the greatness of the sacrifice Jesus made for our deliverance and freedom.

📖 *John 15:13 NKJV*
"Greater love has no one than this, than to lay down one's life for his friends."

📖 *Isaiah 53:3 AMPC*
"He was despised and rejected and forsaken by men, a Man of sorrows and pains, and acquainted with grief and sickness; and like One from Whom men hide their faces He was despised, and we did not appreciate His worth or have any esteem for Him."

> **The cross is the greatest expression of love because Jesus gave up His life so we could live. We understand He did that for us, but I wonder if we fully comprehend everything His sacrifice involved.**

The cross is the greatest expression of love because Jesus gave up *His* life so we could live. We understand He did that for us, but I wonder if we fully comprehend everything His sacrifice involved. As we press on, let us again ask God to open our eyes to see, know, and understand the mystery of the cross. Lord God, please give us revelation that causes us to esteem and appreciate the worth of Jesus Christ and Him crucified.

DEATH HAS OCCURRED

As we look, the first thing to establish is that a death has occurred. We will soon dig into the intent and purpose of that death and the means by which God achieved it, but for now, let's prove from the Scriptures *what* died at Calvary in the body of Jesus.

📖 *Galatians 2:20 NKJV*
"*I have been crucified* with Christ; *it is no longer I who live*, but Christ lives in me; and the life which I now live in the flesh I live by faith in the Son of God, who loved me and gave Himself for me."
📖 *Galatians 2:20 AMPC*
"*I have been crucified* with Christ [in Him I have shared His crucifixion]; it is no longer I who live, but Christ (the Messiah) lives in me; and the life I now live in the body I live by faith in (by adherence to and reliance on and complete trust in) the Son of God, Who loved me and gave Himself up for me."
📖 *Galatians 2:19b-20a GNT*
"*I have been put to death* with Christ on his cross, so that it is no longer I who live, but it is Christ who lives in me."

> **You died! According to the word of God, you HAVE BEEN put to death with Christ on His cross.**

You died! According to the word of God, you HAVE BEEN put to death with Christ on His cross. You WERE crucified with Christ and Christ is now the One living in you. Do you clearly see this death and new life in these verses? I have been crucified with Christ. That means I died with Him on His cross and I no longer live. Yet, the Bible says, "the life that I now live," which means I have a new life that I'm living. You may not fully see or grasp it yet, but the word says, "it is no longer I who live, but Christ lives in me." I died and have a new life! Let's see what else the Bible says to help us understand.

📖 *Galatians 5:24-25 NKJV*
"*And those who are Christ's have crucified the flesh* with its passions and desires. If we live in the Spirit, let us also walk in the Spirit."

📖 *Galatians 5:24-25 GNT*

"And those who belong to Christ Jesus <u>have put to death their human nature</u> with all its passions and desires. The Spirit has given us life; he must also control our lives."

📖 *Galatians 5:24 AMP*

"And those who belong to Christ Jesus <u>have crucified the sinful nature</u> together with its passions and appetites."

> *You are not dying to your sinful nature (the flesh), but it HAS BEEN crucified and already put to death. The past tense is clear, and we need to believe God and take Him at His word.*

Now we are seeing that our death, on the cross with Christ, had something to do with our sinful, human nature. Take note that the word says, "have crucified" and "have put to death." You are not dying to your sinful nature (the flesh), but it HAS BEEN crucified and already put to death. The past tense is clear, and we need to believe God and take Him at His word. We also see here that the *flesh* is the same as the *human* nature, which is the same as the *sinful* nature. Though "flesh" can be referring to our body in the Bible, this verse is referring to it as the sinful nature. At the cross, our flesh, along with all its passions and desires, was crucified in the body of Christ. We now belong to Christ; it is His Spirit that lives in us. We are to learn to let Him control our new lives in Christ Jesus, setting our minds on Him.

📖 *Colossians 3:2-4 NKJV*

"Set your mind on things above, not on things on the earth. <u>For you died,</u> and your life is hidden with Christ in God. When Christ who is our life appears, then you also will appear with Him in glory."

📖 *Colossians 3:3 KJV*

"<u>For ye are dead</u>, and your life is hid with Christ in God."

You are dead, you died, you have died, declares the word of God. It is not that Christ is WITH our life, but Christ now IS our life. The blood paid the price and cleansed us from the activities of our old life. The cross brought about the death of our sinful nature (our old man, the flesh) which produced those sins. The resurrection brought in the

New Man (Christ's very life), and now we are to keep our minds fixed on Him in a growing relationship with Him. The reason we now set our minds on Him is because we died. Did you see that? The word said, "set your mind on things above, not on things on the earth." Then it gave the reason, "*for* you died," or because you died. The word "for" is the same as saying "because," giving us the *why* for setting our minds on Him who now lives in us.

   📖 *Colossians 3:9-11 NKJV*
"Do not lie to one another, <u>since you have put off the old man</u> with his deeds, and have put on the new man who is renewed in know-ledge according to the image of Him who created him, where there is neither Greek nor Jew, circumcised nor uncircumcised, barbarian, Scythian, slave nor free, but Christ is all and in all."

We don't lie to each other, SINCE we have put off the old man. Christ in us will never lie. By being included in Christ and Him crucified, our old man has been put off, and we have been clothed with a new life (Christ in me, and I in Christ)—the *new creation* man. My new life is hidden with Christ in God. This new life will grow fuller in knowing Him and being conformed to His image in every way as I walk with Him. I am now in the process of being renewed and re-molded into the likeness of Him who created me.

> *This new life is not measured by where you are from, what you do for work, your skin color, or your education, but by Christ and Christ alone living in you.*

📖 *Colossians 3:9-11 TLB*
"Don't tell lies to each other; it was <u>your old life</u> with all its wickedness that did that sort of thing; <u>now it is dead and gone</u>. You are living a brand new kind of life that is continually learning more and more of what is right, and trying constantly to be more and more like Christ who created this new life within you. In this new life one's nationality or race or education or social position is unimpor-tant; such things mean nothing. Whether a person has Christ is what matters, and he is equally available to all."

Your old life is dead and gone, and you are living a brand-new kind of life. This new life is not measured by where you are from, what you do for work, your skin color, or your education, but by Christ and Christ alone living in you. We are just establishing that a death has occurred in the body of Christ on the cross. We will soon learn how to walk and grow in this new life God has given us in Him. We will learn to walk in the freedom He secured for us when He crucified our sinful nature at Calvary. The cross is God's means to deliver a fatal blow to our old nature. This was so we could receive His new nature and a new life from Him.

📖 *Colossians 3:9-10 RSV*
"Do not lie to one another, seeing <u>that you have put off the old nature</u> with its practices and have put on the new nature, which is being renewed in knowledge after the image of its creator."

Christ crucified our old nature in His body on the cross. Death HAS occurred, and that is good news! He put to death the sin nature that produced sins and spoiled the bodies God originally created for His own purpose. The cross was not an accident or afterthought. It was always God's intentional design, from the foundation of the world, to redeem and deliver fallen man from sin. I believe it is critical to see what God was devising and intending to do when He came up with the idea of the cross to be the means for our deliverance from the sin nature. Let's spend some time allowing the Scriptures, and the Holy Spirit, to bear witness of the primary reason and function of the cross of Jesus Christ.

GOD'S INTENTION AND PURPOSE FOR THE CROSS

Intention is an aim or plan in the mind; a conception formed by directing the mind towards an object. *Purpose* is the reason for which something is done or created; to design for a particular use. When sin entered the world, God aimed His concentration towards this problem, which banished His people from His presence and condemned them to death and eternal separation from Him. He conceived in His mind, by reason of His love and goodness, a multi-faceted plan to deliver mankind from sin (and its activities and consequences), which now dwelled in them. He deliberately devised and crafted a hidden wisdom for every instrument of His deliverance. He formed a plan to rescue and restore mankind from the grips of sin and its evil hold on them. The cross was God's idea, and its particular use was to terminate and remove the sinful nature that plagues everyone born of the flesh. Jesus came to *take away* the sin of the world.

> 📖 *John 1:29 NKJV*
> "The next day John saw Jesus coming toward him, and said, 'Behold! The Lamb of God who <u>takes away the sin</u> of the world!'"

> *The cross was God's idea, and its particular use was to terminate and remove the sinful nature that plagues everyone born of the flesh.*

Take note it says He takes away the "sin" of the world. It is the **sin** (life in man) that produces the **sins** (activities of man). To take away only the sins, and not the producer of the sins, would result in more sins being produced. Thus, a life without victory over sin and continual separation from the presence of God. It is not accidental God uses the word "sin" to describe His purpose for sending the Lamb of God to the cross. To take away something is to remove it from where it is and deprive it of its effect in its previous location. *Take away* means removed and no longer available for use. The purpose of the cross was to take away the sin of the world by means of death, and to remove it and make it no longer available for use.

> 📖 *Romans 6:6-7 NKJV*
> "knowing this, that <u>our old man was crucified</u> with Him, <u>that the body of sin might be done away with</u>, that we should no longer be slaves of sin. For he who has died has been freed from sin."

> 📖 *Romans 6:6 KJV*
> "Knowing this, that our old man is crucified with him, <u>that the body of sin might be destroyed</u>, that henceforth we should not serve sin."

The word "that" is the same as saying "so that" or "in order that." Like if I say, "I withdrew $100 from the bank today THAT I may go and buy a new pair of shoes." The reason I withdrew money out of the bank was *in order that* I could buy some new shoes. Previously, we saw that our old man was crucified with Him THAT we should no longer be slaves of sin. Now we see, in the same verses, the old man was crucified in the body of Christ, SO THAT the body of sin might be destroyed and done away

The purpose of the cross was to take away the sin of the world by means of death, and to remove it and make it no longer available for use.

with. Do you see it? By means of the cross, we were freed from the power of sin (the life we were joined to) which enslaved us and produced sins and unrighteousness in and through us. The entire body of sin was destroyed at Calvary. Its very nature and all its passions and desires were done away with at the cross of Christ. This reality was activated on your behalf when you repented and believed on the Lord Jesus Christ, thanks be to God. Already in the passages we have read, we consistently see God's intention for the cross was to deal with the problem of sin in man. He sent Jesus to take away sin, to put to death and put away sin, and to have sin done away with and destroyed. Let's continue to explore.

📖 *Hebrews 10:4-10 NKJV*

"For it is not possible that the blood of bulls and goats could take away sins. Therefore, when He came into the world, He said; 'Sacrifice and offering You did not desire, but a body You have prepared for Me. In burnt offerings and sacrifices for sin You had no pleasure. Then I said, 'Behold, I have come- in the volume of the book it is written of Me- to do Your will, O God.' Previously saying, 'Sacrifice and offering, burnt offerings, and offerings for sin You did not desire, nor had pleasure in them' (which are offered according to the law), then He said, 'Behold, I have come to do Your will, O God.' He takes away the first that He may establish the second. By that will we have been sanctified through the offering of the body of Jesus Christ once for all."

179

> **He prepared a body for His Son to crucify and take away the first nature we were born with, so He could establish the second nature we can be reborn with through faith in Jesus Christ.**

Jesus Christ came to do the will of God, which was to deal with and take away the first life we were born with, in order that the second life can be established. Did you see the will and intention of the Father? Jesus shed His blood as the payment for our sins. The offering of the sinless life He lived on earth, as a Man, in total subjection and complete obedience to His Father. However, the blood was not designed or intended to put to death and remove the sin nature in man. The flesh (sin nature) that constantly produced those sins would keep doing so even after sins are forgiven. God devised the cross as His means for Jesus to become the final offering for sin. He prepared a body for His Son to crucify and take away the first nature we were born with, so He could establish the second nature we can be reborn with through faith in Jesus Christ. He actually appeared for the very purpose and intention of putting away sin forever.

📖 *Hebrews 9:24-28 NKJV*
"For Christ has not entered the holy places made with hands, which are copies of the true, but into heaven itself, now to appear in the presence of God for us; not that He should offer Himself often, as the high priest enters the Most Holy Place every year with blood of another- He then would have had to suffer often since the foundation of the world; but now, once at the end of the ages, He has appeared to put away sin by the sacrifice of Himself. And as it is appointed for men to die once, but after this the judgment, so Christ was offered once to bear the sins of many. To those who eagerly wait for Him He will appear a second time, apart from sin, for salvation."

Here is another passage using both sin and sins in what Christ accomplished for us. He appeared to put away sin in His body. His blood was the means to deal with our sins, but Jesus appeared and went to the cross for the purpose of putting away *sin* by the sacrifice of Himself. To "put away" is similar to the language of "take away", but let's look at some other versions to get a better idea of what it means.

GNT *"he has appeared once and for all, to remove sin"*
TLB *"to put away the power of sin forever by dying for us"*
AMPC *"appeared to put away and abolish sin by His sacrifice"*
CEV *"so he could be a sacrifice that does away with sin"*
MSG *"the final solution of sin"*

Putting away is final and definite. This was the intention and purpose of the cross as designed by our Father in heaven. Jesus came to suffer the death of the cross for this very reason. It is a permanent abolishing and removal that does away with the power of sin forever. It is the place where we were crucified with Christ.

📖 *1 Peter 2:24 AMP*
*"He personally carried our sins in His body on the cross [willingly offering Himself on it, as on an altar of sacrifice], **so that** we might die to sin [becoming immune from the penalty and power of sin] and live for righteousness; for by His wounds you [who believe] have been healed."*

The cross was God's intended means and final solution for the problem of sin in man. All who repent and turn to God, believing on the Lord Jesus Christ, are sanctified by God through the offering of Christ. The *blood* of Christ sanctifies and brings forgiveness, and the *cross* of Christ (where we died to sin) frees us from the old man (the flesh, the sinful nature). This work of the cross opens the door (makes way) for God's means of the resurrection provision of *Christ in us* to become our new life. God designed the cross to be the instrument by which He does away with the sin nature, the entire body of its works, and to release us from the power of sin.

📖 *Romans 6:6-7 AMPC*
"We know that our old (unrenewed) self was nailed to the cross with Him in order that [our] body [which is the instrument] of sin might be made ineffective and inactive for evil, that we might no longer be the

slaves of sin. For when a man dies, he is freed (loosed, delivered) from [the power of] sin [among men]."

Our body, of itself, is not sinful; it's just an earthen vessel. The body is a container used by whatever life dwells in it. The purpose of the cross was to crucify the old life we were born with; the life that defiled our bodies by its activities and ways of living. We were slaves to sin living in us. Sin used our bodies to make us effective and active for evil and everything that is contrary to the knowledge of God. God created the body to be inhabited by the life *He* breathed into it. But it was corrupted by the life of sin that came in at the disobedience of Adam. When sin entered the world, we became slaves to that nature. The work of the cross, however, crucified us and set us free. We died with Christ, and now He lives in us, and we live by Him. Hallelujah!

> **God designed the cross to be the instrument by which He does away with the sin nature, the entire body of its works, and to release us from the power of sin.**

📖 **Romans 6:6-8 NLT**
"We know that our old sinful selves were crucified with Christ so that sin might lose its power in our lives. We are no longer slaves to sin. For when we died with Christ <u>we were set free</u> from the power of sin. And since we died with Christ, we know we will also live with him."

📖 **Romans 6:6-7 JBP**
*"Let us never forget that our old selves died with him on the cross **that** the tyranny of sin over us might be broken- for a dead man can safely be said to be immune to the power of sin"*

Have you died with Christ, or does sin still exercise its tyranny over you from within? You will know if you have experienced the death of the cross, if sin no longer has dominion over your life. This is because a dead man can safely be said to be immune to the power of sin. Jesus was crucified to cause our relationship with sin, and its tyranny over us, to be broken forever.

📖 **Romans 6:10 NLT**

"When he died, he died once <u>to break the power of sin</u>. But now that he lives, he lives for the glory of God."

📖 **Romans 6:10 AMPC**

"For by the death He died, He died to sin [ending His relation to it] once for all; and the life that He lives, He is living to God [in unbroken fellow-ship with Him]."

> **You will know if you have experienced the death of the cross, if sin no longer has dominion over your life.**

He died once to break the power of sin. At the cross, your old life (who you used to be) died with Him, and you are now in a new relationship with Christ living in you. If you are in Christ, sin doesn't have power over you because sin has no power over dead people.

📖 **Romans 6:6-7 CEV**

"We know that the persons we used to be were nailed to the cross with Jesus. This was done, so our sinful bodies would no longer be the slaves of sin. We know that sin doesn't have power over dead people."

My friend, I know we saw the problem of sin in Chapter 6. In it we had opportunities to repent and pray to God. But I want to encourage you, as we progress along the Way, to be sensitive to the Holy Spirit. If He taps you on your shoulder and says that you have not experienced this death of the cross, please stop, humble yourself, and beg God that He will grant you the full experience of this death, so you can be loosed and delivered from the power of sin. The cross is God's means to break the power of sin, and to grant you the possibility of unbroken fellowship with Him, by putting the life of Christ inside you. In Him, you are not gradually being set free from sin, but you *have been* set free from sin, by the instrument of death God provided in the cross of Christ.

📖 **Romans 6:17-18 NKJV**

*"But God be thanked that though **you were** slaves of sin, yet you obeyed from the heart that form of doctrine to which you were*

delivered. And _having been set free from sin_, you became slaves of
righteousness."

TLB "And now you are free from your old master, sin; and you have become slaves to your new master, righteousness"

Are you believing the word of God? Again, as we read the Scriptures, we must notice the tenses used in the words.

> **Please stop, humble yourself, and beg God that He will grant you the full experience of this death, so you can be loosed and delivered from the power of sin.**

📖 **Romans 6:20-23 NKJV**
"For **when you were** slaves of sin, **you were** free in regard to righteousness. What fruit **did you have then** in the things of which you are now ashamed? For the end of those things is death. But **now having been set free from sin**, and **having become** slaves of God, you have your fruit to holiness, and the end, everlasting life. For the wages of sin is death, but the gift of God is eternal life in Christ Jesus our Lord."

We used to be in a union with sin producing fruits that brought us shame. We were free in regard to righteousness because the life in us was _un_righteous by nature. That was when WE WERE slaves of sin. BUT NOW we HAVE BEEN set free from sin and have become slaves of God, _by our choice,_ through faith in Jesus Christ. In Romans 6, we have seen Paul describing the death of the old man that occurred at the cross. As he continues into Romans 7, he uses an illustration to help the Jews he was speaking to understand this mystery better.

📖 **Romans 7:1-4 NKJV**
"Or do you not know, brethren (for I speak to those who know the law), that the law has dominion over a man as long as he lives? For the woman who has a husband is bound by the law to her husband as long as he lives. But if the husband dies, she is released from the law of her husband. So then if, while her husband lives, she marries

another man, she will be called an adulteress; but if her husband dies, she is free from that law, so that she is no adulteress, though she has married another man. Therefore, my brethren, you also have become dead to the law through the body of Christ, that you may be married to another- to Him who was raised from the dead, that we should bear fruit to God."

Paul didn't transition into a marriage teaching here. He was still explaining the mystery of the cross and the death that occurred. As a good teacher, he wanted to bring an illustration that would help them understand what died at the cross. He was speaking to Jews who understood the law, so he used their understanding of the law concerning marriage to help them to see more clearly. He said, "the law has dominion over a man as long as he lives." We all know and understand that if we die having unpaid legal fines, the law cannot come to us and demand we pay them, because we are dead. God was not looking for our natural death to free us from the law though, because the Bible says in Hebrews, "It is appointed for men to die once, but after this the judgment." So, if I die while still having the sin nature (in me), it will result in me going to judgment with that sin and condemned eternally.

> *Paul makes it clear, that as long as that life is in us, as long as we are joined to sin, we will never be free to be joined to Jesus, even if we have said we believe in Him.*

Paul then says, "a woman who has a husband is bound by law to her husband as long as he lives." This is to illustrate that we were bound by law (yoked) to the sin nature we were born (one flesh) with. He was like our husband and our head, and we were the weaker vessel. No matter how much we wanted out of that (marriage) union, we couldn't escape it as long as that old man was still alive. If we tried to marry (be joined to) Jesus while still being joined to sin, we would be called an adulteress. And besides, Jesus Himself will not commit adultery by marrying someone who is already married to another (to sin in them).

📖 *John 2:23-25 NKJV*

"Now when He was in Jerusalem at the Passover, during the feast, <u>many believed in His name</u> when they saw the signs which He did. But <u>Jesus did not commit Himself to them</u>, because He knew all men, and had no need that anyone should testify of man, <u>for He knew what was in man</u>."

Paul makes it clear, that as long as that life is in us, as long as we are joined to sin, we will never be free to be joined to Jesus, even if we have said we believe in Him, like those in this scripture. Paul went on to say, "But if the husband dies, she is released from the law of her husband...she is free from that law, so that she is no adulteress, though she has married another man." It's as if she was never married. God's purpose for the cross was to bring about the death of our old man and release us from our life union with him. This death occurred in the body of Christ and freed us from the law of our first husband (the flesh, sin), making a way for us to be married to another, the Lord Jesus Christ. The cross terminates our old union to sin living in us, by crucifying the sinful nature (our first husband) at Calvary. Paul then says, "Therefore, my brethren, you also have become dead to the law through the body of Christ, THAT you may be married to another- to Him who was raised from the dead, that we should bear fruit to God." This is the reason for the cross.

📖 *Romans 8:2 NKJV*
"For the law of the Spirit of life in Christ Jesus has made me free from the law of sin and death."
📖 *Romans 8:2 GNT*
"For the law of the Spirit, which brings us life in union with Christ Jesus, has set me free from the law of sin and death."
📖 *Romans 8:2 AMPC*
"For the law of the Spirit of life [which is] in Christ Jesus [the law of our new being] has freed me from the law of sin and of death."

The cross was to crucify and remove our old man in the body of Christ. It was to release us from that law that bound us to sin and death, so we may be free to marry Jesus Christ. This was in order that His life could come and dwell in us, and by that new union, we would start bearing fruit to God. This is the *new creation* life which the cross prepares the way for.

📖 *2 Corinthians 5:14-17 NKJV*

"For the love of Christ compels us, because we judge thus: that if One died for all, then all died; and He died for all, that those who live should live no longer for themselves, but for Him who died for them and rose again. Therefore, from now on, we regard no one according to the flesh. Even though we have known Christ according to the flesh, yet now we know Him thus no longer. Therefore, if anyone is in Christ, he is a new creation; old things have passed away; behold, all things have become new."

📖 *2 Corinthians 5:17 GNT*

"Anyone who is joined to Christ is a new being; the old is gone, the new has come."

We are a new creation, a new being as a result of the death and resurrection of Jesus. Did you see God's intention for the work of the cross? It was at the cross where we all died. The cross is the place where old things have passed away and are gone. It was the gateway to the resurrection where all things become new. When we repented and believed on Jesus, God imputed this work to us, and we became joined to Christ in a new and living way (union).

Up to this point, the Scriptures have told us that God condemned, subdued, and overcame sin in the body of Christ. Our old man *was crucified* with Christ on the cross. We *have been* put to death with Him, and it is *no longer* we who live but Christ lives in us. The flesh (sinful nature) was crucified, and we have put off the old man with his passions, desires, and deeds;

> *It was at the cross where we all died. The cross is the place where old things have passed away and are gone. It was the gateway to the resurrection where all things become new.*

now he is dead and gone. We died and have received a brand-new life.

Jesus Christ came and took away the sin of the world. He took the body of sin we were yoked to and had no way of escaping and destroyed and did away with it. Jesus made His body an offering for sin and appeared on earth to put away sin by the sacrifice of Himself. He appeared to abolish and remove sin, and He went to the cross as God's means for the final solution of sin. The next time He comes it won't be for sin but for salvation. For we who are born again, He has broken the power of sin over our lives, ending our relation to it so we could be in an intimate relationship with Him. We died at the cross in the body of Christ, and our new life, with a new nature from God, is hidden with Christ in God. We are a new creation; Jesus Christ now lives in us, to the glory and praise of the Father who intended it to be this way, and who devised the means by which it is possible. By the death of the cross, the old is gone and the new has come. Now, let's dig deeper to discover *how* God brought this death about.

THE BAPTISM INTO CHRIST

📖 *Mark 16:14-16 NKJV*

"Later He appeared to the eleven as they sat at the table; and He rebuked their unbelief and hardness of heart, because they did not believe those who had seen Him after He had risen. And He said to them, 'Go into all the world and preach the gospel to every creature. He who believes and is baptized will be saved; but he who does not believe will be condemned.'"

Jesus said, "he who believes and is baptized will be saved." I know we can say, "Okay, that means water baptism," but we need to look at other Scriptures to see if that's true. If it is, where would that leave the thief on the cross whom Jesus said would be with Him in Paradise that day? The way Jesus said it presents it as a mandatory part of being saved. He didn't say, "he who believes and later on decides to get baptized in water will be saved," but "he who believes AND is baptized will be saved." This means we need to see what He's talking about concerning this kind of baptism.

📖 *Romans 6:1-7 NKJV*

"What shall we say then? Shall we continue in sin that grace may abound? Certainly not! How shall we who died to sin live any longer in it? Or do you not know that as many of us as <u>were baptized into Christ Jesus were baptized into His death</u>? Therefore we were buried with Him through baptism into death, that just as Christ was raised from the dead by the glory of the Father, even so we also should walk in newness of life. For if we have been united together in the likeness of His death, certainly we also shall be in the likeness of His resurrection, knowing this, that our old man was crucified with Him, that the body of sin might be done away with, that we should no longer be slaves of sin. For he who has died has been freed from sin."

Somehow, some way, we were baptized INTO Christ Jesus—we were included in His death. 'Therefore, we were buried with Him through baptism into death.' Before we could ever be buried with Him, we had to be baptized (put into) Him. The "therefore" is saying that the first thing to happen was we were baptized INTO Christ Jesus. As a result of that, because we were IN Him, we were baptized into His death at the cross. And, as a result of that, we were then buried with Him by means of *that* baptism (into His body) into death. It was permanent.

> **When Jesus died on the cross, we all died with Him because we were in Him by this baptism (complete and permanent immersing of every one of us) into Christ.**

John the Baptist baptized people in water as a symbol of repentance, forgiveness, and cleansing from sin; believing on the One who would come. But to deal with deliverance from the old sinful nature of man that produced those sins, we had to be baptized (put into) Christ Jesus, so we could be carried to the cross for the death and burial of that corrupt life. When Jesus died on the cross, we all died with Him because we were in Him by *this* baptism (the complete and permanent immersing of every one of us) into Christ.

📖 **2 Corinthians 5:14-15 NKJV**
"For the love of Christ compels us, because we judge thus: that if One died for all, then all died; and He died for all, that those who live should live no longer for themselves, but for Him who died for them and rose again."

As good as water baptism is as a symbol, the baptism that brings you into actual deliverance from the sin nature is not just water. We had to be submerged completely into Christ and into His death. All of us died in His body at Calvary.

In Romans 6, we saw Paul say, "How shall we who DIED to sin live any longer in it?" He said, "Or do you not know that as many of us as were baptized into Christ Jesus were baptized into His death? Therefore we were buried with Him through baptism into death." Paul was reminding them of what happened at the cross. You don't bury someone who's not dead. So, when Jesus died on the cross, everything in Him also died. If a snake swallows a rat completely, the rat is fully submerged in the snake. If the snake dies, everything in the snake, including the rat, also dies. So, in His wisdom, God decided to deal with the life (nature) we were joined to at birth, by baptizing (putting us into) Christ, and having Him carry us to the cross to accomplish the death that can make way for the resurrected (new) life.

> *It was there He put away sin by the sacrifice of Himself. It was there He took away the sin of the world.*

It was there He put away sin by the sacrifice of Himself. It was there He took away the sin of the world. And it was there, at the cross in His body, that when He died, we all died. When He was buried, we were buried with Him. And when we believed, it was applied to us— our old man (sin) was left behind, and we were raised with Him into an entirely new creation life. This was all God's means to set us free from the sin nature we were born with, and to grant us a new life in

Christ. Maybe you are thinking, "but how did God do this?", and that is a good question. But first, let's settle the matter that it is indeed God who did it.

📖 *1 Corinthians 1:30-31 NKJV*

"But <u>of Him</u> you are in Christ Jesus, who became for us wisdom from God- and righteousness and sanctification and redemption- that, as it is written, 'He who glories, let him glory in the Lord.'"

OF HIM you are in Christ Jesus. Of Him I was put in Christ Jesus to go to the cross with Him. I died because I was baptized into Christ by God, and as a result, I was brought into union with Him and included in His death.

📖 *1 Corinthians 1:30-31 GNT*

"But God has brought you into union with Christ Jesus, and God has made Christ to be our wisdom. By him we are put right with God; we become God's holy people and are set free. So then, as the scripture says, 'Whoever wants to boast must boast of what the Lord has done.'"

That's good. It said, "God has brought you into union with Christ Jesus." The first thing God did to secure our deliverance from sin, was to baptize us into Jesus and into His death. You can't be buried with Him if you're not with (in) Him when He dies. This is what the Lord our God has done to save us. Do you remember *where* it happened, where God put us into Christ so He could carry us to the cross? It was in the garden at the Mount of Olives.

📖 *Luke 22:39-44 NKJV*

"Coming out, He went to the Mount of Olives, as He was accustomed, and His disciples also followed Him. When He came to the place, He said to them, 'Pray that you may not enter into temptation.' And He was withdrawn from them about a stone's throw, and He knelt down and prayed, saying, 'Father, if it is Your will, take this cup away from Me; nevertheless not My will, but Yours be done.' Then an angel appeared to Him from heaven, strengthening Him. And being in agony,

He prayed more earnestly. Then His sweat became like great drops of blood falling down to the ground."

📖 ***2 Corinthians 5:21 NKJV***
"For He made Him who knew no sin to be sin for us, that we might become the righteousness of God in Him."

It's important to know this was God's idea. It was the Father's plan (with Jesus in agreement) to pour the entire nature of the Adamic race into Jesus and crucify it on the cross at Calvary. This was in order that we "might" become the righteousness of God in Him. The word "might" is used because being raised from the dead with Jesus, and escaping the condemnation of sin, is only for those who repent and believe on Him.

> *It was the Father's plan (with Jesus in agreement) to pour the entire nature of the Adamic race into Jesus and crucify it on the cross at Calvary.*

📖 ***John 3:18 NKJV***
"He who believes in Him is not condemned; but he who does not believe is condemned already, because he has not believed in the name of the only begotten Son of God."

Jesus drank that cup and carried our sin to the cross, experiencing much abuse along the way. On the cross He supervised the death of that life until He said, "**It is finished**." This was the arrangement between the Father and the Son according to God's good will and His planned means for our deliverance. This is the intercession Christ made on our behalf. His intercession was not just prayer, but a living sacrifice, carrying the sin nature in the body His Father prepared for Him. The Father made Him to *be* sin, not to be *like* sin. There's a difference between being "like something" and actually being made to "be something." Jesus *became* sin when He drank that cup. He was crying tears of blood because of what was getting ready to happen when He accepted the cup His Father presented to Him for *our* deliverance. His tears weren't because of the physical brutality of the cross. He came to earth with the knowledge He would die on

192

the cross, even spoke of it often. What pained Him most was that He was about to be separated from His Father, once He drank that cup filled with sin, and as a result became sin.

📖 **2 Corinthians 5:21 TLB**
"For God took the sinless Christ and poured into him our sins. Then, in exchange, he poured God's goodness into us!"

He cried out on the cross, "My God, My God, why have You forsaken Me." The idea of separation from His Father was the searing pain that caused Jesus to shed tears of blood before He ever came near the cross. That was the agony He suffered which far exceeded any physical pain the death of the cross would bring. That is the depths of His love for us and how He interceded on our behalf to rescue us from sin. Are you seeing what God put in that cup which made Jesus to be sin when He drank it? It was our nature, the sin nature, the iniquity of us all, the whole embodiment of sin. That's what happened. God took the sinless Christ and poured our old, sinful life into Him. That's how Paul can say, "I have been crucified with Christ." God's intention was to deal once and for all with sin that lived in us, and the cross was His way to accomplish it.

> *The idea of separation from His Father was the searing pain that caused Jesus to shed tears of blood before He ever came near the cross.*

Consider that in Jesus' life up until the garden, the powers of darkness could never lay a hand on Him. They tried tempting Him, they wanted to throw him off a cliff, but nothing ever worked because of the Life that is Light that dwelled in Him. Darkness was eager to destroy this Jesus, but they always found themselves unable to do anything to Him, and they could not comprehend it. But the moment He drank that cup, the moment the iniquity of us all was poured into Him, He became sin. Not *like* sin, but He actually became sin. At that moment they were immediately able to beat Him, to grab Him, and to abuse and publicly shame Him in every way. Why? Because the life (sin) that darkness could handle and overpower was now dwelling in Jesus, who never knew sin. It is note-worthy that the devil never stopped to think, 'Why is this suddenly so easy for me to attack this Man, who I have never been able to touch before?" Jesus had been wrecking his works for three and a half years, and the devil was unable to do anything about it. But now, because of sin dwelling in Jesus, the powers of darkness were cele-brating their supposed victory over Him, dragging Him through the streets. They didn't know what God was doing, for had they known, they would not have crucified the Lord of glory. But Satan's rage blinded Him. We will see later what the cross did to defeat him speci-fically, but for now, we are looking at how God made Him (Jesus) who knew no sin to actually become sin.

   📖 *Corinthians 5:21 GNT*
"Christ was without sin, but for our sake God made him share our sin in order that in union with him we might share the righteousness of God."
   📖 *2 Corinthians 5:21 JBP*
"For God caused Christ, who himself knew nothing of sin, actually to be sin for our sakes, so that in Christ we might be made good with the goodness of God."

In the garden, we were baptized (put) into Christ when He drank that awful cup. Can you picture it? The Father presenting the cup to Jesus. The vile cup of sin, the sin of the whole world, necessary to drink if we could ever have a chance at being made right with God, if we could ever be made good with the goodness of God (which is Christ in us). That is the agony we see from Jesus in the garden when He prayed three times to God, asking if there is another way. Jesus was facing the reality, that for the first time ever, He would be disconnected from the Father. That His Father would look away from Him, forsake Him, and pour out His wrath upon Him. That is how bitter that cup was. My friends, this is what Jesus Christ did for you. This is how far He was willing to go to rescue you and bring you back to God. Can you take a moment and thank the Father and the Lord Jesus Christ for what they have done for you? Please thank the Holy Spirit for opening your eyes to see what Jesus did by dying for us and what God did by baptizing us into Him and into His death.

The idea of baptism by *drinking in* a life (a nature) is not an unfamiliar concept in Scripture. Let's keep looking at baptism.

📖 *1 Corinthians 12:12-14 NKJV*
"For as the body is one and has many members, but all the members of that one body, being many, are one body, so also is Christ. For by one Spirit we were all baptized into one body- whether Jews or Greeks, whether slaves or free- and have all been made to drink into one Spirit. For in fact the body is not one member but many."

"Of Him you are in Christ Jesus," Paul said in 1 Corinthians 1:30. Are you seeing more clearly what Jesus was saying when He said, "He who believes AND is baptized will be saved?" We were baptized into Christ Jesus when He drank the cup in the garden. He became sin because of us in Him. He carried that life to the cross and supervised its execution. He was buried, and all of us were buried with Him. Then, when we heard the Gospel and responded, we were made to drink into one Spirit, who made us a part of the body of Christ and gave us our portion of the resurrection provision, Christ in us, the hope of glory. Do you

> *That is how bitter that cup was. My friends, this is what Jesus Christ did for you. This is how far He was willing to go to rescue you and bring you back to God.*

see the exchange? God poured us into Christ (by Him drinking us in) so He could in turn pour Christ into us (by us drinking Him in). God did all of this by His Spirit. This is the message of the cross. The necessary death and burial of our old man so we can be born again by the Spirit of Christ coming to live in us. Praise God for His means for our deliverance and His means for our salvation.

📖 *1 Corinthians 12:13 AMPC*
*"For by [means of the personal agency of] one [Holy] Spirit we were all, whether Jews or Greeks, slaves or free, baptized [**and** by baptism united together] into one body, and all made to drink of one [Holy] Spirit."*

Do you see the two things here? All of mankind was baptized into His body, AND we were made to drink into one Spirit. The first was in the garden, being baptized (put into) Jesus and, thus, into His death (where we all died) and His burial (because we were in Him). The second was when you came to Christ; everything God did to save you was activated and imputed to you, and you were made to drink into one Spirit.

📖 *Romans 10:10-13 NKJV*
"For with the heart one believes unto righteousness, and with the mouth confession is made unto salvation. For the Scripture says, 'Whoever believes on Him will not be put to shame.' For there is no distinction between Jew and Greek, for the same Lord over all is rich to all who call upon Him. For 'whoever calls on the name of the LORD shall be saved.'"

Through your faith, the work of the blood was applied to your sins, and the work of the cross was applied to your sin. You were made to drink of His Holy Spirit so the work of the resurrection could be applied and give you a brand-new life in the resurrected Christ. You became a member of the body of Christ by the Holy Spirit. One day, the disciples James and John came to Jesus asking a question, that came with a related answer.

📖 *Mark 10:37-40 NKJV*
"They said to Him, 'Grant us that we may sit, one on Your right hand and the other on Your left, in Your glory.' But Jesus said to them, 'You do not know what you ask. Are you able to drink the cup that I drink, and be baptized with the baptism that I am baptized with?' They said to Him, 'We are able.' So Jesus said to them, 'You will indeed drink the cup that I drink, and with the baptism I am baptized with you will be baptized; but to sit on My right hand and on My left is not Mine to give, but it is for those for whom it is prepared.'"

What James and John wanted was only possible if they were to drink the cup Jesus drank. They had to be baptized with the baptism Jesus was baptized with. They didn't understand what any of that meant when Jesus was telling them this, even though they said, "we are able." The mystery of the cross was that the life of sin, which dwelled in all of us, was going to be poured into Jesus for Him to crucify and bury forever. Our old life was going to be baptized with the baptism He was baptized with, and we would die to sin forever. Remember how Paul said it in Romans 6 when he said, "Shall we continue in sin that grace may abound?"

📖 *Romans 6:2-3 AMP*

"Certainly not! How can we, the very ones who died to sin, continue to live in it any longer? Or are you ignorant of the fact that all of us who have been baptized into Christ Jesus were baptized into His death?"

> **God didn't take adultery, stealing, dishonesty, and other sinful activities and put them in Jesus. He put the whole body of sin into Jesus.**

📖 *Romans 6:2-3 GNT*

"Certainly not! We have died to sin-how then can we go on living in it? For surely you know that when we were baptized into union with Christ Jesus, we were baptized into union with his death."

📖 *Romans 6:2-3 TLB*

"Of course not! Should we keep on sinning when we don't have to? For sin's power over us was broken when we became Christians and were baptized to become a part of Jesus Christ; through his death the power of your sinful nature was shattered."

God didn't take adultery, stealing, dishonesty, and other sinful *activities* and put them in Jesus. He put the whole *body of sin* into Jesus, and He put sin to death in Christ. We died to sin because of that death. The nature of Adam (separated from God) that does all those things was crushed. The life every man was joined to from birth, since Adam disobeyed, died. All because Jesus was willing to drink that cup. We didn't do anything. It was God who devised it and put us into Christ, and it was Christ who carried us to the cross, and it was Christ that died, resulting in our corresponding death. We became sons and daughters of God through faith in Christ Jesus alone. And because we were baptized into Christ, we have put on Christ.

📖 *Galatians 3:26-28 NKJV*
"For you are all sons of God through faith in Christ Jesus. For as many of you as were baptized into Christ have put on Christ. There is neither Jew or Greek, there is neither slave nor free, there is neither male nor female; for you are all one in Christ Jesus.

📖 *Galatians 3:26-28 GNT*
"It is through faith that all of you are God's children In union with Christ Jesus. You were baptized into union with Christ, and now you are clothed, so to speak, with the life of Christ himself. So there is no difference between Jews and Gentiles, between slaves and free people, between men and women; you are all one in union with Christ Jesus."

📖 *Galatians 3:27 NLT*
"And all who have been united with Christ in baptism have put on Christ, like putting on new clothes."

As many of you as were baptized into Christ, have put on Christ. It's a baptism into death. We were in a union with sin living in us and now we are in a union with Christ. We were put into Him in order that He could be put into us. We were put into Him so He could carry us to the cross and deal with the life that deserved death; the life we were never meant to have and never able to deliver ourselves from. Our old union with sin is dead and gone. Our new union with Christ (Him living in us) is here and alive forevermore. By this necessary baptism, God took the sinless Christ and made Him to be sin *FOR US*. Hallelujah! Praise be to God.

CHRIST MADE TO BE SIN FORESHADOWED

We're going to pass through some Old Testament Scriptures now, and in them we will see a foreshadowing of this work of the cross. These Scriptures are for our learning so let's fix our minds on the word of God and trust Him to help us see and learn what He wants to show us.

📖 **Romans 15:4 NKJV**
"For whatever things were written before were written for our learning, that we through the patience and comfort of the Scriptures might have hope."

📖 **Colossians 2:17 AMPC**
"Such [things] are only the shadow of things that are to come, and they have only a symbolic value. But the reality (the substance, the solid fact of what is foreshadowed, the body of it) belongs to Christ."

We've established it was the LORD God who made Christ to be sin for us. In fact, it was His pleasure to do so; to bruise Him, to crush Him, and to put Him to death when He sent Him to be an offering for sin.

> *For our deliverance from the sin nature, it was going to require a righteous judgment to be applied to a Man on behalf of sinful man.*

📖 **Isaiah 53:10 NKJV**
"Yet it pleased the LORD to bruise Him; He has put Him to grief. When You make His soul an offering for sin, He shall see His seed, He shall prolong His days, and the pleasure of the LORD shall prosper in His hand."

AMP *"the LORD was willing to crush Him"*
NLT *"it was the LORD's good plan to crush him"*
ESV *"it was the will of the LORD to crush him"*

Do you know this was their agreement? God is holy. God is always righteous and just, and He never reduces His requirements. For our deliverance from the sin nature, it was going to require a righteous judgment to be applied to a Man on behalf of sinful man. Let me ask you, do you think it pleased the Father to hurt Jesus, who never disobeyed Him? Of course not. Jesus is the Son of His love. Jesus is His only beloved Son, in whom He is well pleased with. So, what do you think the Father was pleased to crush when the Bible says, "it pleased the LORD to bruise Him?" What would cause a good Father to want to put His Child to grief and crush Him? Even good natural parents would never have a desire, or take pleasure, in crushing their children. But it was the Father's pleasure to crush Jesus, because of what was inside of Him after He drank that cup in the garden. Jesus, in His offering to the Father, became sin (the entire embodiment of that nature) for us. Thus, He became the very object of God's wrath, because God hates sin and what sin does to His creation. So, when Jesus willingly drank that cup and became the last Adam, the Father was pleased to crush Him and put that nature to death once and for all. He was very pleased to crush and fatally wound the life that made us slaves. He did that by pouring it into Jesus Christ, who took it to the cross.

> *So, when Jesus willingly drank that cup and became the last Adam, the Father was pleased to crush Him and put that nature to death once and for all.*

This is wonderful news, and it gets better. That same Isaiah 53:10 can be read like this, "It pleased the Father to bruise Jesus; the Father has put Jesus to grief. When Jesus makes His soul an offering for sin, the Father shall see (look upon and accept) Jesus' seed (His offspring, those who believe in Him), the Father shall prolong Jesus' days (raise Jesus from the dead), and the pleasure of the Father shall prosper in Jesus' hand."

The death of the old man had to come first in the body of Jesus Christ at the cross of Calvary. Jesus became the object of God's wrath by the life of sin He carried in His body. The Father accepted His offering, poured out His judgment on Him, and then raised Him from the dead. In their agreement, anyone who will look unto Jesus for salvation and receive Him will receive His Seed and live forever. This was the Father's plan, and His pleasure now prospers in the hands of the risen Christ.

Let's continue looking to see what else the LORD has done for us by making Jesus to be sin for us.

📖 **Numbers 21:4-9 NKJV**

"Then they journeyed from Mount Hor by the Way of the Red Sea, to go around the land of Edom; and the soul of the people became very discouraged on the way. And the people spoke against God and against Moses: 'Why have you brought us up out of Egypt to die in the wilderness? For there is no food and no water, and our soul loathes this worthless bread. So the LORD sent fiery serpents among the people, and they bit the people; and many of the people of Israel died. Therefore the people came to Moses, and said, 'We have sinned, for we have spoken against the LORD and against you; pray to the LORD that He take away the serpents from us.' So Moses prayed for the people. Then the LORD said to Moses, 'Make a fiery serpent, and set it on a pole; and it shall be that everyone who is bitten, when he looks at it, shall live.' So Moses made a bronze serpent, and put it on a pole; and so it was, if a serpent had bitten anyone, when he looked at the bronze serpent, he lived."

Do you see the work of the cross in the shadow of this story? The people sinned against God. God's judgment was to send serpents among them and the serpents bit the people which resulted in many deaths. In the beginning, man sinned against God and sin entered the world. Sin bit every man ("for all have sinned and fall short of the glory of God") and God's judgment on the wages of sin is death ("for in the day you eat of it you shall surely die"). God's solution for the children of Israel in the wilderness was to take the image of the fiery serpent, nail it to a pole, and lift it up from the earth. Everyone who looked at that serpent on the pole would live, even though they had been bitten.

> *This was the Father's plan, and His pleasure now prospers in the hands of the risen Christ.*

God's solution for mankind was to put the sinful nature (all of us; the entire Adamic race) in the body of Jesus Christ, nail Him to the cross, and lift Him up for all to see.

📖 *John 12:31-33 NKJV*

"'Now is the judgment of this world; now the ruler of this world will be cast out. And I, if I am lifted up from the earth, will draw all peoples to Myself.' This He said, signifying by what death He would die."

📖 *John 12:32 AMPC*

"And I, if and when I am lifted up from the earth [on the cross], will draw and attract all men [Gentiles as well as Jews] to Myself."

Everyone who looks upon Jesus in faith, lifted up on the cross, will be delivered from the life of sin and made alive with Him through His resurrection. At the cross, the venom of the evil nature the serpent injected in the first man (that nature which passed down to everyone born of the flesh) is put to death and removed forever when anyone looks and sees Jesus Christ and Him crucified. This was the will and purpose of God in creating the means of the cross. He did it so those who will "look and see" with their own eyes, believing on His Son, may be raised from the dead and have everlasting life.

📖 *John 6:40 NKJV*

"And this is the will of Him who sent Me, that everyone who sees the Son and believes in Him may have everlasting life; and I will raise him up at the last day."

Do you see how God made Christ, who knew no sin, to be sin for us, by putting our sinful nature into Him? This is His divine strategy to deal with the life we inherited which brought death to us. Are you not blown away at what the Father and the Son were willing to do so you could live forever with them? Are you taking this wondrous work for granted? We need to praise God and give thanks to Him, who was willing to let His only beloved Son be made to be sin, so that He could crush it forever by crushing Jesus. What great love our Father has shown us. What an amazing God!

📖 *Isaiah 53:4-6 NKJV*

"Surely He has borne our griefs and carried our sorrows; yet we esteemed Him stricken, smitten by God, and afflicted. But He was wounded for our transgressions, He was bruised for our iniquities; the chastisement for our peace was upon Him, and by His stripes we

are healed. All we like sheep have gone astray; we have turned, every one, to his own way; and the LORD has laid on Him the iniquity of us all."

A transgressor commits transgressions, a sinner commits sins, the flesh does deeds of the flesh, and iniquity produces iniquities. These are all referring to the same sinful nature we are all born with. In the first two verses, we see the activities (transgressions and iniquities) which Jesus shed His blood to deal with. Wounding involves blood, bruising involves blood, and chastisement and stripes involve the shedding of blood. We praise God for the blood. But here we are looking at how God made Jesus to be sin for us, and we see *how* in the last verse. It says we have all gone astray, every one of us turning to our own way. That is the sinful nature in man we studied in Chapter 7. God's devised means to deal with that iniquity (singular) of us all was to lay it on Jesus.

> *A transgressor commits transgressions, a sinner commits sins, the flesh does deeds of the flesh, and iniquity produces iniquities. These are all referring to the same sinful nature we are all born with.*

📖   **Isaiah 53:6 AMP**
"All of us like sheep have gone astray, we have turned, each one, to his own way; but the LORD has caused the wickedness of us all [our sin, our injustice, our wrongdoing] to fall on Him [instead of us]."

Jesus came and appeared on earth to take away, put away, remove and abolish sin. The Father laid on Him the iniquity of us all. He poured that very life, all of it, the iniquity (sin, flesh, sinful nature) of every single one of us, into the body of Christ, who carried that wicked life all the way to the cross, to crucify it and bury it forever. Look what Jesus did when that happened.

📖 **Isaiah 53:7 NKJV**
"He was oppressed and He was afflicted, yet He opened not His mouth; He was led as a lamb to the slaughter, and as a sheep before its shearers is silent, so He opened not His mouth."

Jesus deliberately kept silent. Do you know why? From the time in the garden all the way to the cross, He was on a mission. It wasn't time to defend Himself. He was now carrying the life of iniquity that even the powers of darkness realized they had access to. They even heard Him ask God why He had forsaken Him. When Jesus was made to be sin, darkness was able to lay hands on Him for the first time. The cross, and the blood of the cross, was God's intentional, planned means to deliver us INDEED from sin and from sins; from iniquity which produces iniquities. It is the glorious plan God devised in dealing with iniquity, the problem in man.

Let's look at another shadow of the cross. One day, God was prophesying through Jeremiah, how He would bring His people out of their captivity and back to Himself.

📖 *Jeremiah 33:7-11 NKJV*
*"'And I will cause the captives of Judah and the captives of Israel to return, and will rebuild those places <u>as at the first</u>. I will cleanse them <u>from all their iniquity **by which** they have sinned against Me</u>, and I will pardon <u>all their iniquities</u> by which they have sinned and by which they have transgressed against Me. Then it shall be to Me a name of joy, a praise, and an honor before all nations of the earth, who shall hear all the good that I do to them; they shall fear and tremble for all the goodness and all the prosperity that I provide for it. Thus says the LORD: Again there shall be heard in this place- of which you say, 'It is desolate, without man and without beast'- in the cities of Judah, in the streets of Jerusalem that are desolate, without man and without inhabitant and without beast, the voice of joy and the voice of gladness, the <u>voice of the bridegroom and the voice of the bride</u>, the voice of those who will say: 'Praise the LORD of hosts, for the LORD is good, for His mercy endures forever'- and of those who will bring the sacrifice of praise into the house of the LORD. For I will cause the captives of the land <u>to return as at the first,</u>' says the LORD."*

Wow! I have to believe the Lord is opening your eyes to see the glory of the cross of Christ in these Scriptures. At the first (in the beginning), God designed man to be with Him, breathed His life into him, and gave him access to His presence. Man sinned against God and sin entered the man He created, along with the death God promised would happen if he ate from the tree he was told not to eat of. As a result, man was banished out of the presence of God. He became a captive to sin and was under the wrath of God by the new nature now in him.

📖 *Ephesians 2:3b AMPC*
"We were then by nature children of [God's] wrath and heirs of [His] indignation, like the rest of mankind."

But in Jeremiah, we are getting a glimpse of what God was planning to do to return mankind to Himself (as at the first). He said, "I will pardon all their iniquities." That is a foreshadowing of His intended purpose for the blood in dealing with our sins, as we've studied. But please take note again, we see *iniquities* and *iniquity*. He said, "I will cleanse them from all their iniquity." The word cleanse here means to purge and to purify. He also said, "from all their iniquity BY WHICH they have sinned against Me." When you use "by which," it implies that it is iniquity that is the source by which man has sinned against God in committing iniquities. By making Jesus to be sin for us, God made a way for us to be cleansed, purged, and purified from the sin nature we were born with. Praise the Lord! In this passage, God is telling us how He, by His goodness and mercy, will make a way for all of captivity (all souls) to return to Him as at the first, when He originally created man. By the cross, He dealt with the iniquity (sin) of man by putting it to death forever and removing it. This makes way for the new life of Christ, God's breathed in life, to inhabit us and give us eternal life (rather than eternal death). We were each joined to the Bridegroom in a new life union, and we were brought into the Body of Christ, which *is* the Father's household. This is all activated

> *God is telling us how He, by His goodness and mercy, will make a way for all of captivity (all souls) to return to Him as at the first, when He originally created man.*

and imputed to us when we repent and believe on the Lord Jesus Christ. There's more to see.

📖 **Zechariah 3:8-10 NKJV**

"'Hear, O Joshua, the high priest, you and your companions who sit before you, For they are a wondrous sign; for behold, I am bringing forth My Servant the BRANCH. For behold, the stone that I have laid before Joshua: upon the stone are seven eyes. Behold, I will engrave its inscription,' says the Lord of hosts, 'and I will remove the iniquity of that land in one day. In that day,' says the Lord of hosts, 'everyone will invite his neighbor under his vine and under his fig tree.'"

God said, "I will remove the iniquity of that land **in one day**." In all of history, there's never been a day when all the iniquity (sinful nature in man) of a land has been removed. There was only one day that ever happened, and that was on the cross at Calvary in the body of Jesus Christ. God sent His Servant, Jesus, as the Branch He extended to offer deliverance and salvation from sin to all who will look on Him. In the garden, God made Him who knew no sin to be sin for us, so that at the cross, He could remove the iniquity of the land in one day by the sacrifice of Jesus. Jesus died for all, and all died, and thus He became the Savior of all men, especially those who believe.

Death is the only solution for the sin that eternally separates mankind from God. Jesus became the whole embodiment of sinful man when He was made to be sin by His Father. When that happened, He became that which deserves death, and God executed His judgment upon Him. Let's press on and keep looking at this mystery as we see Moses explaining the laws God gave the children of Israel.

📖 **Deuteronomy 21:18-23 NKJV**

"If a man has a stubborn and rebellious son who will not obey the voice of his father or the voice of his mother, and who, when they have chastened him, will not heed them, then his father and his mother shall take hold of him and bring him out to the elders of his city, to the gate of his city. And they shall say to the elders of his city, 'This son of ours is stubborn and rebellious; he will not obey our voice;

he is a glutton and a drunkard.' Then all the men of his city shall stone him to death with stones; so you <u>shall put away the evil from among you</u>, and all Israel shall hear and fear. 'If a man has committed a sin deserving of death, and he is put to death, and you hang him on a tree, his body shall not remain overnight on the tree, but you shall surely bury him that day, so that you do not defile the land which the LORD your God is giving you as an inheritance; for he who is hanged is accursed of God.'"

NIV *"anyone who is hung on a pole is under God's curse"*
TLB *"anyone hanging on a tree is cursed of God"*

When Jesus drank in the sin of man, He became filled with the nature of the stubborn and rebellious son who refuses to obey. The life that is a glutton and a drunkard, and where chastening has no effect, was put into Him by God. That nature is evil, deserving of death, and needs to be put away. Did you recognize the words "put away?" We have seen how Jesus came to "**take away** the sin of the world,' and that "the body of sin might be **done away with**," and Jesus "appeared **to put away sin** by the sacrifice of Himself." In this passage, we see the rebellious son was to be put to death in order that the evil may be *put away* from among the people. That is what Christ did, when He carried you and I in His body to the cross. We were *in* Him, and because of sin in us, sin was in Him. Jesus hung from the cross as a cursed Man, because the nature that was cursed was fully in Him. It wasn't random for Jesus to be crucified on that tree. The Jews were following their own law. Jesus became something that brought a curse worthy of death.

📖 **Proverbs 26:2 KJV**
"As the bird by wandering, as the swallow by flying, so the curse causeless shall not come."

> *When Jesus drank in the sin of man, He became filled with the nature of the stubborn and rebellious son who refuses to obey. The life that is a glutton and a drunkard, and where chastening has no effect, was put into Him by God.*

📖 *Galatians 3:13 NKJV*

"Christ has redeemed us from the curse of the law, having become a curse for us (for it is written, 'Cursed is everyone who hangs on a tree')"

MSG "Christ redeemed us from that self-defeating, cursed life by absorbing it completely into himself"

A curse cannot come without a cause. Jesus baptized us into Himself by drinking the cup His Father gave Him to drink. He became a curse for us by absorbing the cursed life of sin completely into Himself. He swallowed into Himself all of the sinful, Adamic nature In each one of us, took it to the cross, and put it to death forever. Christ and Him crucified made *a way* for us to be saved by the life of Christ coming to dwell in us. So, let's continue to see what God did to completely dispose of the nature that was crucified by Christ. In Chapter 6, we saw that if someone has a bad heart that needs to be replaced, the surgeon doesn't just put the new heart next to the old one. In the same way, God doesn't just put the new life (nature) into us next to the old one, but He cuts out the old so the new can come. This is the last element of the cross that is activated for us when we believe on the Lord Jesus.

THE CIRCUMCISION OF CHRIST

📖 *Colossians 2:11-14 NKJV*

"In Him you were also circumcised with the circumcision made without hands, by putting off the body of the sins of the flesh, <u>by the circumcision of Christ,</u> buried with Him in baptism, in which you also were raised with Him through faith in the working of God, who raised Him from the dead. And you, being dead in your trespasses and the uncircumcision of your flesh, He has made alive together with Him, having forgiven you all trespasses, having wiped out the handwriting of requirements that was against us, which was contrary to us. And He has taken it out of the way, having nailed it to the cross."

AMP "the stripping off of the body of the flesh [the sinful carnal nature]"
CEV "just as circumcision removes flesh from the body"

Circumcision is a surgical removal of the flesh. In the natural, when a child is circumcised, the fleshly covering (of skin) is surgically removed, never to return again, never to have any effect on the body again. What is removed is no longer attached and that fleshly skin dies. It cannot be reattached. Circumcision is the cutting away of something that covers. Circumcision is final. It is the permanent removing of flesh from the body. The Bible says we were dead because of our trespasses (sins) AND because of the *un*circumcision of our flesh (sinful nature). But that all changed when we believed on the Lord Jesus Christ and Him crucified.

> *The Bible says we were dead because of our trespasses (sins) AND because of the uncircumcision of our flesh (sinful nature).*

📖 **Colossians 2:11-13 NLT**

"When you came to Christ, you were "circumcised," but not by a physical procedure. Christ performed a spiritual circumcision—the cutting away of your sinful nature. For you were buried with Christ when you were baptized. And with him you were raised to new life because you trusted the mighty power of God, who raised Christ from the dead. You were dead because of your sins and because your sinful nature was not yet cut away. Then God made you alive with Christ, for he forgave all our sins."

All of the work of Christ is complete, but none of it was activated for us until we came to Him. And we won't touch the reality of it until we see and agree with what He did. When you came to Christ, He performed a spiritual circumcision by cutting away your sinful nature. That was the flesh that covered your life and couldn't be removed by human effort.

Earlier we saw the difference between the *natural* baptism (in water)—that is done by human hands (which doesn't save but is symbolic)—and our *spiritual* baptism of being baptized into Christ, which caused us to die to sin. In the same way, the *physical* operation of circumcision—performed by human hands, which cuts away the flesh (foreskin) from the natural body—is only external and symbolic and has no power to deliver from the flesh (the sinful nature) inside. But in the *spiritual* circumcision of Christ, Jesus completely removed, stripped off, and permanently cut away our sinful nature when we believed. It was the internal work of the Spirit of God. The cross of Christ is God's divine scalpel to cut away and remove the flesh, in order that He, Himself, could come and live inside of us. Death has to occur first, then burial, then the circumcision (upon our faith), and ultimately the provision of the resurrection life which makes us the true children of God by Christ coming to live IN us.

> *The cross of Christ is God's divine scalpel to cut away and remove the flesh, in order that He, Himself, could come and live inside of us.*

📖 **Romans 2:28-29 NKJV**
"For he is not a Jew who is one outwardly, nor is circumcision that which is outward in the flesh; but he is a Jew who is one inwardly; and circumcision is that of the heart, in the Spirit, not in the letter; whose praise is not from men but from God."

📖 **Romans 2:28-29 GNT**
"After all, who is a real Jew, truly circumcised? It is not the man who is a Jew on the outside, whose circumcision is a physical thing. Rather, the real Jew is the person who is a Jew on the inside, that is, whose heart has been circumcised, and this is the work of God's Spirit, not of the written Law. Such a person receives praise from God, not from human beings."

Being a member of the household of God is not based on any outward appearances. Being born a Jew in the natural is not a qualification for being in God's family. All must repent and come to God through faith in Jesus Christ. A person must experience the death of the cross before they can be brought into God's family through the resurrection. Only those who have died with Christ can be born again and live with Christ through faith in God, who raised Him from the dead. Only those who have had God remove (cut away) that sinful, carnal nature, which covered their heart, can receive the new life of Christ. Did you actually experience the death of the cross yet? Has this surgery taken place for you? Are you able to worship God in the Spirit and in the truth of the cross? Do you want to agree with Him now that you see, and experience the reality of this working? Please talk to Him about it right now.

📖 *Philippians 3:1-3 NKJV*
"Finally, my brethren, rejoice in the Lord. For me to write the same things to you is not tedious, but for you it is safe. Beware of dogs, beware of evil workers, beware of the mutilation! For we are the circumcision, who worship God in the Spirit, rejoice in Christ Jesus, and have no confidence in the flesh,"

📖 *Philippians 3:3 NLT*
"For we who worship by the Spirit of God are the ones who are truly circumcised. We rely on what Christ Jesus has done for us. We put no confidence in human effort,"

The sinful nature that covers every man's heart is a barrier between them and God. The message of the cross delivers us from any confidence in the flesh, any outward appearances, and any trust in ourselves or our own abilities. This is so crucial for all to see because the cross is the place where the death and burial of our old man occurred, and where our sinful nature was cut away when we believed.

As we near the end of this chapter, let's look once more and learn from the Old Testament Scriptures to see how God was foreshadowing the work of the cross relating to this circumcision.

📖 *Joshua 5:6-9 NKJV*
"For the children of Israel walked forty years in the wilderness, till all the people who were men of war, who came out of Egypt, were consumed, because they did not obey the voice of the LORD- to whom the LORD swore that He would not show them the land which the LORD had sworn to their fathers that He would give us, 'a land flowing with milk and honey.' Then Joshua circumcised their sons whom He raised up in their place; for they were uncircumcised, because they had not been circumcised on the way. So it was, when they had finished circumcising all the people, that they stayed in their

places in the camp till they were healed. Then the LORD said to Joshua, 'This day I have rolled away the reproach of Egypt from you.' Therefore the name of the place is called Gilgal to this day."

GNT *"Today I have removed from you the disgrace of being slaves in Egypt"*
CEV *"But now I have taken away that disgrace"*
AMP *"I have rolled away the reproach (derision, ridicule) of Egypt from you"*
NLT *"Today I have rolled away the shame of your slavery in Egypt"*

Did you notice the language "rolled away?" It is the repeated theme of the work of the cross: take away, put away, done away with, and rolled away. Here, the Holy Spirit uses the word *reproach* to describe the problem. A reproach is a disgrace and a shame because of a condition. It is what makes the failings of someone more apparent. That is what the sinful nature does. The flesh is a reproach to God. It puts us in a condition that brings shame and disgrace to our lives. God said in 1 Corinthians 1:29, "that no flesh should glory in His presence." We see the cross in this story when it says, "This day I have rolled away," again pointing to the day when Jesus Christ took our reproach to the cross.

> **The flesh is a reproach to God. It puts us in a condition that brings shame and disgrace to our lives.**

The children of Israel were walking in the wilderness for forty years until all the men of war, who did not obey the voice of the LORD, were consumed. Before Christ came, mankind was wandering the earth (in the wilderness of sin and separation from God) until they all died in the body of Christ at Calvary. The men of war in Israel, who came out of Egypt, were prohibited from seeing or entering the promised land which God swore to their fathers. In the same way, all who are born of the flesh have a nature that is disobedient and at war with God. We all carried a life inside of us that cannot see or enter the promised kingdom of God, regardless of our genealogy or human effort for righteousness. That life prohibits us from receiving the promises of God for our salvation and eternal life with Him.

> *This circumcision of the flesh is what prepares the way for the Spirit of Christ to come and dwell in the hearts of men, enabling them (by His life) to love the Lord and obey Him.*

God's solution for the children of Israel was to circumcise them on the way to the place He wanted to take them. For us, God's solution was to circumcise us with the circumcision of Christ, removing the flesh that covers us and prohibits us from entering His kingdom. This was to make the way possible for us to receive our new life in Christ, by the word of our Father. His first deliverance for the children of Israel was to remove them from their bondage to slavery in Egypt. Then He circumcised them on the way so that they could enter the land of promise. At the cross, the death that occurred separated us from our old life of slavery. And when we personally came to Christ, God rolled away the reproach (sinful nature) that made us slaves in the first place. He rolled away the reproach of sin. That old slave-driving life that ruled us was rolled away when He circumcised us. This circumcision of the flesh is what prepares the way for the Spirit of Christ to come and dwell in the hearts of men, enabling them (by His life) to love the Lord and obey Him.

📖 *Deuteronomy 30:1-6 NKJV*
"Now it shall come to pass, when all these things come upon you, the blessing and the curse which I have set before you, and you call them to mind among all the nations where the LORD your God drives you, and you return to the LORD your God and obey His voice, according to all that I command you today, you and your children, with all your heart and with all your soul, that the LORD your God will bring you back from captivity, and have compassion on you, and gather you again from all the nations where the LORD your God has scattered you. If any of you are driven out to the farthest parts under heaven, from there the LORD your God will gather you, and from there He will

bring you. Then the LORD your God will bring you to the land which your fathers possessed, and you shall possess it. He will prosper you and multiply you more than your fathers. And the LORD your <u>God will circumcise your heart</u> and the heart of your descendants, to love the LORD your God with all your heart and with all your soul, that you may live."

No matter how far a person has traveled away from the Lord, there is always hope. There is always the possibility of being brought back from captivity, if they return to the Lord and obey His voice. There is no sin which God cannot forgive and cleanse by the blood of Christ. And He is fully able to cut away the sinful nature when anyone comes to faith in His Son, Jesus Christ. Again, in Deuteronomy 30, we are seeing repentance, a bringing out of captivity, and a circumcision done by God to cut away the nature that covered us from birth.

> *No matter how far a person has traveled away from the Lord, there is always hope. There is always the possibility of being brought back from captivity, if they return to the Lord and obey His voice.*

The circumcision of Christ happened so God could pour the Spirit of Christ into us, give us a new spirit and a new heart, and enable us (by Christ) to truly love the Lord our God with all our heart and soul.

📖 *Jeremiah 4:1-4 NKJV*
"'If you will return, O Israel,' says the LORD, 'return to Me; and if you will <u>put away your abominations out of My sight</u>, then you shall not be moved. And you shall swear, 'The LORD lives,' in truth, in judgment, and in righteousness; the nations shall bless themselves in Him, and in Him they shall glory.' For thus says the LORD to the men of Judah and Jerusalem: 'Break up your fallow ground, and do not sow among thorns. Circumcise yourselves to the LORD, and take away the foreskins of your hearts, you men of Judah and inhabitants of Jerusalem, <u>lest My fury come forth</u> like fire, and burn so that no one can quench it, because of the evil of your doings."

The cross of Christ "put away" the abomination of our sinful nature that draws the wrath and fury of God. We put away that evil and circumcise ourselves to the LORD by believing on the finished work of Jesus Christ and putting our faith in God. What Christ accomplished at Calvary was the termination of the life inside of man which caused us to live a life that followed the impulses and imaginations of the evil nature we were born with. All who come to the cross to die with Jesus, by faith in what He did, will be raised together with Him into an entirely new life in Christ. A life which is not subject to a love for sin and selfish desires. As we continue with Jesus (being led by and obedient to His Spirit) our minds will be increasingly renewed in the knowledge of Him and His ways. We will discover our appetites, desires, and impulses being subdued by His life and replaced with His own as we yield to and obey His Spirit. I want to ask again, has this death become your reality? Now is the time to settle this matter once and for all. Let's pray.

Our Father in heaven, You are worthy of all praise and honor and glory. We want to thank You for the cross of Jesus Christ, and how You used it to permanently put to death and remove our sinful nature. We thank You for opening our eyes to see Jesus and Him crucified, and for giving us understanding of what this message means. Thank You for helping us to see the death of our old man, the cutting away of our sinful nature, and the new life of Christ You have put into us in return. We ask You, Father, to continue unveiling the glory of the cross to us as we proceed. Father, please help us to walk in the reality of this death that occurred, and to live according to the truth of Christ in us. Teach us Your Way, Oh Lord, that we may know You, and that we may walk in Your Way. Father, I pray for those who have not experienced the death of the cross. As they cry out to you for this experience, I ask You to grant it to them. I ask You to give them assurance of this death in the way You choose, and to be pleased to reveal Your Son in them. Thank You, precious Lord, for hearing us, for we are praying to You in the wonderful name of Jesus Christ. Amen.

THE EFFECTS OF THE CROSS

W e will now rely on God's help to dig further in order to see the fullness of deliverance He has accomplished for us in the finished work of the cross of Christ. In previous chapters, we discovered extensively our deliverance from the power of *sin* and from the consequences of *sins*, which our old union with the sinful nature brought forth. Now we will examine many more dimensions of the wisdom and effects of the cross which God has supplied for our deliverance.

📖 ***Ephesians 3:9-12 NKJV***
"...to make all see what is the fellowship of the mystery, which from the beginning of the ages has been hidden in God who created all things through Jesus Christ; to the intent that <u>now the manifold wisdom of God</u> might be made known by the church to the principalities and powers in the heavenly places, according to the eternal purpose which He accomplished in Christ Jesus our Lord, in whom we have boldness and access with confidence through faith in Him."

Manifold means many sided and varied; having many different aspects, forms, or elements; multifaceted. The work of Christ crucified is a mystery which comes by revelation from God. The practical deliverance, freedom, power, and resurrection life that proceeds from the cross, must be learned and revealed by God from faith to faith, as we walk with Jesus and study the word of God.

Think of it like buying a brand-new smartphone which you have never used before. You have acquired something loaded with many (manifold) functions, applications, and benefits which you now must learn in order to maximize your experience with it. But, if you never learn how to operate the phone, or only learn the mere basics, it may only be useful to you as an instrument to make phone calls and send texts. The truth is, within that new phone, there are many things to deliver your life from unnecessary burdens and bring great help to you, but you could end up living the same way, not tapping into what's available because you have not seen or understood the multifaceted dimensions of it. The work of the cross is similar. All the benefits of it are only fully realized, applied, and experienced when we gain increasing wisdom, understanding, and knowledge of what has truly happened at Calvary. So, let's look at more of the manifold wisdom of God for our deliverance.

THE CROSS FOR OUR DELIVERANCE FROM THE DEVIL

📖 *1 Corinthians 2:7-8 NKJV*
"But we speak the wisdom of God in a mystery, the hidden wisdom which God ordained before the ages for our glory, which none of the rulers of this age knew; for had they known, they would not have crucified the Lord of glory."

KJV *"which none of the princes of this world knew"*

What was it about the cross, that if the devil had really known what would happen to him, he would not have crucified the Lord of glory? It is a wisdom the Lord hid from everyone (especially Satan) before the set time to make it known came.

218

At the cross the devil was judged.

  📖 *John 16:5-11 NKJV*
"But now I go away to Him who sent Me, and none of you asks Me, 'Where are You going?' But because I have said these things to you, sorrow has filled your heart. Nevertheless I tell you the truth. It is to your advantage that I go away; for if I do not go away, the Helper will not come to you; but if I depart, I will send Him to you. And when He has come, He will convict the world of sin, and of righteousness, and of judgment: of sin, because they do not believe in Me; of righteousness, because I go to My Father and you see Me no more; of judgment, because the ruler of this world <u>is judged</u>."
  📖 *John 16:11 AMPC*
"About judgment, because the ruler (evil genius, prince) of this world [Satan] is judged and condemned and sentence already is passed upon him."

Here is Jesus, before the cross, telling His disciples Satan is already judged and condemned. That means, at some point in time, God determined beforehand the sentence He would execute on the devil and all the disobedient angels that followed him. This is important to understand as we study to see how deliberate God was in carrying out His sentence on the principalities, rulers, and powers of this world. It is important to see how He used the cross as the instrument for the devil's demise.

> *What was it about the cross, that if the devil had really known what would happen to him, he would not have crucified the Lord of glory?*

  📖 *John 12:30-33 NKJV*
"Jesus answered and said, 'This voice did not come because of Me, but for your sake. Now is the judgment of this world; now the ruler of this world will be cast out. And I, if I am lifted up from the earth, will draw all peoples to Myself.' This He said, signifying by what death He would die."

📖 *John 12:30-32 TLB*

"Then Jesus told them, 'The voice was for your benefit, not mine. The time of judgment for the world has come- and the time when Satan, the prince of this world, shall be cast out. And when I am lifted up on the cross, I will draw everyone to me.'"

God already determined the kind of judgment to execute upon Satan (and the principalities and powers he set up for his unauthorized rule in the world). God set an appointed time for that sentence to be carried out, and for the prince of this world to be overthrown and cast out. That time was when Jesus was lifted up on the cross. Knowing this, we need to see all God did to the devil and how that relates to our new life in Christ.

> *God set an appointed time for that sentence to be carried out, and for the prince of this world to be overthrown and cast out. That time was when Jesus was lifted up on the cross.*

At the cross the devil was disarmed.

📖 **Colossians 2:13-15 NKJV**

"And you, being dead in your trespasses and the uncircumcision of your flesh, He has made alive together with Him, having forgiven you all trespasses, having wiped out the handwriting of requirements that was against us, which was contrary to us. And He has taken it out of the way, having nailed it to the cross. Having disarmed princi-palities and powers, He made a public spectacle of them, triumphing over them in it."

All principalities and powers were disarmed, defeated, and made a public spectacle of at the cross of Calvary—in the body of Christ and by the resurrection of Christ. Jesus defeated them by bearing in His body the sinful nature of man, whom Satan had dominion over. He carried that life and nailed it to the cross, along with all the written records of our deeds against God. At the cross, God disarmed the devil by destroying his ability to exercise sway over mankind and his power to keep them in captivity. At the cross, God disarmed the devil by stripping away his ability to accuse us of all the violations against the law we had committed; having nailed that extensive list to the cross. Jesus came to crucify our old man, which was subject to Satan, and to come live in us by the Spirit of God. Now, because of Christ in us, the enemy has no sway nor power over our lives, because he has no sway nor power over Christ's life.

📖 *Hebrews 2:14 NKJV*
"Inasmuch then as the children have partaken of flesh and blood, He Himself likewise shared in the same, that through death He might destroy him who had the power of death, that is, the devil,"
📖 *Hebrews 2:14b AMP*
"so that through [experiencing] death He might make powerless (ineffective, impotent) him who hud the power of death- that is, the devil"

At Calvary, Jesus disarmed (destroyed) the devil, who had the power of death, making him powerless. He did this at the cross, where the nature in man was terminated in Jesus' earthly body, which rendered the devil ineffective and impotent to rule over anyone who is born again. The word "destroy" means to render entirely idle and useless or to deprive of force. God raised Jesus from the dead to show His power over death, then He put that resurrected life of Christ into the heart of all who believe. He did this in order to demonstrate to the principalities and powers the manifold wisdom of His power over them through His church. God had a plan all along. He manifested Jesus to destroy the devil and the works he produced in sinful man on the earth. His judgment was planned from the beginning. God was going to do what He had purposed as the means for our deliverance.

> *Now, because of Christ in us, the enemy has no sway nor power over our lives, because he has no sway nor power over Christ's life.*

📖 *1 John 3:8 NKJV*
"He who sins is of the devil, for the devil has sinned from the beginning.

221

For this purpose the Son of God was manifested, <u>that He might de-</u>
<u>stroy the works of the devil."</u>
📖 *1 John 3:8b AMPC*
"The reason the Son of God was made manifest (visible) was to undo
(destroy, loosen, and dissolve) the works the devil [has done]"

Our sins, and the nature within us that produced them, caused us to be under the power of the devil. He was easily able to use his strength against us in order to keep us in bondage to his will and the desires of his wicked heart. Jesus came to "cut away" that sinful nature by bearing it in His body and taking it to the cross to remove it forever. That sacrifice brought forgiveness for our sins, the erasing of all the record of our sins, the removal of our sinful nature, and through the resurrection, a new life in Christ—to all who believe. God disarmed all principalities and powers who used to rule over us. He gave us victory through Christ and Him crucified, and by the daily experience of Christ in us. As we continue in obedience to Jesus, we are completely free from all strength the devil can ever try to exert against us. It is no longer we who live, but Christ who lives in us. The devil's power was dissolved and destroyed, according to the plan and purpose of God in executing His judgment at the appointed time. Since we died and Christ is now the life in us, *by Him* the wicked one can no longer lay his hands on us, and *by Him* we can live above sin as we yield to His Spirit in everyday life. Praise God for the cross of Christ!

📖 *1 John 5:18 AMPC*
"We know [absolutely] that anyone born of God does not [deliber-
ately and knowingly] practice committing sin, but the One Who was
begotten of God carefully watches over and protects him [Christ's
divine presence within him preserves him against the evil], and the
wicked one does not lay hold (get a grip) on him or touch [him]."

It is Christ Himself living in us, by the Spirit of God, who keeps us safe as we abide in Him. We have been delivered from the power of the devil by the work of Christ and Him crucified. This is God's hidden wisdom which the devil, if he knew, would never have compelled men to crucify the Son of God. This was part of God's elaborate, secret plan to judge the devil and to strip the principalities and powers of their authority over man.

> **This was part of God's elaborate, secret plan to judge the devil and to strip the principalities and powers of their authority over man.**

📖 *Colossians 2:15 AMPC*
"[God] disarmed the principalities and powers that were ranged against us and made a bold display and public example of them, in triumphing over them in Him and in it [the cross]."

📖 *Colossians 2:15 MSG*
"He stripped all the spiritual tyrants in the universe of their sham authority at the Cross and marched them naked through the streets."

The cross was the hidden wisdom of God to strip all the spiritual tyrants of their sham authority over man (and their authority on the earth). But we also see another element of the fierceness of the wrath of God towards the devil and his army. God made a bold display and public example of their defeat at the cross, exhibiting them as captives and defeated foes.

📖 *Colossians 2:15 AMP*
"When He had disarmed the rulers and authorities [those supernatural forces of evil operating against us], He made a public example of them [exhibiting them as captives in His triumphal procession], having triumphed over them through the cross."

At the cross the devil was defeated and made to be a public spectacle.

To help us understand this better, we need to look at some Old Testament stories, which are a shadow of God's deliverance for us at the cross. In the Old Testament, the natural accounts of God's dealings with the children of Israel (and their enemies), provide us a glimpse into the manifold deliverance God has provided for us in Christ Jesus. They serve as a shadow of the reality which is in Christ. If we look carefully, with the help of the Holy Spirit, we can see the devil at work in the heart of the enemies of God's people. These accounts reveal the heart of Satan and foreshadow the work of the cross for our total deliverance from him.

In Exodus, when God was delivering His people from the land of slavery (Egypt) and Pharaoh its leader, we see a glimpse into Satan's venom, arrogance, and blind rage. God sent 10 devastating plagues into Egypt, telling Pharaoh to let His people go, through His servant Moses. Pharaoh's heart was hard; he kept refusing to release the children of Israel until God sent the tenth plague which struck dead all the firstborn in the land of Egypt. The children of Israel were saved because (according to the word of God) they killed the Passover lamb and dwelled in their homes with the blood of the lamb on the door-posts. Then God executed His judgment on the gods of Egypt.

> *God made a bold display and public example of their defeat at the cross, exhibiting them as captives and defeated foes.*

📖 *Exodus 12:12 NKJV*
"For I will pass through the land of Egypt on that night, and will strike all the firstborn in the land of Egypt, both man and beast; and against all the gods of Egypt I will execute judgment: I am the LORD."

📖 *Exodus 12:12 AMPC*
"For I will pass through the land of Egypt this night and will smite all the firstborn in the land of Egypt, both man and beast; and against all the gods of Egypt I will execute judgment [proving their helplessness]. I am the Lord."

That night, all the gods of Egypt who Pharaoh and the Egyptians thought could protect them, were rendered useless and powerless as they saw their firstborns killed. Judgment was executed and death occurred. As a result, Pharaoh let the people of Israel go. But his heart would quickly change his mind, and he soon pursued destroying them again. This prideful, evil heart was revealed in the song Moses sang after God's great deliverance of Israel.

📖 *Exodus 15:9 NKJV*

"The enemy said, 'I will pursue, I will overtake, I will divide the spoil; my desire shall be satisfied on them. I will draw my sword, my hand shall destroy them.'"

Do you see how Satan (using Pharaoh) was in ruthless pursuit and so sure of himself? Do you see the blind rage in his heart which overlooked all the great sufferings and setbacks that came from the ten plagues, yet he still wanted to destroy God's people? This is a shadow of the judgment God executed upon Satan and the powers of darkness at Calvary. And just like God judged the devil at the cross, making a public spectacle of him, we need to see in Exodus how God made a public spectacle of Pharaoh and his army. As the children of Israel came to the sea and could proceed no further, God told Moses to set up camp by the sea. Then He said:

📖 *Exodus 14:3-4 NKJV*

"For Pharaoh will say of the children of Israel, 'They are bewildered by the land; the wilderness has closed them in.' Then I will harden Pharaoh's heart, so that he will pursue them; and I will gain honor over Pharaoh and over all his army, that the Egyptians may know that I am the LORD.' And they did so."

Look at the intention of God for this deliverance. He planned it so the Egyptians will KNOW that *He* is the LORD and no one else. Likewise, at the cross and resurrection of Jesus Christ, God deliberately brought judgment to the devil and his army, so they would KNOW that *He* is the LORD, and no one else. As Pharaoh gathered his army in violent pursuit of God's people, they finally came within sight of the children of Israel. The people of Israel became afraid and started complaining to Moses.

📖 *Exodus 14:13-14 NKJV*

"And Moses said to the people, 'Do not be afraid. Stand still, and see the salvation of the LORD, which He will accomplish for you today. For the Egyptians whom you see today, you shall see again no more forever. The LORD will fight for you, and you shall hold your peace.'"

This is important because our deliverance is dependent on our *seeing* what Jesus Christ accomplished at the cross. If we saw Jesus die on the cross for our sins, repented and believed that He came from God, and received Him into our heart, we became born again. But if we haven't seen what He did to the sin nature, and what that means in relation to the devil, we won't *practically* walk in the reality of that deliverance. God knows we must see (with our own eyes of understanding) the judgment and public ruin of the enemy of our souls in order for us to walk in the truth. So, as the children of Israel were instructed to "stand still, and see the salvation of the LORD," God began to show them their deliverance.

> *This is important because our deliverance is dependent on our seeing what Jesus Christ accomplished at the cross.*

📖 *Exodus 14:26-31 NKJV*
*"Then the LORD said to Moses, "Stretch out your hand over the sea, that the waters may come back upon the Egyptians, on their chariots, and on their horsemen." And Moses stretched out his hand over the sea; and when the morning appeared, the sea returned to its full depth, while the Egyptians were fleeing into it. So the LORD overthrew the Egyptians in the midst of the sea. Then the waters returned and covered the chariots, the horsemen, and all the army of Pharaoh that came into the sea after them. Not so much as one of them remained. But the children of Israel had walked on dry land in the midst of the sea, and the waters were a wall to them on their right hand and on their left. So the LORD saved Israel **that day** out of the hand of the Egyptians, <u>and Israel saw</u> the Egyptians dead on the seashore. Thus Israel saw the great work which the LORD had done in Egypt; so the people feared the LORD, and believed the LORD and His servant Moses."*

The work of Christ on the cross was the place (on that day) God publicly judged, defeated, and made a display of His defeat of Satan and all the evil principalities and powers forever. Israel of old saw this splendid work and how Egypt (the land of slavery) would never be able to harm them again. They were free indeed! Today, anyone who looks on this deliverance of the cross, which God accomplished, and believes on His Servant Jesus Christ, is delivered from all the power of Satan. The life of sin Satan was able to rule over was crucified in Christ. God used the aggressive nature of the devil to bring about his own destruction. God, through Moses, made a public display of the utter destruction of Israel's enemy, who had enslaved them all their life. The result was the people feared the LORD and believed the LORD and His servant Moses. This is a shadow of how God, through Jesus Christ, utterly destroyed and made a public spectacle of Satan and all the powers of darkness by using the devil's own aggressive, murderous nature to bring about his defeat.

> *This is a shadow of how God, through Jesus Christ, utterly destroyed and made a public spectacle of Satan and all the powers of darkness by using the devil's own aggressive, murderous nature to bring about his defeat.*

As we continue, we can again see a shadow of the strategy of the cross played out in God's deliverance of His people in the book of Esther. In those days, there was a man named Haman who became the chief adviser to King Ahasuerus of the vast Persian empire. Haman hated the Jews because Mordecai (a Jewish man) would not bow down to him and pay homage to him as the king's second in command.

📖 *Esther 3:5-6 NKJV*

"When Haman saw that Mordecai did not bow or pay him homage, Haman was filled with wrath. But he disdained to lay hands on Mordecai alone, for they had told him of the people of Mordecai. Instead, Haman sought to destroy all the Jews who were throughout the whole kingdom of Ahasuerus- the people of Mordecai."

Do you see the devil, as Haman plotted and schemed to carry out his murderous desires? Haman proceeded to deceive the king, convincing him to give permission to remove the Jewish people from the provinces, as it seemed good to Haman, which was total elimination. Haman built wooden gallows 75-feet high in order to publicly shame and hang Mordecai. But Haman's evil plot was exposed to the king, who cancelled his plans to kill and destroy all the Jews. The king instead ordered that Haman (the enemy of the Jews) and his sons be hanged on the gallows he had built to kill Mordecai.

📖 *Esther 9:24-25 NKJV*
"because Haman, the son of Hammedatha the Agagite, the enemy of all the Jews, had plotted against the Jews to annihilate them, and had cast Pur (that is, the lot), to consume them and destroy them; but when Esther came before the king, he commanded by letter that this wicked plot which Haman had devised against the Jews should return on his own head, and that he and his sons should be hanged on the gallows."

In Haman, you can see the rage and hatred of Satan against the people of God. You see how he was overly confident in preparing to execute Mordecai publicly, for all to see, and to wipe out all Jews in one day. This is another picture of God's hidden wisdom of the cross, where He disarmed and defeated Satan completely, and revealed His intention to make a public display of his defeat. This was in order for all to see that He alone is the LORD. Do you see the strategic, manifold wisdom of God being displayed through His people to the rulers and authorities on the earth? God used the aggressive, evil behavior of the enemy, the blind rage of the wicked one, to bring about his own defeat, even on the very gallows (cross) of his choosing. God is always in charge, strategically bringing about total victory. Praise be to the Lord God for our deliverance from the devil through Christ and Him crucified.

> **God is always in charge, strategically bringing about total victory.**

One last example of this strategy is in the book of Joshua. In it, God gave Israel a great victory over the city of Jericho, along with instructions to abstain from taking accursed things from that city.

However, a man named Achan secretly took some of the accursed things, and the anger of the LORD burned against the children of Israel. As Joshua led Israel to the next city to conquer, called Ai, he sent about 3,000 men to fight.

📖 *Joshua 7:4-5 NKJV*
"So about three thousand men went up there from the people, but they fled before the men of Ai. And the men of Ai struck down about thirty-six men, for they chased them from before the gate as far as Shebarim, and struck them down on the descent; therefore the hearts of the people melted and became like water."

This defeat baffled Joshua, and he and the elders fell to the earth on their faces asking the Lord what happened. God said:

📖 *Joshua 7:11-12 NKJV*
"Israel has sinned, and they have also transgressed My covenant which I commanded them. For they have even taken some of the ac-cursed things, and have both stolen and deceived; and they have also put it among their own stuff. Therefore the children of Israel could not stand before their enemies, but turned their backs before their enemies, because they have become doomed to destruction. Neither will I be with you anymore, unless you destroy the accursed from among you."

Before we proceed, please note that sin causes a person to be un-able to stand before their enemies and dooms them to destruction. In the natural, the accursed things here were in relation to what the children of Israel took from Jericho and put in their own stuff. But spiritually, the sin nature is the accursed thing in men that separates them from God, brings them under the power of their enemies, and brings eternal destruction to their life. The cross is the means by which Christ dealt with that accursed life and delivered us from our enemies when we believed.

After the Lord spoke to the children of Israel, they dealt with the sin problem, and the Lord gave them a strategy for gaining the victory over Ai. Joshua put a troop behind the city to ambush it at the right time—when the enemy would be most vulnerable. Then Joshua would approach the city in plain view with another troop. When the king came after them, Joshua and the men of Israel would flee, relying on the king's aggressive behavior to pursue them, falsely assured because of his previous victory over them. But this king did not know his city would soon be ambushed and set ablaze, and that his public defeat was imminent.

📖 *Joshua 8:13-18,26,29 NKJV*

"And when they had set the people, all the army that was on the north of the city, and its rear guard on the west of the city, Joshua went that night into the midst of the valley. Now it happened, when the king of Ai saw it, that the men of the city hurried and rose early and went out against Israel to battle, he and all his people, at an appointed place before the plain. But he did not know that there was an ambush against him behind the city. And Joshua and all Israel made as if they were beaten before them, and fled by the way of the wilderness. So all the people who were in Ai were called together to pursue them. And they pursued Joshua and were drawn away from the city. There was not a man left in Ai or Bethel who did not go out after Israel. So they left the city open and pursued Israel. Then the Lord said to Joshua, 'Stretch out the spear that is in your hand toward Ai, for I will give it into your hand.' And Joshua stretched out the spear that was in his hand toward the city."... "For Joshua did not draw back his hand, with which he stretched out the spear, until he had utterly destroyed all the inhabitants of Ai".... "And the king of Ai he hanged on a tree until evening. And as soon as the sun was down, Joshua commanded that they should take his corpse down from the tree, cast it at the entrance of the gate of the city, and raise over it a great heap of stones that remains to this day."

Do you see the hidden, manifold wisdom of the cross? Satan and all his devils were tricked by God to crucify the Son of Man. And just like the king of Ai, when Satan saw Jesus in plain sight, he assumed he could go out to meet him and kill him by taking Him to the cross. He did not know that he was being ambushed by God with a divine, unseen strategy. Jesus made as if He was beaten before Satan, not putting up a fight or saying anything as he was taken to the hill of

Calvary. Satan thought he was winning when he aggressively pursued beating and crucifying the Son of God. He was so arrogant as he paraded Jesus through the streets, beaten and bloodied, to try and publicly shame Him and display his power over Him. But he did not know God was allowing his rage and hatred toward God, Jesus, and mankind to be his undoing. He didn't know the cross would be the hidden wisdom by which he would lose all his power. He didn't know God would put his defeat on display for all to see that he has been destroyed, and that the Lord alone is God.

And just like the king of Ai, when Satan saw Jesus in plain sight, he assumed he could go out to meet him and kill him by taking Him to the cross. He did not know that he was being ambushed by God with a divine, unseen strategy.

This is why, if the devil knew what would happen at the cross, he would *not* have crucified the Lord of glory. His rage blinded him, and God used it to bring about his own destruction and disarming. God's divine strategy to save men from sin and the grip of Satan, was to allow Satan to plan and participate in his own destruction, demise, and public defeat without knowing it. At the cross, Satan and all his authority was stripped away. His kingdom was publicly defeated and remains defeated to this day. This overthrowing of Satan and his army was prophesied about in Ezekiel.

📖 *Ezekiel 21:25-27 NKJV*

"Now to you, O profane, wicked prince of Israel, whose day has come, whose iniquity shall end, thus says the Lord God: 'Remove the turban, and take off the crown; nothing shall remain the same. Exalt the humble, and humble the exalted. Overthrown, overthrown, I will make it overthrown! It shall be no longer, until He comes whose right it is, and I will give it to Him.'"

At the cross, on THAT DAY, Satan (the wicked prince of Israel) and all his sham authority over earth and mankind was removed from him. Nothing shall ever remain the same for the defeated devil; he has been overthrown. God Himself has declared three times, "Over-thrown, overthrown, I will make it overthrown!" Now the risen Christ has taken His rightful place, whose right it is as given by God. He is Lord of all and King of all, and no one who continues in Christ will come under the authority of Satan ever again. He who is in you is greater than he who is in the world.

The Risen Christ is given all authority.

The devil and all authorities are subject to the Life of Christ in the new creation man and have no power whatsoever against Him. They have been placed by the Father under the authority of Jesus. We can see what happened to the devil, and his dominion, in the book of Daniel, when he prophesied of the resurrected Christ being brought back to God after His victory at the cross.

📖 *Daniel 7:12-14 NKJV*

"As for the rest of the beasts, they had their dominion taken away, yet their lives were prolonged for a season and a time. 'I was watch-ing in the night visions, and behold, One like the Son of Man, coming with the clouds of heaven! He came to the Ancient of Days, and they brought Him near before Him. Then to Him was given dominion and glory and a kingdom, that all peoples, nations, and languages should serve Him. His dominion is an everlast-ing dominion, which shall not pass away, and His kingdom the one which shall not be destroyed.'"

> **The disciple of Jesus Christ, who abides in Him and obeys Him, will have no fear of the devil because the Lord is with him (Christ is in him).**

The Father has given Jesus (the Son of Man) dominion that is an everlasting dominion. All who have come to the cross, who are born again and relo-cated by God, brought out from under the power of darkness and into the kingdom of God's dear Son, have been delivered from the authority and power of the devil who was disarmed. The disciple of Jesus Christ, who abides in Him and obeys Him, will have no fear of the devil because the Lord is with him

(Christ is in him). They will be able, by Christ, to carry out God's assignment on earth, to be fruitful with this life of Christ and multiply it by making disciples. They will be able to subdue the land and exercise dominion over it for the purpose and glory of the kingdom of God. Every defense the devil has enacted to keep souls in captivity, and in his possession (in order to promote darkness), has departed from him. His dominion has been stripped from him because of the work of Jesus Christ and Him crucified. You can now walk in the reality of this deliverance from the devil because Jesus says:

📖 *Luke 10:19-20 NKJV*
"Behold, I give you the authority to trample on serpents and scorpions, and over all the power of the enemy, and nothing shall by any means hurt you. Nevertheless do not rejoice in this, that the spirits are subject to you, but rather rejoice because your names are written in heaven."

THE CROSS FOR DELIVERANCE FROM OUR LOCATION UNDER THE POWER OF DARKNESS

📖 *Colossians 1:12-14 NKJV*
"giving thanks to the Father who has qualified us to be partakers of the inheritance of the saints in the light. He has delivered us from the power of darkness and conveyed us into the kingdom of the Son of His love, in whom we have redemption through His blood, the forgiveness of sins."

In Chapter 6, we saw one of the problems between man and God is his location *under* the powers of darkness. We were trapped under the sway of the wicked one because of the nature we were born with, inherited from Adam. At the cross, that nature controlled by the evil one was crucified. When you came to Christ, the flesh was removed, and Christ came to dwell in you. As a result, you were delivered from your previous location. His very nature (and kingdom) is *above* the principalities and powers of darkness. God delivered us from the power of darkness and conveyed us into the kingdom of the Son of His love, through faith in the cross and resurrection of

Jesus Christ. *Conveying* means transporting or carrying to a place. It is a movement from one location to another.

📖 *Colossians 1:13 KJV*
"Who hath delivered us from the power of darkness, and hath translated us into the kingdom of his dear Son:"
📖 *Colossians 1:13 AMP*
"For He has rescued us and has drawn us to Himself from the dominion of darkness, and has transferred us to the kingdom of His beloved Son,"

The word "translated" means to move from one place to another. It is a shifting of location. We were under the dominion of darkness and now we have been rescued and transferred into the light of the kingdom of God's beloved Son. This is a complete deliverance from our previous location, and it was foreshadowed in God's dealings with the children of Israel.

📖 *Deuteronomy 6:20-23 NKJV*
"When your son asks you in time to come, saying, 'What is the meaning of the testimonies, the statutes, and the judgments which the LORD our God has commanded you?' then you shall say to your son: 'We were slaves of Pharaoh in Egypt, and the LORD brought us out of Egypt with a mighty hand; and the LORD showed signs and wonders before our eyes, great and severe, against Egypt, Pharaoh, and all his household. Then He brought us out from there, that He might bring us in, to give us the land of which He swore to our fathers.'"

> **This deliverance of the cross is a bringing out from the land of bondage and into the land of His promise (Christ).**

This deliverance of the cross is a bringing out from the land of bondage and into the land of His promise (Christ). We were slaves to the devil and located under the powers of darkness. The Bible said we were children of darkness, children of wrath, and children of the night. God sent Christ to crush that condemned life at the cross, and to make a way to be brought *up* and *into* His beloved Son.

📖 *Ephesians 2:4-6 NKJV*
"But God, who is rich in mercy, because of His great love with which He loved us, even when we were dead in trespasses, made us alive together with Christ (by grace you have been saved), and raised us up together, and made us sit together in the heavenly places in Christ Jesus,"

> **The devil and his army do not want you to know this. He would rather keep you blinded from this dimension of the mystery of the cross of Christ.**

God raised us up with Christ and located us in the heavenly places *in* Him. The devil and his army do not want you to know this. He would rather keep you blinded from this dimension of the mystery of the cross of Christ. He wants you to fear him and give him more attention than he deserves as a defeated and lower foe. He does not want you to see the death and removal of the nature he could control, nor see the glory of the very life of Christ Himself dwelling in you.

📖 *Ephesians 2:5 AMPC*
"Even when we were dead (slain) by [our own] shortcomings and trespasses, He made us alive together in fellowship and in union with Christ; [He gave us the very life of Christ Himself, the same new life with which He quickened Him, for] it is by grace (His favor and mercy which you did not deserve) that you are saved (delivered from judgment and made partakers of Christ's salvation)."

The cross obliterated the enemy's shackles on our life by destroying the life and nature we were each born with. For all who believe, the Bible says, you died, and Christ now lives in you. Your life is hidden with Him in God, far above the rulers, authorities, principalities, and powers of darkness.

📖 *Colossians 3:3 NKJV*
"For you died, and your life is hidden with Christ in God."

THE CROSS FOR DELIVERANCE FROM THE WORLD SYSTEM

📖 *Galatians 6:14-16 NKJV*

"But God forbid that I should boast except in the cross of our Lord Jesus Christ, by whom the world has been crucified to me, and I to the world. For in Christ Jesus neither circumcision nor uncircumcision avails anything, but a new creation. And as many as walk according to this rule, peace and mercy be upon them, and upon the Israel of God."

📖 *Colossians 3:3 AMPC*

"For [as far as this world is concerned] you have died, and your [new, real] life is hidden with Christ in God."

The Scripture says, "you died." It is not referring to a daily progress-ive death, but the death that *already* occurred at Calvary's cross in the body of Christ. The old man HAS BEEN crucified and the new creation life of Christ dwells in us. It says, the world has been cruci-fied to me by Christ. This is the rule to live by and walk according to, now that you belong to Christ. The old Adamic nature previously in you was part of the world and sub-ject to the rulers, regulations, and demands of the world. It has been put to death with Christ. It is no long-er you who live, but Christ who now lives in you.

> *I have been set free from all the spiritual forces of this world. I am not bound to live according to its principles for life, its systems of operations, and its concepts of right and wrong.*

📖 *Colossians 2:20-23 NKJV*

"Therefore, if you died with Christ from the basic principles of the world, why, as though living in the world, do you subject yourselves to regulations- "Do not touch, do not taste, do not handle," which all con-cern things which perish with the using- according to the commandments and doctrines of men? These things indeed have an appearance of wisdom in self-imposed

religion, false humility, and neglect of the body, but are of no value against the indulgence of the flesh."

The cross terminated the life of the flesh we were born with. It delivered us from the world system and all the hooks it had in our life. Because Christ lives in me (and not the sin nature), I have been set free from all the spiritual forces of this world. I am not bound to live according to its principles for life, its systems of operations, and its concepts of right and wrong. Christ in me is the One who determines all those things for my life in union with Him. In the above passage, we see the world is something that comes (at least in part) by the commandments and doctrines of man. Let's dig deeper to discover more about *the world* and why God needed to deliver us from it, and how it could only happen by the cross.

What is the world?

📖 *Psalm 24:1 NKJV*
"The earth is the LORD's, and all its fullness, the world and those who dwell therein."

First of all, the world is not the earth. There is a clear distinction between the earth and the world in this Scripture. The earth has all its wonderful fullness (trees, plants, mountains, fruits, gold, diamonds, oil, etc.), which God has created for man to use and enjoy for His purpose. But the world, on the other hand, is a system. A *system* is a set of things working together as parts of a whole mechanism. It is an interconnecting network designed to produce the desired results of the one who creates it. The world is a system with principles, philosophies, and mechanisms for life on earth, that man (under the power and coercion of the devil) creates and dwells in according to the thoughts and intents of his own heart. This system is according to the appetites and desires of his own belly, in order to produce a life (and lifestyle) independent of God. The world is the place where sinful people congregate in various locations, creating cultures, making laws, and establishing their own way of life, outside of the will, counsel, purpose, and pleasure of God. The world, com-

prised of men and women (in whom sin dwells and rules), is displeasing to God and arouses His anger.

📖 *Genesis 6:5-7 NKJV*
*"Then the LORD saw that the wickedness of man was great in the
earth, and that every intent of the thoughts of his heart was only evil
continually. And the LORD was
sorry that He had made man on
the earth, and He was grieved in
His heart. So the LORD said, 'I will
destroy man whom I have created from the face of the earth,
both man and beast, creeping
thing and birds of the air, for I am
sorry that I have made them."*

> **The world is the place
> where sinful people
> congregate in various
> locations, creating
> cultures, making laws,
> and establishing their
> own way of life, outside of
> the will, counsel, purpose,
> and pleasure of God.**

After the fall of Adam, when sin
entered the world (into mankind), all men and women became totally corrupted by the
sinful nature and were brought
under the power of the wicked one. The devil then took over the
authority Adam relinquished to him (through his disobedience) and
became the ruler and god of this world—which was comprised
completely of people born in sin. God abhorred that nature in man
so much that He flooded the earth to destroy its influence. He left
Noah, who found favor in God's sight, and his family so there would
still be a path for His Son, Jesus Christ, to come redeem and save
souls. But He wiped out the world (man and all his created systems
for living apart from God) from the earth. He did this to temporarily
slow down the progression of this evil (in man) until Jesus came to
deal with it permanently.

📖 *2 Peter 3:5-6 NKJV*
*"For this they willfully forget: that by the word of God the heavens
were of old, and the earth standing out of water and in the water, by
which the world that then existed perished, being flooded with
water,"*

In the flood, the earth didn't perish, it was still standing when the waters receded. But the world completely perished. That is to say, the people who inhabited the earth, who created the systems to live by and the cultures within those systems, perished from the face of the earth, except the eight the Lord preserved. When Adam disobeyed God, the devil gained temporary access to influence, control, and impart to man his rebellious ways which separate man from God. Jesus acknowledged the devil's position in the world when He was talking to His disciples before He went to the cross.

📖 *John 14:30 NKJV*
"I will no longer talk much with you, for the ruler of this world is coming, and he has nothing in Me."

Jesus overcame the devil because of the life that was in Him. The devil could never come and find a place to rest in Jesus, or establish a way of thinking in Him that would damage His union with the Father. When Adam sinned, the devil gained access to manipulate and teach man the selfish and sinful ways of life that are contrary to and hostile to God. That became the system man lived under which promotes the life of selfishness and self-rule and denies God and His way. The same kind of life that caused the devil to fall from heaven.

The apostles John and Paul both described what life is like (on earth) for all those who are only born of the flesh (children of the world) and have not yet become born again (children of God) through faith in the finished work of Jesus Christ.

📖 *1 John 5:19 NKJV*
"We know that we are of God, and the whole world lies under the sway of the wicked one."
📖 *Ephesians 2:2 AMPC*
"In which at one time you walked [habitually]. You were following the course and fashion of this world [were under the sway of the tendency of this present age], following the prince of the power of the air. [You were obedient to and under the control of] the [demon] spirit that still constantly works in the sons of disobedience [the

careless, the rebellious, and the unbelieving, who go against the purposes of God]."

All who are born of the flesh are born with a spirit of disobedience, under the sway of the wicked one, and subject to the powers of darkness operating over them, and even within them. They are bound to the kind of life that walks habitually according to the course (ways, paths, and practices) of the world and its ruler, the devil. The world, and those who dwelled in it, became corrupt and evil (because of sin), necessitating a solution to deliver man from it by the sacrifice of Jesus Christ. The world was and still is evil.

> *The world, and those who dwelled in it, became corrupt and evil (because of sin), necessitating a solution to deliver man from it by the sacrifice of Jesus Christ. The world was and still is evil.*

📖 *Galatians 1:3-5 KJV*
"*Grace to you and peace from God the Father, and from our Lord Jesus Christ, who gave himself for our sins, that he might deliver us from this <u>present evil world</u>, according to the will of God and our Father: to whom be glory for ever and ever. Amen.*"

AMPC "*in order to rescue and deliver us from this present wicked age and world order*"

The world is intentionally ordered and constructed to oppose and obscure God, His ways, and His Christ. It says things like "all religions are the same" and "there is more than one way to heaven." This is strategic in order to deny the Lord's Christ who said, "I am the Way, the Truth, and the Life. No one comes to the Father except through Me." Consider the bumper sticker you see on some cars that says COEXIST. The world presents it as an attempt at unity, saying it represents indigenous spirituality: Hinduism, Judaism, Buddhism, Islam, Unitarian Universalism, and Christianity. This is all veiled under the idea of unity, but the spiritual (demonic) purpose behind that veil is to obscure God's Christ. It is to make Him One of many answers and not God's only solution on earth for the people of the world to be saved.

📖 *John 3:17 NKJV*
"For God did not send His Son into the world to condemn the world, but that the world through Him might be saved."

The world is *mankind*. It is where sinful men and women (by nature) gather and create communities and standards by which they agree to live by. They determine what is acceptable and what is not acceptable, and what the punishments are for violating what they have established. This is all done according to their own commandments, their own wisdom, and not according to God. The world is hostile to God and tries to diminish God and His Christ in everything it does. The world imprisons those who live in it to condemnation. It separates its inhabitants from knowing God, and it will eventually lead all who dwell in it to eternal separation from God; just as its ruler desires. God sent Jesus to save the world from these horrible outcomes and to reconcile souls back to Himself.

This is all veiled under the idea of unity, but the spiritual (demonic) purpose behind that veil is to obscure God's Christ; to make Him One of many answers and not God's only solution on earth for the people of the world to be saved.

📖 *2 Corinthians 5:19 NKJV*
"that is, that God was in Christ reconciling the world to Himself, not imputing their trespasses to them, and has committed to us the word of reconciliation."

Christ didn't come to save the *earth* but the *souls* of sinful men and women (the world). So, when the Bible says, "reconciling the world" or "the world through Him might be saved," we can clearly see it is referring to mankind. The world system is completely constructed by sinful men. It is set up and established to promote the selfish, sinful nature of man and his own way of life. And we have all been trapped in it.

241

What does God say about the world system?

📖 *1 John 2:15-17 NKJV*

"Do not love the world or the things in the world. If anyone loves the world, the love of the Father is not in him. For <u>all that is in the world</u>- the lust of the flesh, the lust of the eyes, and the pride of life- <u>is not of the Father</u> but is of the world. And the world is passing away, and the lust of it; but he who does the will of God abides forever."

📖 *1 John 2:15 TLB*

"Stop loving this evil world and all that it offers you, for when you love these things you show that you do not really love God."

None of the world is of the Father! All of it is wholly instituted by the desires, ideas, and intelligence of natural, evil man under the power and dominion of darkness. The world appeals to the senses and feelings of people, using the material things that are visible, to make the unseen and spiritual things of God obscure, irrelevant, and unreal to them. The world creates idols (riches, celebrities, fame, recreation, intellectualism, etc.) to engage the affections of the human heart and turn them away from God—even Christians. Anyone who loves the world, or the things in the world, is demonstrating the reality that they don't really have the love of the Father in them. The world's philosophies and advertisements promote and tap into the cravings of the sinful nature, and the advancement of the kingdom of darkness (the absence of God's rule) on the face of the earth. The kingdom of God has a lifestyle, a way of living on earth that is the lifestyle of Jesus Christ. The world has its own lifestyle, designed to make the way of Christ undesirable, too difficult, unreasonable, and burdensome. It deceives souls concerning the way of God, which is in Christ Jesus, and carries them off as spoil. You as a Christian

> *The world appeals to the senses and feelings of people, using the material things that are visible, to make the unseen and spiritual things of God obscure, irrelevant, and unreal to them.*

must be careful not to be caught up in the world's ways now that Christ has saved you.

📖 **Colossians 2:8 AMPC**
"See to it that no one carries you off as spoil or makes you yourselves captive by his so-called philosophy and intellectualism and vain deceit (idle fancies and plain nonsense), following human tradition (men's ideas of the material rather than the spiritual world), just crude notions following the rudimentary and elemental teachings of the universe and disregarding [the teachings of] Christ (the Messiah)."

> *We had to be delivered from the world system because we were all caught in its web—trained by it, educated by it, and grew up to love and participate in it (and its ways) in every way.*

We had to be delivered from the world system because we were all caught in its web—trained by it, educated by it, and grew up to love and participate in it (and its ways) in *every* way. Selfish ambition (a way of the world) thrived in us and by nature we chose to be the god of our own lives, being the one to choose what we would do, where we would live, and how we would decide what was right and wrong for our own life. We loved the world and the things the world offered us, or at least enticed us with, to try and compel us to acquire and obtain them. Its principles and desires were embedded in us, not the desires for the things of God and for Him to rule our lives. We loved ourselves, and what the world dangled before us, more than we loved God and doing His will. We were friends of the world and not friends of God.

📖 **James 4:4-5 NKJV**
"Adulterers and adulteresses! Do you not know that friendship with the world is enmity with God? Whoever therefore wants to be <u>a friend of the world makes himself an enemy of God</u>. Or do you think

that the Scripture says in vain, 'The Spirit who dwells in us yearns jealously?'"

📖 *James 4:4 AMP*

"You adulteresses [disloyal sinners- flirting with the world and breaking your vow to God]! Do you not know that being the world's friend [that is, loving the things of the world] is being God's enemy? So whoever chooses to be a friend of the world makes himself an enemy of God."

Everyone born into the world is, by nature, an enemy of God and under His wrath. The life inside must be removed and replaced If there is to be any hope for that person to be a friend of God. The cross was God's means to deliver us from the sinful nature that made us enemies of God and slaves to the world system. The cross delivered us from the spirit of the world and made way for us to receive a new spirit, and God's Spirit, to live in us.

What has God done to deliver us?

📖 *1 Corinthians 2:11-12 NKJV*

"For what man knows the things of a man except the spirit of the man which is in him? Even so no one knows the things of God except the Spirit of God. Now we have received, not the spirit of the world, but the Spirit who is from God, that we might know the things that have been freely given to us by God."

Being born again, we no longer have the spirit of the world, but we have the Spirit who is from God. The Spirit of Christ teaches us to love God (not the world), and to love His provisions in Christ Jesus, and not the world's. God brought us out of the control of the devil and the world system and into His kingdom to be His people. Look at the shadow of this deliverance, when Moses talked to the children of Israel about God's deliverance from Egypt.

📖 *Deuteronomy 4:20 NKJV*

"But the Lord has taken you and brought you out of the iron furnace, out of Egypt, to be His people, an inheritance, as you are this day."

We were brought out of the iron furnace of the world system by the cross of Christ, where Jesus condemned sin in His flesh. That system forged its ways into our inner man. It imposed on us its agenda to support, regulate, and promote the life of sin in men. At the cross, Jesus executed judgment upon the world, by crushing the life in man which brought him under its power, and by casting out the devil's access to all who believe in Christ and receive His life in them. Jesus announced this before it came to pass.

📖 *John 12:31-32 NKJV*
"Now is the judgment of this world; now the ruler of this world will be cast out. And I, if I am lifted up from the earth, will draw all peoples to Myself."

📖 *John 12:31-32 AMP*
"Now the judgment is upon this world [the sentence is being passed]. Now the ruler of this world (Satan) will be cast out. And I, if and when I am lifted up from the earth [on the cross], will draw all people to Myself [Gentiles, as well as Jews]."

> **As Jesus was going to the cross, He was declaring that the world was coming to judgment, and sentence was going to be passed on it and its ruler.**

As Jesus was going to the cross, He was declaring that the world was coming to judgment, and sentence was going to be passed on it and its ruler. The world order was about to suffer a devastating defeat as Jesus was going to terminate the nature that it so loves to control. The world would soon learn that all those who are disciples of Jesus Christ have a life inside of them the world cannot entice or control anymore. The Spirit of God in the new creation man creates new desires for the things of God. He helps and teaches *that* man to reject the things of the world, empowering him to overcome all its ways, and to obey God through continuing faith in Jesus Christ.

📖 *1 John 5:3-5 NKJV*
"For this is the love of God, that we keep His commandments. And His commandments are not burdensome. For whatever is born of God overcomes the world. And this is the victory that has overcome

the world- our faith. Who is he who overcomes the world, but he who believes that Jesus is the Son of God?"

📖 **1 John 5:4 AMP**

"For everyone born of God is victorious and overcomes the world; and this is the victory that has conquered and overcome the world- our [continuing, persistent] faith [in Jesus the Son of God]."

The expectation for everyone who is born again by the Spirit of God, is that they will follow Jesus, obey all His commands through communion with and faith in Him, and increasingly grow in intimately knowing Him. This is the will of God and the only way to encounter daily victory over the lust that is in the world.

> **The expectation for everyone who is born again by the Spirit of God, is that they will follow Jesus, obey all His commands through communion with and faith in Him, and increasingly grow in intimately knowing Him.**

📖 **2 Peter 1:2-4 NKJV**

"Grace and peace be multiplied to you in the knowledge of God and of Jesus our Lord, as His divine power has given to us all things that pertain to life and godliness, through the knowledge of Him who called us by glory and virtue, by which have been given to us exceedingly great and precious promises, that through these you may be partakers of the divine nature, having escaped the corruption that is in the world through lust."

Jesus delivered us from the pollutions and corruption of the world by crucifying the nature we were born with. He fatally wounded the sin nature that produced the corruption that made us captives. Now your job is to be with Jesus and to grow in knowing Him, obeying Him, and daily walking with Him by the Spirit of God that now dwells in you. Can you pause for a minute and please ask God to help you follow Jesus and to grow in knowing Him? And can you take a moment to give God the glory for delivering you from the world system by the finished work of Jesus Christ and Him crucified?

THE CROSS FOR DELIVERANCE FROM THE POWER OF THE FEAR OF DEATH

📖 *Hebrews 2:14-15 NKJV*
"Inasmuch then as the children have partaken of flesh and blood, He Himself likewise shared in the same, that through death He might destroy him who had the power of death, that is, the devil, and release those who through fear of death were all their lifetime subject to bondage."

All who are born of the flesh are born with a fear of death. They are subject to a lifetime of bondage to that fear. This fear enslaves the heart of men and women. It is often not seen in youth because of the natural vigor, health, and stamina the age of youth generally produces. However, if the threat and presence of death comes knocking (cancer, accident, sick relative, aging, etc.) the fear of death will arise from within and bring about drastic measures to avoid it. Without Christ, the idea of death, and what happens when one dies, will haunt people over the entire course of their lives.

📖 *Hebrews 2:15 AMPC*
"and also that He might deliver and completely set free all those who through the [haunting] fear of death were held in bondage throughout the whole course of their lives."

Because of God's sentence of death upon all who sin, it is an underlying fear in every man—for the wages of sin is death, and all have sinned and fall short of the glory of God. Anyone still in union with sin faces a certain death and judgment that follows.

> **However, if the threat and presence of death comes knocking (cancer, accident, sick relative, aging, etc.) the fear of death will arise from within and bring about drastic measures to avoid it.**

📖 *Hebrews 9:27-28 NKJV*
"And as it is appointed for men to die once, <u>but after this the judgment,</u> so Christ was offered once to bear the sins of many. To those who eagerly

247

wait for Him He will appear a second time, apart from sin, for sal-
vation."

The devil had the power of death because of the life of sin living in man which he could control and exercise sway over. He knew that if we die in our sin, God will judge us, and we will be eternally con-demned to hell. Natural man, under this fear, is always seeking out ways to preserve and extend his life and to battle the certainty of death. God set us free from that fear through faith in Jesus, who died for us and took our judgment upon Himself. God raised Him from that death in order to show the devil that God alone has power over death.

📖 *2 Timothy 1:10 NKJV*
"but has now been revealed by the appearing of our Savior Jesus Christ, who has abolished death and brought life and immortality to light through the gospel,"

The cross made the way for the resurrection of Christ, where Jesus proved His power over death. Men were enslaved to the powers of darkness and filled with the fear of death because of their sins and because of sin in them. By the cross, Jesus abolished the devil's pow-er of death by bearing in His body the sin nature which produces that fear within us. Our death, in the body of Christ at Calvary, brought us into a brand-new life in Christ, which is immune to eternal death and separation from God.

📖 *2 Timothy 1:10 AMPC*
"[It is that purpose and grace] which He now has made known and has fully disclosed and made real [to us] through the appearing of our Savior Christ Jesus, Who annulled death and made it of no effect and brought life and immortality (immunity from eternal death) to light through the Gospel."

All who are born of the Spirit through faith in Jesus receive this new life of Christ in them. This new creation man is delivered and com-pletely set free from the fear of death that haunted them in their old life. If a disciple of Jesus is still tormented by the fear of death, it is because they have either heard the truth and refused to believe and live according to it, or they have not yet heard, seen, or understood the truth of what Jesus did on the cross. You have died and your life is now hidden with Christ. This revelation in the knowledge of the truth sets God's people free and brings forth the fullness of the provision of the cross and resurrection into their lives. Jesus abolished death and took away the devil's power to threaten death and hell to all who believe on Him and have received His life. Do you see and know this reality, and do you live in the knowing of it every day?

> *This revelation in the knowledge of the truth sets God's people free and brings forth the fullness of the provision of the cross and resurrection into their lives.*

📖 **Romans 6:6-11 NKJV**

"knowing this, that our old man was crucified with Him, that the body of sin might be done away with, that we should no longer be slaves to sin. For he who has died has been freed from sin. Now if we died with Christ, we believe that we shall also live with Him, knowing that Christ, having been raised from the dead, dies no more. Death no longer has dominion over Him. For the death that He died, He died to sin once for all; but the life that He lives, He lives to God. Likewise you also, reckon yourselves to be dead indeed to sin, but alive to God in Christ Jesus our Lord."

Reckon means to take this truth into account at all times; always remember and apply it in everything you do. Death no longer has dominion over you because you died and have been set free from sin; Christ now lives in you. Continue KNOWING this and walk with Jesus according to this truth. Make Him your treasure and He will daily and eternally deliver you from every fear of death.

📖 **Proverbs 11:4 AMPC**

"Riches provide no security in any day of wrath and judgment, but righteousness (uprightness and right standing with God) delivers from death."

Nothing delivers man from death, and the wrath and judgment that awaits natural man after that death, except the work of Jesus Christ and Him crucified. Right standing with God and deliverance from death come only through faith in Jesus, who Himself is the righteousness of God. Deliverance from fear is through faith in His finished work (with understanding) through daily knowing we died, remembering Christ is the life in us, and letting Him live His life through us for the glory of God.

> *Deliverance from fear is through faith in His finished work (with understanding) through daily knowing we died, remembering Christ is the life in us, and letting Him live His life through us for the glory of God.*

THE CROSS FOR DELIVERANCE FROM THE WRATH TO COME

📖 *Ephesians 2:1-3 NKJV*

"And you He made alive, who were dead in trespasses and sins, in which you once walked according to the course of this world, according to the prince of the power of the air, the spirit who now works in the sons of disobedience, among whom also we all once conducted ourselves in the lusts of our flesh, fulfilling the desires of the flesh and of the mind, and were by nature children of wrath, just as the others."

AMP *"We were, by nature, children [under the sentence] of [God's] wrath, just like the rest [of mankind]"*
NIV *"we were by nature deserving of wrath"*
NLT *"By our very nature we were subject to God's anger, just like everyone else"*

All men are born with a sinful nature, inherited from Adam through his disobedience to God. We became sinners because sin came to dwell in us and produced the fruit of his life—sins.

    📖 ***Romans 5:19 NKJV***

"For as by one man's disobedience many were made sinners, so also by one Man's obedience many will be made righteous."

That nature makes all people deserving of wrath and subject to God's anger. The sin-life is hostile to God and follows its own impulses and desires. It walks according to the prince of the power of the air, and it is a life of darkness (from within) that does not submit to or obey God in spirit and in truth. This life cannot participate in or enter into the kingdom of God. It is a life that draws the wrath of God upon it by its very nature and what it produces through us.

    📖 ***Ephesians 5:5-8 NKJV***

"For this you know, that no fornicator, unclean person, nor covetous man, who is an idolater, has any inheritance in the kingdom of Christ and God. Let no one deceive you with empty words, for because of these things the wrath of God comes upon the sons of disobedience. Therefore do not be partakers with them. For <u>you were once darkness</u>, but now you are light in the Lord. Walk as children of light."

Man was without hope of escaping the wrath of God. He had no power to deliver himself because the nature he was born with was not discardable in his own strength. Deliverance from the wrath of God would only be available to those who hear the Gospel of Jesus Christ, repent of their sins, and believe in Him.

    📖 ***John 3:35-36 NKJV***

"The Father loves the Son, and has given all things into His hand. He who believes in the Son has everlasting life; and he who does not believe the Son shall not see life, but the wrath of God abides on him."

The wrath of God abides on all who are born of the flesh. That life, no matter how good the person tries to live, has the wrath of God hanging over their head. It abides with them everywhere they go, until the day God judges all men by the Lord Jesus Christ; the day the wrath of God will be released on all who refused to believe in His Son.

However, God made a way for deliverance from His wrath through faith in the finished work of Jesus Christ and Him crucified. At the cross, Jesus put to death the Adamic nature that caused us to be in darkness and eternally prohibited us from entering the kingdom of God.

> *That life, no matter how good the person tries to live, has the wrath of God hanging over their head. It abides with them everywhere they go, until the day God judges all men by the Lord Jesus Christ.*

Christ Jesus, who knew no sin, became sin for us, and God poured out His wrath upon Him and upon the life of disobedience that was poured into Him. Jesus carried to the cross and crucified the life of sin that brought us under the condemnation and wrath of God. Then, God raised Him from the dead, and through the resurrected Christ we became filled with the life of Christ, who Himself becomes our salvation and deliverance from wrath.

   📖 *1 Thessalonians 1:9-10 NKJV*
"For they themselves declare concerning us what manner of entry we had to you, and how you turned to God from idols to serve the living and true God, and to wait for His Son from heaven, whom He raised from the dead, even Jesus who delivers us from the wrath to come."
   📖 *1 Thessalonians 1:10b JBP*
"the Son Jesus, whom God raised from the dead, and who personally delivered us from the judgment which hung over our heads."

Our deliverance from the wrath of God is not a *thing*, but the very Person and life work of Jesus Christ. The judgment of God, which hung over our heads, was placed over His head at the cross and executed fiercely upon Him *("My God, My God, why have You forsaken Me?")*. Praise the Lord for the sacrifice of our Savior, through whom we are saved from the wrath of God *now,* and through whom we shall be saved from the wrath to come *then.*

📖 ***Romans 5:9-10 NKJV***
"Much more then, having now been justified by His blood, we shall be saved from wrath through Him. For if when we were enemies we were reconciled to God through the death of His Son, much more, having been reconciled, we shall be saved <u>by His life</u>."

Our salvation, our deliverance from the wrath to come, is because His life now dwells in us. Christ can never be under the wrath of God. Not only are we saved from the wrath to come, but His very life in us *daily* delivers us from sin's dominion, because sin no longer abides in us.

📖 ***Romans 5:10b AMPC***
"it is much more [certain], now that we are reconciled, that we shall be saved (daily delivered from sin's dominion) through His [resurrection] life."

TLB *"what blessings he must have for us now that we are his friends and he is living within us!"*
GNT *"how much more will we be saved by Christ's life!"*

THE CROSS FOR DELIVERANCE FROM THE LAW FOR RIGHTEOUSNESS

📖 ***Romans 7:4 NKJV***
"Therefore, my brethren, you also have become dead to the law through the body of Christ, that you may be married to another-to Him who was raised from the dead, that we should bear fruit to God."
📖 ***Colossians 3:3-4 NKJV***
"For you died, and your life is hidden with Christ in God. When Christ who is our life appears, then you also will appear with Him in glory."

The cross is where our old man was crucified. Remember, you died with Christ in the body of Christ, and Christ is now your life. He is who you have been joined to in the new birth. Therefore, you also died to the law (the old code and ways) because a dead man cannot obey the law. Imagine a man who owes $300 to the city for unpaid fines. But the man dies of a heart attack and has never paid the debt the law demands. The city doesn't know he is dead, a warrant has been issued for his arrest, and police officers come to his house. They can knock for 10 hours, and that man will never open the door to greet them. They can go to his grave, stand over it and demand he pay his fines, but he will not come out to give them what they want. That is what the cross of Christ did to our relationship with the Law. We are no longer under its demands because we have died to the law through the body of Christ. Now we can submit to Christ in us, who is God's righteousness.

📖 *Romans 10:1-4 NKJV*
"Brethren, my heart's desire and prayer to God for Israel is that they may be saved. For I bear them witness that they have a zeal for God, but not according to knowledge. For they being ignorant of God's righteousness, and seeking to establish their own righteousness, have not submitted to the righteousness of God. For Christ is the end of the law for righteousness to everyone who believes."

Man has no ability to make himself right with God. He cannot establish his own righteousness by outward acts, trying to please God. No matter how sincerely and energetically he seeks to be right with God in his own strength, he will always fall short and be unable to attain right standing or the salvation of God. Only faith in the work of Christ crucified can make someone right with God and end his relationship to the law as a means for righteousness. You must submit to the righteousness of God, which is Christ and nothing else. Obeying and following Jesus, submitting your life to Him who dwells in you, and giving Him all your devotion, is now your daily duty to God.

> *No matter how sincerely and energetically he seeks to be right with God in his own strength, he will always fall short and be unable to attain right standing or the salvation of God.*

📖 *Romans 10:1-4 GNT*
"My friends, how I wish with all my heart that my own people might be

saved! How I pray to God for them! I can assure you that they are deeply devoted to God; but their devotion is not based on true knowledge. They have not known the way in which God puts people right with himself, and instead, they have tried to set up their own way; and so they did not submit themselves to God's way of putting people right. For Christ has brought the Law to an end, so that everyone who believes is put right with God."

Only the righteousness that comes from God, through the finished work of Christ, will make way for a man to enter the kingdom of heaven. Sincere devotion and extraordinary zeal, without this knowledge being mixed with faith in the heart, can never deliver a man from the demands of the Law. Praise the Lord and give Him all the glory. For the work of the cross has caused us (who believe) to become dead to the law (and its demands) for righteousness, and to find our righteousness in Christ alone.

> *Sincere devotion and extraordinary zeal, without this knowledge being mixed with faith in the heart, can never deliver a man from the demands of the Law.*

📖 *1 Corinthians 1:30-31 NKJV*
"But of Him you are in Christ Jesus, who became for us wisdom from God- and righteousness and sanctification and redemption- that, as it is written, 'He who glories, let him glory in the LORD.'"

THE CROSS FOR DELIVERANCE FROM EVERY CURSE

📖 *Jeremiah 17:5-6 NKJV*
"Thus says the LORD: Cursed is the man who trusts in man and makes flesh his strength, whose heart departs from the LORD. For he shall be like a shrub in the desert, and shall not see when good comes, but shall inhabit the parched places in the wilderness, in a salt land which is not inhabited."

Any trust in man, or in the strength of the flesh of man, brings with it a curse. The reason the cross delivers us from this kind of curse is because it destroyed the flesh (the sinful nature) as the source of strength to rely on from within. Death has come to our old, self-dependent life and as we carry the reality of that death in our daily walk with Jesus, we shall learn to rely on Him *alone* for our strength. Jesus became a curse for us by absorbing the sinful, Adamic nature of man entirely into Himself. He did this so we (through faith) could be delivered from the curse of the law of sin and death, which was upon us in our union with sin.

📖 *Galatians 3:13 NKJV*
"Christ has redeemed us from the curse of the law, having become a curse for us (for it is written, 'Cursed is everyone who hangs on a tree')."
📖 *Galatians 3:13 MSG*
"Christ redeemed us from that self-defeating, cursed life by absorbing it completely into himself. Do you remember the Scripture that says, 'Cursed is everyone who hangs on a tree'? That is what happened when Jesus was nailed to the cross: He became a curse, and at the same time dissolved the curse."

The old man (the sin nature we were yoked to by law) was cursed by God, sentenced to death and eternal separation from Him. The wages of sin is death, and that declaration hangs over the head of everyone born of the flesh. Jesus became cursed for us when He went to the cross with that cursed life inside of Him. It was there He delivered us from that self-defeating, cursed life that was under the law of sin and death the moment we believed on Him. He dealt with the stubborn, rebellious, and disobedient life of sin we were born with, in order to give us a new, obedient life in Him. Let's look at an Old Testament law that is a shadow of the work of the cross in dealing with the life which was cursed to death.

> *Jesus became cursed for us when He went to the cross with that cursed life inside of Him.*

📖 *Deuteronomy 21:18-23 NKJV*
"If a man has a stubborn and rebellious son who will not obey the voice of his father or the voice of his mother, and who, when they have chastened him,

will not heed them, then his father and his mother shall take hold of him and bring him out to the elders of his city, to the gate of his city. And they shall say to the elders of his city, 'This son of ours is stubborn and rebellious; he will not obey our voice; he is a glutton and a drunkard.' Then all the men of his city shall stone him to death with stones; so you shall put away the evil from among you, all Israel shall hear and fear. If a man has committed a sin deserving of death, and he is put to death, and you hang him on a tree, his body shall not remain overnight on the tree, but you shall surely bury him that day, so that you do not defile the land which the LORD your God is giving you as an inheritance; <u>for he who is hanged is accursed of God.</u>"

The Adamic nature is a disobedient life that will not obey the voice of the God who created him. Even after discipline he will not listen to or obey God. It is a stubborn and rebellious nature, too sick to be healed, and only worthy of death. All men, born into this world, inherited that nature from Adam and were under the curse of the sentence of death and rejection by God. Jesus Christ *became* that stubborn and rebellious Son, who God put to death, when He drank into Himself the Adamic nature and became sin; when He became the last Adam. He came to take the place of our stubborn and rebellious selves by becoming the embodiment of that whole, corrupt carnal nature, and taking it to the cross to crucify it.

   📖 *2 Corinthians 5:21 NKJV*
"For He made Him who knew no sin to be sin for us, that we might become the righteousness of God in Him."
   📖 *2 Corinthians 5:21 JBP*
"For God caused Christ, who himself knew nothing of sin, actually to be sin for our sakes, so that in Christ we might be made good with the goodness of God."

God poured our sinful, Adamic nature into Jesus and He bore it in order to be hanged on a tree (the cross). He became a curse for us and delivered us from every curse when He took that life to the grave. For those who are born again, there is no longer a life inside that can be cursed. Christ dwells in you, and He cannot be cursed because a curse must have a cause for it to come.

📖 **Proverbs 26:2 NKJV**
"Like a flitting sparrow, like a flying swallow, so a curse without cause shall not alight."

AMP "the curse without cause does not come and alight [on the undeserving]"
TLB "an undeserved curse has no effect"
NLT "an undeserved curse will not land on its intended victim"

> *For those who are born again, there is no longer a life inside that can be cursed.*

Even if all the evil spirits came to surround a man born of the Spirit of God, they would not be able to lay one single curse upon that man as he abides in Jesus. The life of Christ inside of him *cannot* be cursed and is greater than all those outside of him put together. The same is true for what they call generational curses that are passed down the natural family lineage. When you came to Christ, you were removed from that lineage by the work of the cross, and you were brought into the lineage of God by the resurrection of Christ. The life of mere flesh that was in you, that could receive a curse passed down from your ancestors, was terminated and re-moved. All generational curses ceased and ended at the cross, for the one who is born again. Christ, in a person, is their strength and protection from all curses of the enemy. Christ delivered us from every curse by going to the cross to crucify that old, sin-cursed life.

THE CROSS FOR DELIVERANCE FROM THE LUSTS AND DESIRES OF THE FLESH

📖 **Galatians 5:24-25 NKJV**
"And those who are Christ's have crucified the flesh with its passions and desires. If we live in the Spirit, let us also walk in the Spirit."
📖 **Galatians 5:24 AMP**
"And those who belong to Christ Jesus have crucified the sinful na-ture together with its passions and appetites."

The cross terminated the sinful nature. As a result, all of its passions, desires, and appetites were done away with. A dead man cannot produce desires and passions. Think of it like this. You have a boss who is always yelling at you and forcing you to do what he wants, ruling you according to his desires. You are subject to his ways, operations, and desires by way of your employment. But if that boss dies, none of his passions or desires will be active in your life; they perish with him. Likewise, your flesh (sinful nature) was crucified with Christ, along with all his appetites and ways. Now you belong to Jesus Christ, and as you walk with Him by His Spirit, you will be discovering and experiencing *His* passions, *His* desires, and *His* appetites re-placing your old ones. We are not BEING delivered from the flesh but HAVE BEEN delivered. You are no longer in the flesh but in the Spirit.

> *The cross terminated the sinful nature. As a result, all of its passions, desires, and appetites were done away with. A dead man cannot produce desires and passions.*

📖 *Romans 8:8-9 NKJV*
"So then, those who are in the flesh cannot please God. But <u>you are not in the flesh</u> but in the Spirit, if indeed the Spirit of God dwells in you. Now if anyone does not have the Spirit of Christ, he is not His."

It is clear that those who are "in the flesh" cannot please God. We all agree with the word of God. However, I perceive many people think this means those who "let the flesh be in charge" or those who "obey the flesh". But that is not what Paul used to define what "in the flesh" means. The qualification for being "in the flesh" was not the activities you do or don't do, but *if* the Spirit of God dwells in you or not. Did you see that? It would read differently if it said, "you are not in the flesh, but in the Spirit, if indeed you do what the Spirit says and not the flesh." Then you would ascribe being "in the flesh" with what activities you are doing. But the Bible says, "you ARE NOT in the flesh" if the Spirit of God dwells in you.

According to the Scripture, at the cross, Christ crucified the flesh (the sinful nature) and you who belong to Christ are not in the flesh any longer. Look at further evidence to strengthen the case.

📖 *Romans 7:5 NKJV*

"For <u>when we were</u> in the flesh, the sinful passions which <u>were</u> <u>aroused </u>by the law <u>were at work</u> in our members to bear fruit to death."

📖 *Ephesians 2:3 NKJV*

"among whom also <u>we all once</u> conducted ourselves in the lusts of our flesh, fulfilling the desires of the flesh and of the mind, <u>and were</u> by nature children of wrath, just as the others."

📖 *Colossians 2:11 AMPC*

"In Him also you were circumcised with a circumcision not made with hands, but in a [spiritual] circumcision [performed by] Christ stripping off the body of the flesh (the whole, corrupt, carnal nature with its passions and lusts)."

You have been delivered from the flesh, and the power of its lusts and desires, by the glorious work of Christ at Calvary. You once conducted yourselves (*past tense*) in the lusts of the flesh. You WERE in the flesh, which USED to be at work in your members to bear fruit to death. That nature is no longer in you, but Christ is in you, and you *can* walk with Him as you yield to His Spirit. You will now carry yourself to Christ (in you) when you find wrong desires and appetites arising from within your heart. As you do that, you will be remembering that you died to sin and that nature no longer dwells in you; it is only old ways left behind from that union. You will be turning to Christ and asking Him what to do and how to respond to these old desires, and He will give you grace and enable you to understand and carry out His instructions which will bring life and godliness. As you learn to live this way, in the realities of the manifold deliverance of the cross, you will become a living testimony to the principalities and powers in the heavenly places, that they are defeated, because now you *know* they are defeated.

> **The qualification for being "in the flesh" was not the activities you do or don't do, but if the Spirit of God dwells in you or not.**

📖 *Ephesians 3:10 AMPC*

"[The purpose is] that through the church the complicated, many-sided wisdom of God in all its infinite variety and innumerable aspects might now be made known to the angelic rulers and authorities (principalities and powers) in the heavenly sphere."

> *You will be turning to Christ and asking Him what to do and how to respond to these old desires, and He will give you grace and enable you to understand and carry out His instructions which will bring life and godliness.*

As we have been traveling through these pages, God is helping us to see and understand how extensive and powerful the Gospel of Jesus Christ is, and how wonderful the message of the cross is to we who are being saved. We have seen, by the grace of God, the manifold deliverance and effects of the cross, and what God has done to deliver us *completely*. We are now ready to proceed and look at His provision of the resurrection of Jesus Christ. But first, let's take a moment to thank God and pray and plead with Him to open our eyes of understanding to see Jesus more fully.

Our God and Father, we praise You for the manifold deliverance of the cross which Christ secured for us who have believed. Thank You for further opening our eyes of understanding and enlarging our capacity to see the mystery of Jesus Christ and Him crucified. Please help us to practically live according to these truths in our everyday life with Jesus. Now Father, we ask that You keep showing us great and mighty things concerning our Lord Jesus Christ and the resurrection provision You have given us in Him. Thank You for hearing us, Father, for we are praying to You in the name of Jesus Christ. Amen.

CHAPTER 11

THE RESURRECTION OF JESUS CHRIST

📖 *1 Corinthians 15:17 NKJV*
"And if Christ is not risen, your faith is futile; you are still in your sins!"
📖 *1 Corinthians 15:17 AMPC*
"And if Christ has not been raised, your faith is mere delusion [futile, fruitless], and you are still in your sins [under the control and penalty of sin];"

As wonderful as the blood and cross of Christ are, they are of no use to our life if they are not connected to the resurrection provision from God. Our faith will be empty and fruitless, because we will not have the right kind of life inside of us. The resurrection of Jesus Christ is God's devised means to give us hope and to fulfill the desires of His heart by putting His very life in us.

📖 *Galatians 1:11-12 NKJV*
"But I make known to you, brethren, that the gospel which was preached by me is not according to man. For I neither received it from

man, nor was I taught it, but it came through the revelation of Jesus Christ."

The resurrected Christ comes into our life by believing the word of God and by the revelation (manifestation) of Jesus Christ to us. Many who call on the name of the Lord have not come to a revelation in the knowledge of what Christ has done, both in the cross (the death and removal of the old man) and in the resurrection (the pouring in of the New Man—Jesus Christ). This blindness has led to a vague and powerless life without much victory over sin, self, the world, and the devil. Many Christians look like ordinary men of the world whose lives do not differ from unbelievers in any significant way. God must open our eyes to see this mystery and discover how to walk in it. The reality of the resurrection comes as the Father reveals His Son to us and in us, according to His good pleasure and purpose. God's provision of the resurrection and new life are not *things* to acquire, but the very Person of the Lord Jesus Christ Himself. He IS the resurrection, and He IS the life. Once you believed on Jesus, if you have not seen this or understood this reality, you may be living as if Jesus is not your life. It's possible He is not even in you.

> **Once you believed on Jesus, if you have not seen this or understood this reality, you may be living as if Jesus is not your life.**

📖 **2 Corinthians 13:5 NKJV**
"Examine yourselves as to whether you are in the faith. Test yourselves. Do you not know yourselves, that Jesus Christ is in you?- unless indeed you are disqualified."

📖 **2 Corinthians 13:5 TLB**
"Check up on yourselves. Are you really Christians? Do you pass the test? Do you feel Christ's presence and power more and more within you? Or are you just pretending to be Christians when actually you aren't at all?"

📖 **2 Corinthians 13:5b AMPC**
"Do you not yourselves realize and know [thoroughly by an ever-increasing experience] that Jesus Christ is in you- unless you are [counterfeits] disapproved on trial and rejected?"

There is an authentic biblical test of whether someone is a Christian or not. It is not because they say they have believed in Jesus, but whether or not Christ is *in* them as a result of their faith. Otherwise, their faith is futile, and they are counterfeits. The word of God is not saying for me to examine you, but for you to examine yourselves to make sure you are in the faith, by meeting this one critical test. If Christ is IN you, you will know it by ever-increasing experiences of His presence and power within. If He is not, you are only pretending to be a Christian, and you will be disapproved on trial, rejected by God on that Day, and disqualified from entering into eternal life with Him. So, we are going to spend some time digging into the word of God to better understand this wonderful provision of the resurrected Christ living in you.

CHRIST IN YOU, THE HOPE OF GLORY

📖 *Colossians 1:27-28 AMPC*
"To whom God was pleased to make known how great for the Gentiles are the riches of the glory of this mystery, which is Christ within and among you, the Hope of [realizing the] glory. Him we preach and proclaim, warning and admonishing everyone and instructing everyone in all wisdom (comprehensive insight into the ways and purposes of God), that we may present every person mature (full-grown, fully initiated, complete, and perfect) in Christ (the Anointed One)."

NKJV *"Christ in you, the hope of glory"*
GNT *"the secret is that Christ is in you, which means that you will share in the glory of God"*
MSG *"the mystery in a nutshell is just this: Christ is in you, so therefore you can look forward to sharing in God's glory"*

We have been looking into the mystery of Christ in much detail. The Lord has helped us to better understand the unsearchable riches God has placed in Christ, the blood of Christ, and the cross of Christ. But the *riches* of the glory of this mystery is Christ coming to live within you. This is the pinnacle of all of God's provisions to us in Christ Jesus. This is that which brings us hope of realizing the glory of God in our lives, in our marriages and families, in our occupations, and in our ministries. The Bible says, "that no flesh shall glory in His presence." The cross dealt with the issue of the flesh, and the resurrection is God's means to bring Christ into us, who enables us to share in God's glory as He does the work of God through us. This is a critical understanding, and it only comes by revelation from God. You need to see Jesus actually living in you.

📖 *Galatians 1:15-16 NKJV*
"But when it pleased God, who separated me from my mother's womb and called me through His grace, <u>to reveal His Son in me</u>, that I might preach Him among the Gentiles, I did not immediately confer with flesh and blood,"

It does not say, "to reveal His Son to me," but "to reveal His Son IN me." This must come by revelation from God. Many Christians have been sincerely born again, but because they have never seen the reality of Christ in them, their lives lack power and a considerable level of intimacy with Jesus. There is a difference between seeing the letters of the Bible that say Christ is in you, and the actual revelation experience that comes from God to reveal His Son in you. The cross effectively crucified the life we were born with from our mother's womb. It separated us from that life forever. The resurrection is the way God now brings Christ to live in us and to actually BE our life, everlasting. Jesus shared this reality one day when He was having a conversation with Martha.

> *There is a difference between seeing the letters of the Bible that say Christ is in you, and the actual revelation experience that comes from God to reveal His Son in you.*

📖 *John 11:23-27 NKJV*
"Jesus said to her, 'Your brother will rise again.' Martha said to Him, 'I know that he will rise again in the resurrection at the last day.' Jesus said to her, 'I am the resurrection and the life. He who believes in Me, though He may die, he shall live. And whoever lives and be-

lieves in Me shall never die. Do you believe this?' She said to Him, 'Yes, Lord, I believe that You are the Christ, the Son of God, who is to come into the world.'"

AMPC "shall never [actually] die at all"
MSG "does not ultimately die at all"

Martha told Jesus her understanding concerning the resurrection, but Jesus took it further to show her that He *is* the resurrection and life. He is telling Martha not to put her hope in the resurrection, but to put her hope in Him, who is the resurrection. If you believe in Him and have received His life, even if you physically die, you will be raised from that death and live forever with God because of Christ in you. And if you have believed in Him and God has still allowed you to live on the earth, you will never ultimately die, because Christ is your life, and He will cause you to live forever with God. When you believed on Jesus, you began a new life because Christ came to live inside of you. He didn't just give us a new life; He Himself actually became our resurrection and new life.

📖 **Galatians 2:20-21 NKJV**
"I have been crucified with Christ; it is no longer I who live, but Christ lives in me; and the life which I now live in the flesh I live by faith in the Son of God, who loved me and gave Himself for me. I do not set aside the grace of God; for if righteousness comes through the law, then Christ died in vain."
📖 **Galatians 2:20 AMP**
"I have been crucified with Christ [that is, in Him I have shared His crucifixion]; it is no longer I who live, but Christ lives in me. The life I now live in the body I live by faith [by adhering to, relying on, and completely trusting] in the Son of God, who loved me and gave Himself up for me."

Christ died to come and live in me and do the work of God through me. My job is to be with Him daily; yield-

> **He is telling Martha not to put her hope in the resurrection, but to put her hope in Him, who is the resurrection.**

ing to and obeying Him and letting Him live His life from within me. Anything else I try to do *for* God will be considered frustrating the very grace of Christ's life which God has put in me. All of my own efforts to produce righteousness, apart from allowing Christ to do it, will be me setting aside the grace of God, and treating Christ as meaningless and of minor importance, defeating the very purpose of God for my life in Him. It is no longer we who live, but Christ who lives in us. It is the sweet aroma of His life that God desires to release through us into the world. It is Christ in us who always leads us in victory as we correctly walk with Him.

📖 *2 Corinthians 2:14-15 NKJV*
"Now thanks be to God who always leads us in triumph in Christ, and through us diffuses the fragrance of His knowledge in every place. For we are to God the fragrance of Christ among those who are being saved and among those who are perishing."

As God's people walk according to the reality of Christ living in them, in obedience and submission to Him, their lives (Christ's life) will be diffused (poured out) in such a way that unbelievers, disobedient believers, as well as disciples, will see the riches of the glory of God's good plan for a man's life. God desires to release the fragrance of His life through you. Christ in men is the hope of glory and the plan of God for man to enter eternal life. The life of Christ in man, being allowed to live His life through that man, will release an aroma that brings a true knowledge of God in every place. As we have shared in His crucifixion, we have also shared in His resurrection, and we now live because of and by Christ in us. The hope of realizing (experiencing) the glory of God is located in relying on Christ in us, adhering to Him, and completely trusting in Him in everything we do in this new creation life. God desires you to really come to know this truth in increasing measures, and for you to be filled with all the fullness of God by Christ's life growing in you.

📖 *Ephesians 3:19 AMPC*
"[That you may really come] to know [practically, through experience for yourselves] the love of Christ, which far surpasses mere know-ledge [without experience]; that you may be filled [through all your

being] unto all the fullness of God [may have the richest measure of the divine Presence, and become a body wholly filled and flooded with God Himself]!"

This was always God's objective from the beginning when He created man. He originally designed mankind to be a body wholly filled and flooded with the life of God Himself. That life was what made man in His image. He made the first man from the dust of the earth and breathed His very life into them. His intention was for them to multiply that kind of life on the face of the earth and to deal with the issue of darkness which covered the earth. They were made in the image of God by the life God breathed into them.

   📖 **Genesis 1:27 NKJV**
"So God created man in His own image; in the image of God He created him; male and female He created them."

   📖 **Genesis 2:7 NKJV**
"And the LORD God formed man of the dust of the ground, and breathed into his nostrils the breath of life; and man became a living being."

> **He originally designed mankind to be a body wholly filled and flooded with the life of God Himself. That life was what made man in His image.**

But when Adam sinned, a new kind of life came that was unable to deal with the problem of darkness that covered the earth. A life that was actually darkness itself, and carried with it a *different* image and likeness than God's. In the day God created man, He created him in the image of God, male and female He created them in His own image. But when they sinned against God, they became something different and bore a different image according to the life that was now in them.

   📖 **Genesis 5:1-3 NKJV**
"This is the book of the genealogy of Adam. In the day that God created man, He made him in the likeness of God. He created them male and female, and blessed them and called them Mankind in the

day they were created. And Adam lived one hundred and thirty years, and begot a son in his own likeness, after his image, and named him Seth."

KJV *"and called their name Adam, in the day when they were created"*

Something has changed! Please note the Bible says, "in the day that God created man." That is referring to a singular day; the day when God originally created the first man Adam (the sixth day of creation). That was THE DAY when God created mankind (the male and female) in His own image and likeness. But now we see that Adam (who *was* in the image of God) is now bearing children who are in the image and likeness of man, and not God. I know this challenges the belief of some that all people are children of God who are born in His image. So, let's look into the word of God to see what He says about the concept of children to settle the matter.

Children of the flesh and children of the promise

> *There is a difference between children of the flesh and children of God. Only those who come through the promise of Jesus Christ can be counted as the children (seed) of God.*

📖 **Romans 9:6-8 NKJV**
"But it is not that the word of God has taken no effect. For they are not all Israel who are of Israel, nor are they all children because they are the seed of Abraham; but, 'In Isaac your seed shall be called.' That is, those who are the <u>children of the flesh</u>, these are not the children of God; but the <u>children of the promise</u> are counted as the seed."

There is a difference between children of the flesh and children of God. Only those who come through the promise of Jesus Christ can be counted as the children (seed) of God. Everyone born of the flesh is a son or daughter of disobedience by nature; by the very life and image they inherited from their disobedient father, Adam. That is the life that brought death to us all.

📖 *Ephesians 2:1-3 NKJV*
"And you He made alive, who were dead in trespasses and sins, in which you once walked according to the course of this world, according to the prince of the power of the air, the spirit <u>who now works in the sons of disobedience</u>, *among whom also* <u>we all once conducted ourselves in the lusts of our flesh</u>, *fulfilling the desires of the flesh and of the mind, and were by nature children of wrath, just as the others."*

📖 *Ephesians 2:3 TLB*
"All of us used to be just as they are, <u>our lives expressing the evil within us</u>, *doing every wicked thing that our passions or our evil thoughts might lead us into. We started out bad, being born with evil natures, and were under God's anger just like everyone else."*

📖 *Ephesians 2:2b AMPC*
"[You were obedient to and under the control of] the [demon] spirit that still constantly works in the sons of disobedience [the careless, the rebellious, and the unbelieving, who go against the purposes of God]."

Does any of this sound or look like the image and likeness of God to you? Nature produces and expresses an image that is in its own likeness. The life in a man brings forth a representative resemblance (an observable image) that is the embodiment (likeness) of the nature of the life within.

We started out bad, being born with evil natures that would express (manifest) the evil within us. We were under the control of the wicked spirit that dwelled in us, and we conducted our lives in a selfish manner that looked like, acted like, and disobeyed like sons of disobedience. By nature, we were children of wrath, not children of God; children of the curse, not children of the promise. We became sons of disobedience and children of the devil.

271

Children of the devil and children of God

📖 *1 John 3:10 NKJV*
"In this the <u>children of God</u> and the <u>children of the devil</u> are manifest: Whoever does not practice righteousness is not of God, nor is he who does not love his brother."
📖 *1 John 3:10 TLB*
"So now we can tell who is a child of God and who belongs to Satan. Whoever is living a life of sin and doesn't love his brother shows that he is not in God's family;"

Image and likeness is based on what life is being manifested from inside of a person. The activities (fruits) of that life reveal whose child you are and whether you are in the image of God or in the image of man. This verse clearly says there are children of God and there are children of the devil. It also says we can tell who you belong to by the manifestation of the kind of life you are living. Listen to Jesus.

📖 *Matthew 13:37-39 NKJV*
"He answered them and said to them: 'He who sows the good seed is the Son of Man. The field is the world, the good seeds are the <u>sons of the kingdom</u>, but the tares are the <u>sons of the wicked one</u>. The enemy who sowed them is the devil, the harvest is the end of the age, and the reapers are the angels."

> **There are sons of the kingdom and sons of the wicked one. The determining factor is what life is inside, producing its image through you to be seen by those around you.**

There are sons of the kingdom and sons of the wicked one. The determining factor is what life is inside, producing its image through you to be seen by those around you. What are you like? Is your likeness and conduct like that of God (by Christ in you), or like that of man (by the wicked one)? One day, Jesus dealt with this in Peter (before he was born again on the night of the resurrection). Let's look.

📖 *Matthew 16:21-23 NKJV*

"From that time Jesus began to show to His disciples that He must go to Jerusalem, and suffer many things from the elders and chief priests and scribes, and be killed, and be raised the third day. Then Peter took Him aside and began to rebuke Him, saying, "Far be it from You, Lord; this shall not happen to You!' But He turned and said to Peter, 'Get behind Me, Satan! You are an offense to Me, for you are not mindful of the things of God, but the things of men.'"

AMPC *"for you are minding what partakes not of the nature and quality of God, but of men"*
GNT *"because these thoughts of yours don't come from God, but from human nature"*

Who was Jesus talking to? Was it to Peter or was it to Satan? Both! Peter didn't even realize he was offending God by what he was saying. It was just the nature and quality of life inside of him, engaging his mind and his mouth to utter something contrary to the will of God. Can you imagine it? Basically, Peter was calling Jesus a liar. Jesus told His disciples about things that were getting ready to happen to Him and Peter rebuked Him and said they would not happen. That is a behavior, that proceeds from a nature, that looks like the image of the life of darkness that dwelled in Peter. The life we were born with (the life of the flesh) was in the image of mere man and under the power of Satan. When Jesus delivered Paul from that old life on the road to Damascus and told him what kind of ministry he would be doing, He referred to this problem in mankind.

📖 *Acts 26:17-18 NKJV*

*"I will deliver you from the Jewish people, as well as from the Gentiles, to whom I now send you, to open their eyes, in order to turn them from darkness to light, and from the power of Satan to God, that they may receive forgiveness of sins **and** an inheritance among those who are sanctified by faith in Me."*

Upon hearing the Gospel and repenting, we received forgiveness of sins, and the blood of Christ was applied by God. Then the work of the cross was activated on our behalf to terminate and remove the life inside of us that was in the image of man and under the power of Satan. After that, we were able to receive our inheritance from God, the resurrection provision of Christ coming to live in us. Christ, who is the image of God, became our new life and we became children of God who were reborn into His likeness by the life of Christ in us. We became children of light by His life.

Children of light and children of darkness

📖 *Ephesians 5:6-9 NKJV*
"Let no one deceive you with empty words, for because of these things the wrath of God comes upon the sons of disobedience. Therefore do not be partakers with them. For <u>you were once darkness</u>, but now you are light in the Lord. Walk as children of light (for the fruit of the Spirit is in all goodness, righteousness, and truth),"
📖 *Ephesians 5:8 AMPC*
"For once you were darkness, but now you are light in the Lord; walk as children of Light [lead the lives of those native-born to the Light]."

The Bible says, "you were once darkness.' That is different than only saying you were IN the darkness. Saying we WERE darkness means it was actually our nature; it was what we were like (our likeness), and it was the picture (image) of who we were. We were born children of darkness who produced darkness by the life we were joined to. The Gospel came to deal with the issue that made us darkness, and to make us to be reborn as children of Light. We actually became light in the Lord by Christ's life coming into us.

📖 *1 Thessalonians 5:4-6 NKJV*
"But you, brethren, are not in darkness, so that this Day should overtake you as a thief. You are all sons of light and sons of the day. We are not of the night nor of darkness. Therefore let us not sleep, as others do, but let us watch and be sober."

📖 *1 Thessalonians 5:5 NIV*
"You are all children of light and children of the day. We do not belong to the night or to the darkness."

Thanks be to God! We do not belong to the night nor to the darkness anymore. We have nothing to fear when the Day of judgment comes and overtakes those who are in darkness. This isn't only because we believed on the Lord Jesus, but because of what God did as a result of our faith. He took away that which made us darkness (and made us to dwell in the darkness), and He put in us the life of Christ that is Light. He *made* us children of God. We were not *born* children of God. We became children of God and heirs of the promise because we believed on Jesus. And because we received Jesus to come and live in us, we became *born again*.

📖 *John 1:10-13 NKJV*
"He was in the world, and the world was made through Him, and the world did not know Him. He came to His own, and His own did not receive Him. But as many as received Him, to them He gave the right <u>to become</u> children of God, to those who believe in His name: <u>who were born</u>, not of blood, nor of the will of the flesh, nor of the will of man, but <u>of God</u>."

> **The Gospel came to deal with the issue that made us darkness, and to make us to be reborn as children of Light.**

Upon our faith, God gave us the right to BECOME children of God. The word "become" means to begin to be, to come into existence, to come into being. It is the beginning of something, and it has to do with a new birth. Did you see the word of God say, "who were born of God?" We were first born of the flesh, born of the seed of Adam, born of a woman, and joined to a life of darkness and disobedience. When we came to Christ, God made us to *become* children of God by causing us to be born again with a new life.

📖 *Galatians 3:26 NKJV*
"For you are all sons of God through faith in Christ Jesus."
📖 *Galatians 3:26 AMP*
"For you [who are born-again have been reborn from above-spiritually transformed, renewed, sanctified and] are all children of God [set apart for His purpose with full rights and privileges] through faith in Christ Jesus."

275

We need to spend a little time looking at the idea of being born again. Many people do not understand what this means, and the Lord desires to shed light upon this truth to help our lives.

YOU MUST BE BORN AGAIN

📖 *John 3:3-8 NKJV*

"Jesus answered and said to him, 'Most assuredly, I say to you, unless one is born again, he cannot see the kingdom of God. Nicodemus said to Him, 'How can a man be born when he is old? Can he enter a second time into his mother's womb and be born?' Jesus answered, "Most assuredly, I say to you, unless one is born of water and the Spirit, he cannot enter the kingdom of God. That which is born of the flesh is flesh, and that which is born of the Spirit is spirit. Do not marvel that I said to you, 'You must be born again.' The wind blows where it wishes, and you hear the sound of it, but cannot tell where it comes from and where it goes. So is everyone who is born of the Spirit."

In saying, "you MUST be born again," Jesus presented it as an absolute requirement. The language He uses implies that unless this happens you cannot see or enter the kingdom of God. No flesh shall glory in His presence, so the life of the flesh can never be where God is. Here, Jesus also equates being born again with being born of the Spirit. As He was explaining this to Nicodemus, He emphasized the difference between being born of the *flesh* and being born of the *Spirit*.

Because of where we are at this stage of the book, we know that our first birth came with a nature that had to be put to death and removed. We saw God's means of the blood and the cross to deal with that. The resurrection is His means to cause us to experience the required second birth, being born from *above* by the Spirit of Christ coming to live in us and be our life.

📖 *John 3:7 AMP*

"Do not be surprised that I have told you, 'You must be born again [reborn from above- spiritually transformed, renewed, sanctified].'"

276

Being born again is being born from above. You *were* born from be-low (of the flesh) and now you have been born from above (of the Spirit). You are an entirely different, newly created being because of the life of Christ in you. It is not because your sins are forgiven or because you professed faith in Jesus. Those things are good and necessary first things, but the reason you are born again is because Christ now lives in you.

In talking with Nicodemus to describe what this new life is like, Jesus used an illustration to help him better understand being born again. He said, "*The wind blows where it wishes, and you hear the sound of it, but cannot tell where it comes from and where it goes. So is every-one who is born of the Spirit.*" What did Jesus mean by this? Wind is something you cannot see with your natural eyes. You know it is there and you can feel its effects, but you are unable to trap it with your hands or see it with your physical eyes. So, imagine you are looking out of your window at a tree in the yard and you see its branches and leaves moving about as if they are dancing. It is not the tree itself saying, "I think I want to shake my branches and leaves for a while," but it is the unseen force of the wind that is orchestrating the movement of those branches and leaves. Do you see that? The tree did nothing to initiate its movement but to abide in the place where it was planted and allow the wind to have its way.

> *The resurrection is His means to cause us to experience the required second birth, being born from above by the Spirit of Christ coming to live in us and be our life.*

To be born again is to have the reality of Christ in you. But nobody can *see* Him in you, they can only see your outward man with their natural eyes. As you walk with Jesus, abiding in Him, and learning to let Him live His life from within and through you, the movements of your life will be because of Him (His Spirit) and not you. You will be the branch that moves where He wants to move and does what He wants to do. The unseen force (life) of Christ *in you* will be orchestrating the movements of your life and it will be manifested to those around you. It will become evident to all that you are indeed born again with a different kind of life. You will be born of God and permitted to enter into His kingdom by the new life you have received. Jesus was explaining this born-again necessity one day to His disciples when they came and asked Him, "Who then is the greatest in the kingdom of heaven?"

📖 *Matthew 18:2-4 NKJV*
"Then Jesus called a little child to Him, set him in the midst of them, and said, 'Assuredly, I say to you, unless you are converted and become as little children, you will by no means enter the kingdom of heaven. Therefore whoever humbles himself as this little child is the greatest in the kingdom of heaven."

Converted means to change from one form to another. Jesus again is using the word "unless" to describe the necessary conversion required for the new birth. Unless you are born again, unless you are converted; He is speaking of the same thing. Unless we humble ourselves before the Lord, repent of our sins, believe on the Lord Jesus Christ, and receive Him and become newly born babes in Christ, we will by no means enter the kingdom of heaven. We must be changed from one form of life to another by means of the blood, cross, and resurrection of Christ Jesus. We were born as babies, through the womb of our mother, with a life that manifested itself through us. We grew with that nature, and it was made visible as it orchestrated the movements of our life in union with it. The manifestation of the flesh (sinful nature) was expressed in many ways through each individual person. Some were pure evil, and some really tried to do good, but all were born of the flesh and not children of God's kingdom.

> **Unless we humble ourselves before the Lord, repent of our sins, believe on the Lord Jesus Christ, and receive Him and become newly born babes in Christ, we will by no means enter the kingdom of heaven.**

278

Listen to how Jesus described John the Baptist, who was only born of the flesh.

📖 *Matthew 11:11 NKJV*

"Assuredly, I say to you, among those born of women there has not risen one greater than John the Baptist; but he who is least in the kingdom of heaven is greater than he."

Do you see the difference? Jesus acknowledged that of all the people who have ever been born of women, there has never been one greater than John the Baptist. However, Jesus also said that he who is least in the kingdom of heaven is greater than John. That reveals two distinct kinds of life. It's true, to be born again you have to *first* be born of the flesh. But no matter how great you are or try to be while in the flesh, you are not in the kingdom of heaven because of the life and nature you carry inside. Even the newest born babe in the kingdom of God is greater than the greatest of those who are born of the flesh. That is because of the corruptible seed of life that is in one, and the incorruptible seed of life that is in the other.

> **Even the newest born babe in the kingdom of God is greater than the greatest of those who are born of the flesh.**

📖 *1 Peter 1:22-23; 2:1-3 NKJV*

"Since you have purified your souls in obeying the truth through the Spirit in sincere love of the brethren, love one another fervently with a pure heart, having been born again, not of corruptible seed but incorruptible, through the word of God which lives and abides forever....Therefore, laying aside all malice, all deceit, hypocrisy, envy, and all evil speaking, as newborn babes, desire the pure milk of the word, that you may grow thereby, if indeed you have tasted that the Lord is gracious."

📖 *1 Peter 1:23 AMPC*

"You have been regenerated (born again), not from mortal origin (seed, sperm), but from one that is immortal by the ever living and lasting Word of God."

📖 *1 Peter 1:23 TLB*

"For you have a new life. It was not passed on to you from your parents, for the life they gave you will fade away. This new one will last forever, for it comes from Christ, God's ever-living Message to men."

Being born again is becoming a newborn babe in Christ. Whether you were 14 or 84 years old when you believed, you were converted and became a babe in the Father's house. You received a new heart from God, a new spirit from God, and God has put His Spirit in you. You were regenerated (born again) by the life (seed) of Christ coming to live in you (united with you). The riches of the glory of the mystery of Christ comes from this resurrection provision from God, which is nothing other than Christ in you, the hope of glory. Jesus is the perfect gift given from our Father in heaven. Christ *in* us is the good gift of God coming to dwell in us.

> *You received a new heart from God, a new spirit from God, and God has put His Spirit in you.*

📖 *James 1:17-18 NKJV*

"Every good gift and every perfect gift is from above, and comes down from the Father of lights, with whom there is no variation or shadow of turning. Of His own will He brought us forth by the word of truth, that we might be a kind of firstfruits of His creatures."

📖 *James 1:18 TLB*

"And it was a happy day for him when he gave us our new lives through the truth of his Word, and we became, as it were, the first children in his new family."

God *willed* (greatly desired) to make known the riches of this mystery to us. A pregnant woman brings forth a newborn from her womb, but God brought us forth into His family by His Word, Jesus Christ. We now need to see that the life of Christ we receive at our new birth is a life that is *light* that comes from the Father of lights. He makes us children of light and enables us to carry that light to deal with the darkness which covers the earth and the people of the earth.

📖 *Isaiah 60:1-2 NKJV*

"Arise, shine; for your light has come! And the glory of the LORD is risen upon you. For behold, the darkness shall cover the earth, and deep darkness the people; but the LORD will arise over you, and His glory will be seen upon you."

We have seen that all who are born of women are born with a life that *is* darkness and that is *in* darkness. That deep darkness covers people, oppresses them, and blinds them from seeing the light of the Son of God, who is able to deliver them from the darkness and bring them into the light. The reason you have been born again and given this new life is to shine in the world with the light of the Lord.

📖 *Isaiah 60:1 AMP*

"Arise [from spiritual depression to a new life], shine [be radiant with the glory and brilliance of the LORD]; for your light has come, and the glory and brilliance of the LORD has risen upon you."

The resurrection provision is where God caused us to arise from the spiritual depression we were in, and to enter into a radiant and brilliant new life. That life is a light that is meant to shine and deal with the issue of darkness on the face of the earth. And the light that we are to be radiant with is nothing other than Christ in you, the Light of men.

> *The reason you have been born again and given this new life is to shine in the world with the light of the Lord.*

THE LIFE THAT IS LIGHT

📖 *John 1:1-5 NKJV*

"In the beginning was the Word, and the Word was with God, and the Word was God. He was in the beginning with God. All things were made through Him, and without Him nothing was made that was made. In Him was life, and the life was the light of men. And the light shines in the darkness, and the darkness did not comprehend it."

📖 *John 1:4-5 AMP*
"In Him was life [and the power to bestow life], and the life was the Light of men. The Light shines on in the darkness, and the darkness did not understand it or overpower it or appropriate it or absorb it [and is unreceptive to it]."

From the beginning, God's plan was always to put His life that is light inside of man to deal with the problem of darkness. To fulfill this, His solution for *now* fallen man was to remove the life of darkness, and to put His life-light into all those who will believe in His Son. Jesus Christ is that Light! John the Baptist bore witness to this, and the word of God is crystal clear.

📖 *John 1:6-9 NKJV*
"There was a man sent from God, whose name was John. This man came for a witness, to bear witness of the Light, that all through him might believe. He was not <u>that Light</u>, but was sent to bear witness of that Light. That was the true Light which gives light to every man coming into the world."

📖 *Job 33:29-30 NKJV*
"Behold, God works all these things, twice, in fact, three times with a man, to bring back his soul from the Pit, that he may be enlightened with the light of life."

Do you see that the kind of life and image we are looking at is a life that is Light? It is a life that darkness cannot comprehend or over-power. In fact, darkness runs away from the Light of Life which is Christ. Everywhere He shows up, they are unable to do anything be-cause light always compels darkness to retreat. God's devised means to deliver souls from the Pit of hell is the light of the Gospel of Jesus Christ. The blood to deal with the activities of darkness—the cross to deal with the life of darkness—and the resurrection to enlighten us with the Light of Christ's life. He Himself is the Light. Walking with Him is the key to overcoming every way of darkness that comes against us as we engage the purpose of God in our lives.

📖 *John 8:12 NKJV*
"Then Jesus spoke to them again, saying, 'I am the light of the world. He who follows Me shall not walk in darkness, but have the light of life.'"
　　📖 *John 12:44-46 NKJV*
"Then Jesus cried out and said, 'He who believes in Me, believes not in Me but in Him who sent Me. And he who sees Me sees Him who sent Me. I have come as a light into the world, that whoever believes in Me should not abide in darkness."

Praise the Lord for exchanging our old life that abode in darkness, with the new life that abides in Light. What does Jesus now tell us to do with this new life that is Light?

LET YOUR LIGHT SHINE

📖 *Matthew 5:14-16 NKJV*
"You are the light of the world. A city that is set on a hill cannot be hidden. Nor do they light a lamp and put it under a basket, but on a lampstand, and it gives light to all who are in the house. Let your light so shine before men, that they may see your good works and glorify your Father in heaven."
　　📖 *Matthew 5:14 AMP*
"You are the light of [Christ to] the world. A city set on a hill cannot be hidden;"

Being born again, YOU are now the light of the world because Christ lives in you. You are Christ's representative on the earth. Jesus said, 'let your light so shine before men." *Let* means to allow and not to prevent or forbid. It is a word that places responsibility on us. If I said, "John, did you let your children go outside to play today?" You would know that John is the one who has the authority and ability to make that decision. If he would not allow it, the children would not be permitted to go outside. In the same way, we are

> *Let means to allow and not to prevent or forbid. It is a word that places responsibility on us.*

283

to let (allow) Christ in us to come forth and do what He wants to do. That happens by denying ourselves, remembering that we died, and turning to Christ in us to obediently do what He says. That is our choice, to *let Him* shine through us, or to not let Him shine through us. If we live independently from Him, being in charge of our life and setting aside the grace of God, our lives will not shine. Who we associate with and what we decide to do with this new life will be determining factors in how much light emanates from us for the glory of God.

📖 *2 Corinthians 6:14-16 NKJV*

"Do not be unequally yoked together with unbelievers. For what fellowship has righteousness with lawlessness? And what communion has light with darkness? And what accord has Christ with Belial? Or what part has a believer with an unbeliever? And what agreement has the temple of God with idols? For <u>you are the temple of the living God</u>. As God has said: '<u>I will dwell in them</u> and walk among them. I will be their God, and they shall be My people.'"

📖 *2 Corinthians 6:14-15a JBP*

"Don't link up with unbelievers and try to work with them. What common interest can there be between goodness and evil? How can light and darkness share life together? How can there be harmony between Christ and the devil?"

We see here that a man cannot be a Christian and still have a sinful nature in him that causes him to be in fellowship with darkness; light and darkness cannot share life together. A Chrisitan is a person who has Christ in them; it is as simple as that. As a Christian, if you join yourselves to those who are in darkness, and practice the things they do, you will be covering the Light that is in you and obscuring the testimony of God that saves souls. Light cannot have fellowship with darkness. Only when Christ is in a man can he begin walking with God and learning to obey Jesus and all He says. It is only then that light will begin to come forth out of his life.

📖 *Philippians 2:14-16 NKJV*

"Do all things without complaining and disputing, that you may become blameless and harmless, children of God without fault in the

midst of a crooked and perverse generation, among whom you shine as lights in the world, holding fast the word of life, so that I may rejoice in the day of Christ that I have not run in vain or labored in vain."

KJV *'holding forth the word of life"*
NIV *"shine among them like stars in the sky"*
AMP *"beacons shining out clearly in the world of darkness"*

Christ's life is different! He doesn't look or behave like the children of the world. They are perverse and crooked, and God desires *us* to let the light of Christ's life shine like stars in the sky, giving them direction to find their way back to God. It is not *words* but His *life* that shines, and that life must be developed and matured in us and released through us as we continue with Jesus. The early disciples of Jesus learned this as they handled the life of Christ and were brought to God through Him. John wrote it like this:

📖 *1 John 1:1-3 NKJV*
"That which was from the beginning, which we have heard, which we have seen with our eyes, which we have looked upon, and our hands have handled, concerning the Word of life- the life was manifested, and we have seen, and bear witness, and declare to you that eternal life which was with the Father and was manifested to us- that which we have seen and heard we declare to you, that you also may have fellowship with us; and truly our fellowship is with the Father and with His Son Jesus Christ."

> **One will result in people remaining in darkness, and the other will result in people seeing the good works of Christ in you and glorifying our Father in heaven. Which do you want?**

Jesus always allowed the light of His life to shine among men. It wasn't just His teachings but the way He conducted Himself in every circumstance, no matter what people were doing. The disciples handled His life and saw it with their own eyes. They noticed, by being with Him, it was a good life, unlike theirs, and they described it as the *Word of life*. His life was the Light that shined in the midst of (and overcame) darkness. He always held forth His life by allowing it to shine, and it resulted in people being brought out of the darkness and into the light. That same life now dwells in *you*. You can cover that light by living according to yourself and your own selfish ambitions, or you can let that light shine by yielding to and obeying Christ in you. One will result in people remaining in darkness, and the other will result in people seeing the good works of Christ in you and glorifying our Father in heaven. Which do you want? How much do you shine? I trust the Lord is helping you to see the riches of the glory this mystery, so you will cry out to Him to teach you increasingly how to walk in this reality.

As we continue, I would like to look at some of the ways God reveals His wonderful provision of the resurrection of Jesus Christ.

Further Benefits of the Resurrection

CHRIST IN US: Where We Became a New Creation

📖 *Ephesians 2:14-16 NKJV*
"For He Himself is our peace, who has made both one, and has broken down the middle wall of separation, having abolished in His flesh the enmity, that is, the law of commandments contained in ordinances, so as to create in Himself <u>one new man</u> from the two, thus making peace, and that He might reconcile them both to God in one body through the cross, thereby putting to death the enmity."

AMPC *"that He from the two might create in Himself one new man [one new quality of humanity out of the two]"*
GNT *"in order to create out of the two races one new people in union with himself"*
MSG *"he created a new kind of human being"*

> We have become a new creation with a new life that has ability to hear, obey, and please God.

The resurrection of Jesus Christ made Him to be the firstborn from among the dead. And all who come to Him are recreated by God into an entirely new kind of human being. We have become a new creation with a new life that has ability to hear, obey, and please God. This new creation man is meant to live for God's purpose, to bear fruit unto God, and to reconcile souls back to Him. The new creation man lives only for God and not for himself.

  📖 *2 Corinthians 5:14-17 NKJV*
"For the love of Christ compels us, because we judge thus: that if One died for all, then all died; and He died for all, that <u>those who live should live no longer for themselves, but for Him</u> who died for them and rose again. Therefore, from now on, we regard no one according to the flesh. Even though we have known Christ according to the flesh, yet now we know Him thus no longer. Therefore, if anyone is in Christ, he is a new creation; old things have passed away; behold, all things have become new."

> **It is only Christ in a man that makes him a Christian, and it is only Christ in a man who can do Christian work.**

A Christian is not someone who merely believes one time that Jesus is Lord and goes on to live life according to their own terms. A Christian is one who has received the exchanged life God has offered through the cross and resurrection of Christ. It is only Christ *in* a man that makes him a Christian, and it is only Christ *in* a man who can do Christian work. In this new life, we are to live according to the reality of what happened at the cross, and according to the reality of Christ now living in us. We are not our own, and we are to no longer live for ourselves but for Him who died and rose again for us. This is the new rule to live by if we desire to experience the mercy and peace of God in our everyday life.

  📖 *Galatians 6:15-16 AMPC*
"For neither is circumcision [now] of any importance, nor uncircumcision, but [only] a new creation [the result of a new birth and a new

287

nature in Christ Jesus, the Messiah]. Peace and mercy be upon all who walk by this rule [who discipline themselves and regulate their lives by this principle], even upon the [true] Israel of God!"

The new creation man always remembers that He died with Christ at the cross of Calvary, and now it is Christ who lives in him, who is his life. We must regulate our lives according to this truth, and discipline ourselves to let Christ have His way and rule from within us, shining through us for the glory of God.

CHRIST IN US: Where We Became Heirs of God

📖 ***Romans 8:14-17 NKJV***
"For as many as are led by the Spirit of God, these are sons of God. For you did not receive the spirit of bondage again to fear, but you received the Spirit of adoption by whom we cry out, 'Abba, Father.' The Spirit Himself bears witness with our spirit that we are children of God, and if children, then heirs- heirs of God and joint heirs with Christ, if indeed we suffer with Him, that we may also be glorified together."

We used to carry the spirit of bondage within us, but the resurrecttion provision has given us the Spirit of adoption that makes us children of our Father in heaven. The Spirit of Christ is in us, and He bears witness with our spirit that we are indeed children and heirs of God, even joint heirs with Christ. However, receiving the things of God and His kingdom is not experienced in living a life independent of Christ's rule. Our practical experience and growth in the things of God are in direct relation to being led by the Spirit of His Son in all things.

> *However, receiving the things of God and His kingdom is not experienced in living a life independent of Christ's rule.*

📖   ***Galatians 4:6-7 NKJV***
"And because you are sons, God has sent forth the Spirit of His Son into your hearts, crying out, 'Abba, Father!' Therefore you are no longer a slave but a son, and if a son, then an heir of God through Christ."

📖 *Galatians 4:7 TLB*

"Now we are no longer slaves but God's own sons. And since we are his sons, everything he has belongs to us, for that is the way God planned."

This was always God's plan. An *heir* is an inheritor of something based on the death of the One he receives the inheritance from. Christ's death on the cross met the requirement for release of the inheritance, and God raising Him from the dead is the means for us to receive the inheritance in Him. We have become heirs of God, not heirs of things. God has released and given us *Himself* as our inheritance. We now have access, as sons and daughters, to the fullness of God by the risen Christ whose Spirit has been poured into our hearts. We have been made heirs. But walking in the reality of this is directly related to our communing with Christ in us on a daily basis.

> We have become heirs of God, not heirs of things. God has released and given us <u>Himself</u> as our inheritance.

📖   *Galatians 4:28-31 NKJV*

"Now we, brethren, as Isaac was, are children of promise. But, as he who was born according to the flesh then persecuted him who was born according to the Spirit, even so it is now. Nevertheless what does the Scripture say? 'Cast out the bondwoman and her son, for the son of the bondwoman shall not be heir with the son of the freewoman.' So then, brethren, we are not children of the bondwoman but of the free."

The work of the cross cast out the son of the bondwoman so that the resurrection provision could make me a son of the free. My becoming an heir was based on the finished work of Christ crucified and resurrected. Upon my faith, God put the Spirit of Christ in me, which made me a child of promise with access to the inheritance He has located in Christ for me. Christ, living His life in me, is what makes me and qualifies me to be a child of promise and an heir of God. I can do all things through Christ who is my strength.

CHRIST IN US: Where We Became Clothed with Christ

📖 *Galatians 3:26-27 NKJV*
"For you are all sons of God through faith in Christ Jesus. For as many of you as were baptized into Christ have put on Christ."

📖   *Galatians 3:25-27 MSG*
"But now you have arrived at your destination: By faith in Christ you are in direct relationship with God. Your baptism in Christ was not just washing you up for a fresh start. It also involved dressing you in an adult faith wardrobe- Christ's life, the fulfillment of God's original promise."

> **Every time we do what is right in our own eyes, leaning on our own understanding, and not seeking His instruction from within, we step outside of our covering (clothing) and make ourselves naked and vulnerable.**

To be clothed with something means to be wrapped up and inside it. By baptism, God put us into the body of Christ to die with Him and be buried with Him in His death. And by the means of that baptism, we were raised together with Him (and by Him) into a new life. We are now clothed with Christ because we are in Christ and Christ is in us. And now that we are clothed with Him, we are to let Christ live His life, as it pleases Him, from within us. Every time we do what is right in our own eyes, leaning on our own understanding, and not seeking His instruction from within, we step outside of our covering (clothing) and make ourselves naked and vulnerable. It is only Christ that protects us from the elements and principalities of the world; it is only Christ who can do the work of God; and it is only Christ who can do anything lasting and pleasing to the Father. Staying clothed is abiding in Him. It is in denying self, taking up our daily cross, and following Him as His Spirit leads us.

📖 *Romans 13:11-14 NKJV*
"And do this, knowing the time, that now it is high time to awake out of sleep; for now our salvation is nearer than when we first believed. The night is far spent, the day is at hand. Therefore let us cast off the

works of darkness, and let us put on the armor of light. Let us walk properly, as in the day, not in revelry and drunkenness, not in lewdness and lust, not in strife and envy. But put on the Lord Jesus Christ, and make no provision for the flesh, to fulfill its lusts."

We *were* clothed with the old man (joined to the sinful nature in us from birth), but now we are clothed with Christ (joined to Christ in us by the new birth). To put on the armor of light is to put on the Lord Jesus Christ in everyday activities, by denying ourselves and putting our faith in Him. As we do this, we will discover more of the reality that He is the armor of light that protects us from all evil. We will grow, be renewed, and remolded into His image and in the intimate knowledge of Him increasingly each day.

📖 ***Colossians 3:9-10 AMPC***
"Do not lie to one another, for you have stripped off the old (unregenerate) self with its evil practices, and have clothed yourselves with the new [spiritual self], which is [ever in the process of being] renewed and remolded into [fuller and more perfect knowledge upon] knowledge after the image (the likeness) of Him who created it."

CHRIST IN US: Where We Became Accepted in the Beloved

📖 ***Ephesians 1:3-6 NKJV***
"Blessed be the God and Father of our Lord Jesus Christ, who has blessed us with every spiritual blessing in the heavenly places in Christ, just as He chose us in Him before the foundation of the world, that we should be holy and without blame before Him in love, having predestined us to adoption as sons by Jesus Christ to Himself, according to the good pleasure of His will, to the praise of the glory of His grace, by which He made us accepted in the Beloved."

It is important to see it is God who decided to make us acceptable to Himself *in* Christ Jesus. It is solely His work, according to His good pleasure, to grant us acceptance and allow us to be highly favored in His eyes. The blood brought forgiveness, the cross brought deliverance, and the resurrection brought Christ into us who is well-pleasing to God and makes us accepted by God. Jesus is the Beloved of God, in whom all His good pleasure, favor, and love dwells and is experienced.

📖 **Matthew 3:16-17 NKJV**
"When He had been baptized, Jesus came up immediately from the water; and behold, the heavens were opened to Him, and He saw the Spirit of God descending like a dove and alighting upon Him. And suddenly a voice came from heaven, saying, 'This is My beloved Son, in whom I am well pleased.'"

📖 **Isaiah 42:1 NKJV**
"Behold, My Servant whom I uphold, My Elect One in whom My soul delights! I have put My Spirit upon Him; He will bring forth justice to the Gentiles."

Our experience, in increasing measures, of the delight of God, will be discovered as we continue with Jesus and surrender all to Him.

Lastly,

📖 **2 Corinthians 4:3-7 NKJV**
"But even if our gospel is veiled, it is veiled to those who are perishing, whose minds the god of this age has blinded, who do not believe, lest the light of the gospel of the glory of Christ, who is the image of God, should shine on them. For we do not preach ourselves, but Christ Jesus the Lord, and ourselves your bondservants for Jesus' sake. For it is the God who commanded light to shine out of darkness, who has shone in our hearts to give the light of the knowledge of the glory of God in the face of Jesus Christ. But <u>we have this treasure in earthen vessels</u>, that the excellence of the power may be of God and not of us."

> *Our experience, in increasing measures, of the delight of God, will be discovered as we continue with Jesus and surrender all to Him.*

📖 **2 Corinthians 4:6 AMPC**
"For God Who said, Let light shine out of darkness, has shone in our hearts so as [to beam forth] the Light for the illumination of the knowledge of the majesty and glory of God [as it is manifest in the Person and is revealed] in the face of Jesus Christ (the Messiah)."

The Holy Spirit must open our eyes and ears to see and hear what God has done in sending His Son to die for us, raising Him from the dead, and coming to live in us. The light of revelation must dawn in your heart to see that Jesus Christ (Himself) is *the Treasure* that comes from God. *He* is the image of God and the radiance of His glory, and it is *He* who is meant to beam forth *His* Light from within us.

No one can know God but through Jesus Christ, and no one can experience the glory of God except through revelation in the knowledge of Him, of Him crucified, and of Him resurrected. The Treasure God gives us is the life of Christ which He pours into our earthen vessels (after He removes the old nature). His intention is for us to learn how to let this wonderful Life—*which is the Light of Christ in us*—shine through us and bring a knowledge of God to all those around us.

Jesus is the divine Light of the Gospel. In the beginning of creation, God said, "Let there be light,' and the light came forth and shined in the midst of darkness, and the darkness did not comprehend it. By that Light (which was Christ) God made all things in heaven and in earth, and there was nothing made that was not made through and by and for Him.

Now, God has brought forth that same Light to shine in our hearts, which is the hope of God being glorified in the earth through Christ, who now lives in us. He did this so that the power would be of Him and not of us; the life of Christ simply being allowed to shine forth with His glory. Our job is to walk in a vital union with Jesus (who alone is able to bring glory to God) and learn how to let Him shine from within us, to accomplish the will and purpose of God on earth through us. Would you like to praise God with me for His devised means of the resurrection of Jesus Christ? Can we take a moment to thank Him for opening our eyes of understanding to see the reality of Christ in us?

Our Father in heaven, hallowed and blessed and wonderful is Your name. We want to thank You for sending Jesus Christ to die for us, and we want to praise You for raising Him from the dead to bring us hope. You have delivered us from the tyranny of darkness and brought us into Your kingdom and Your light. You have put the Spirit of Christ in us, and we give You all the glory for your mercy, grace, and longsuffering toward us. You forgave us all our sins, cleansed us from their stain, and delivered us from the life that produced them. We worship You for what You have done in sending Your Son. Thank You Father, for the wonderful gift of Jesus Christ and His Spirit, whom You have poured into us as our inheritance. And now Father, we want to learn how to walk consistently in the power, the victory, and the reality of this new union with Christ in us. Once again, we ask You to enlarge our hearts and increase our capacity to understand Your way more accurately, even as we begin to conclude. Thank You, Father, for hearing us, for we are praying to You in the name of Jesus Christ. Amen.

NECESSARY POWER FOR LIFE AND MINISTRY

📖 *Luke 24:46-51 NKJV*

"Then He said to them, 'Thus it is written, and thus it was necessary for the Christ to suffer and to rise from the dead the third day, and that repentance and remission of sins should be preached in His name to all nations, beginning at Jerusalem. And you are witnesses of these things. Behold, I send the Promise of My Father <u>upon you</u>; but tarry in the city of Jerusalem until you are endued with power from on high. And He led them out as far as Bethany, and He lifted up His hands and blessed them. Now it came to pass, while He blessed them, that He was parted from them and carried up into heaven."

📖 *Acts 1:5 NKJV*

"for John truly baptized with water, but you shall be baptized with the Holy Spirit not many days from now"

N ow that we have seen the wonderful provisions God has given for our deliverance in Christ Jesus—all things in Him, the blood, the cross, and the resurrection—we need to examine the scriptures to understand what it is to be endued with power from on high (the baptism with the Holy Spirit). We need to understand it because Jesus commanded His disciples to go and wait for this Promise; indicating it as something they *must* receive from Him for their life. Please note that the word *Promise* is capitalized in the verse, letting us know this Promise is a Person of the Godhead— the Holy Spirit. As we push forward, we will be deliberate in taking note of the purposes for this enduement (or *baptism*), what it is for, and for every detail we can glean from the word of God. This will bring help into our lives and our service to God. The first understanding I want to emphasize is that Jesus is the Baptizer. Even in the passage above we see Jesus telling them to go and wait in Jerusalem until *He* "sends the Promise of My Father upon you."

Jesus is the One Who Baptizes With the Holy Spirit

📖 *Matthew 3:11 NKJV*
"I indeed baptize you with water unto repentance, but He who is coming after me is mightier than I, whose sandals I am not worthy to carry. He will baptize you with the Holy Spirit and fire."

John the Baptist baptized people in water for repentance and forgiveness of sins. He is telling them to believe on the One who was to come, declaring that *Jesus* is the One who baptizes with the Holy Spirit and fire. It is an authority the Father gave to Jesus after He raised Him from the dead and brought Him back to heaven.

📖 *Acts 2:32-33 NKJV*
"This Jesus God has raised up, of which we are all witnesses. Therefore being exalted to the right hand of God, and having received from the Father the promise of the Holy Spirit, He poured out this which you now see and hear."

📖 *Acts 2:33 TLB*
"And now he sits on the throne of highest honor in heaven, next to God. And just as promised, the Father gave him the authority to send the Holy Spirit- with the results you are seeing and hearing today."

After all Jesus accomplished, and in His glorious, victorious return to heaven, the Father gave Him the authority to send the Holy Spirit. The Promise of the Father is the promise of the Holy Spirit, and God entrusted Jesus to send that Promise where He wills. Peter declared this to the crowd he preached to, after they witnessed what happened to the disciples who were gathered together in the upper room on the Day of Pentecost. Our main goal here is to note that Jesus has been given authority to pour out the promise of the Holy Spirit. There are many teachings concerning the baptism of the Holy Spirit, which have confused God's people to either abuse this gift (by misunderstanding) or refuse this gift (by not believing). Let us therefore press on and trust the Lord to teach us the way of God more accurately. What does the Lord want us to see, in order to help us understand this wonderful provision of power from on high; that which is needed for our faith journey on earth? As He has faithfully opened our eyes of understanding in the previous chapters, we will trust Him to do the same here, in order for us to effectively walk with Jesus according to His designed way.

> *There are many teachings concerning the baptism of the Holy Spirit, which have confused God's people to either abuse this gift (by misunderstanding) or refuse this gift (by not believing).*

📖 *1 John 2:6 NKJV*
"He who says he abides in Him ought himself to walk just as He walked."

Jesus is Our Pattern for Receiving This Power

📖 *Matthew 1:19-20 NKJV*
"Then Joseph her husband, being a just man, and not wanting to make her a public example, was minded to put her away secretly. But while he thought about these things, behold, an angel of the Lord appeared to him in a dream, saying, 'Joseph, son of David, do not be

afraid to take to you Mary your wife, for that which is conceived in her is of the Holy Spirit.'"

The Bible reveals that Jesus was born of the Spirit, and not of the seed of man, and that when we come to Christ, we likewise have to be reborn of the same Spirit. This is the necessity of being *born again*. Also, we see Jesus, in His humanity, continually declaring that He *did* nothing of Himself and *could do* nothing of Himself.

📖 **John 5:19 NKJV**
"Then Jesus answered and said to them, 'Most assuredly, I say to you, the Son can do nothing of Himself, but what He sees the Father do; for whatever He does, the Son also does in like manner.'"

📖 **John 5:30 AMPC**
"I am able to nothing from Myself [independently, of My own accord- but only as I am taught by God and as I get His orders]. Even as I hear, I judge [I decide as I am bidden to decide. As the voice comes to Me, so I give a decision], and my judgment is right (just, righteous), because I do not seek or consult My own will [I have no desire to do what is pleasing to Myself, My own aim, My own purpose] but only the will and pleasure of the Father Who sent Me."

As a Man on earth, Jesus walked in a living union with His Father— who lived *in* Him and who was doing the works of God *through* Him, by this Holy Spirit. Jesus said it like this:

📖 **John 14:10-11 NKJV**
"Do you not believe that I am in the Father, and the Father in Me? The words that I speak to you I do not speak on My own authority; but the Father who dwells in Me does the works. Believe Me that I am in the Father and the Father in Me, or else believe Me for the sake of the works themselves."

NIV *"Rather, it is the Father, living in me, who is doing his work"*
NLT *"but my Father who lives in me does his work through me"*
AMPC *"the Father Who lives continually in Me does (His) works"*

The apostle Paul said it like this.

298

 📖 *2 Corinthians 5:18-19 NKJV*

"Now all things are of God, who has reconciled us to Himself through Jesus Christ, and has given us the ministry of reconciliation, that is, that God was in Christ reconciling the world to Himself, not imputing their trespasses to them, and has committed to us the word of reconciliation."

 📖 *2 Corinthians 5:19 AMPC*

"It was God [personally present] in Christ, reconciling and restoring the world to favor with Himself, not counting up and holding against [men] their trespasses [but canceling them], and committing to us the message of reconciliation (of the restoration to favor)."

As men and women on earth (born of the Spirit) we are now to walk just as Jesus walked, daily—by the same Holy Spirit of God living *in* us, doing the works of God *through* us.

Please note the Bible says *in* Christ and *in* Me. The Spirit of God was IN Jesus from birth, just as He is IN us when we become born-again. We need to see clearly, though, the difference between IN and UP-ON in the Scriptures. These two words indicate locational position-ing. If I say, "your food is *in* the oven," you are not confused about what I am saying. You know that your food is located inside the oven. If I say, "your food is *on* or *upon* the oven," you likewise understand that I am saying your food is located on top of the oven; upon means up on, not inside. Jesus was born of the Spirit, and the Spirit of God was located IN Him; this He received at the time of His birth from the Father who sent Him. With that in mind, let's look at another time the Father sent the Holy Spirit during the life of Jesus.

 📖 *Matthew 3:13-17 NKJV*

"Then Jesus came from Galilee to John at the Jordan to be baptized by him. And John tried to prevent Him, saying, 'I need to be baptized by You, and are You coming to me?' But Jesus answered and said to him, 'Permit it to be so now, for thus it is fitting for us to fulfill all righteousness.' Then he allowed Him. When He had been baptized, Jesus came up immediately from the water; and behold, the heavens were opened to Him, and He saw the Spirit of God descending like a

dove and alighting <u>upon Him</u>. And suddenly a voice came from heaven, saying, 'This is My beloved Son, in whom I am well pleased.'"

Jesus came to be baptized by John; to fulfill all righteousness and to be an example that we are to follow. As He was being raised out of the water, we see the Spirit of God coming down from heaven and alighting UPON Him. Let's consider a few other versions of this Scripture to help us understand "alighting UPON" more fully.

📖 **Matthew 3:16b**

ESV *"descending like a dove and coming to <u>rest on him</u>"*
NLT *"descending like a dove and <u>settling on him</u>"*
LSB *"descending like a dove and <u>coming upon Him</u>"*
MSG *"descending and <u>landing on him</u>"*

> **The Holy Spirit did not come down at this time to dwell IN Jesus because the Spirit was already IN Him. Here, God poured out His Spirit UPON Jesus.**

This experience was a sending of the Spirit to rest ON Jesus; to settle ON Jesus; to come UPON Jesus; and to land ON Jesus. This is not a confusing language. The Holy Spirit did not come down at this time to dwell IN Jesus because the Spirit was already IN Him. Here, God poured out His Spirit UPON Jesus. This was after 30 years of Jesus (in obscurity) walking with God (who was within Him) and growing in stature, in spirit, and in favor with God and man; living the life that was declared acceptable and pleasing to His Father.

At the baptism of John, Jesus was getting ready to enter into His public ministry. This was also the time directly before the Spirit led Him into the wilderness to be tempted by the devil. The Father was *enduing* Jesus with necessary power from on high for the journey ahead.

So, we see from this that one of the reasons for the baptism of the Holy Spirit is for power in ministry, and another reason is for enduring and overcoming the temptations of the devil. These are not the only reasons, but we want to acknowledge them as they come into our line of sight along this path. This baptism experience (being *endued with power from on high*) was prophesied by Isaiah in the Old Testament.

> 📖 *Isaiah 42:1 NKJV*
> *"Behold! My Servant whom I uphold, My Elect One in whom My soul delights! I have put My Spirit upon Him; He will bring forth justice to the Gentiles."*

> 📖 *Matthew 12:17-18 NKJV*
> *"that it might be fulfilled which was spoken by Isaiah the prophet, saying: Behold! My servant whom I have chosen, My Beloved in whom My soul is well pleased! I will put My Spirit upon Him, and He will declare justice to the Gentiles."*

We see from this that one of the reasons for the baptism of the Holy Spirit is for power in ministry, and another reason is for enduring and overcoming the temptations of the devil.

This anointing of the Holy Spirit was, in part, to bring forth and declare justice to the Gentiles. It was God who decided to do this, and it was God who anointed Jesus by the Holy Spirit of God UPON Him.

> 📖 *Acts 10:38 NKJV*
> *"how God anointed Jesus of Nazareth with the Holy Spirit and with power, who went about doing good and healing all who were oppressed by the devil, for God was with Him."*

Jesus was already born of the Spirit. This baptism was a separate divine act for the purpose of God to be accomplished, in the equipping and empowering of His Servant. It is important to see how Jesus was born of the Spirit AND endued with power from on high. This helps us understand the baptism with the Holy Spirit is biblical, and something Jesus Himself received as a Man. Next, we'll see how this was also the experience of the disciples of Jesus.

The Disciples' Experience is Another Example

📖 *John 20:19-22 NKJV*
"Then, the same day at evening, being the first day of the week, when the doors were shut where the disciples were assembled, for fear of the Jews, Jesus came and stood in the midst, and said to them, 'Peace be with you.' When He had said this, He showed them His hands and His side. Then the disciples were glad when they saw the Lord. So Jesus said to them again, 'Peace to you! As the Father has sent Me, I also send you.' And when He had said this, He breathed on them, and said to them, 'Receive the Holy Spirit.'"

This was the night of the resurrection when Jesus came to His disciples to give them the Holy Spirit for the new birth. Please note, this was not the same *Promise of the Father* (being endued with power from on high) that Jesus referred to in Luke 24.

This experience in John 20 was the moment these disciples became born again. *Just* as the Father sent Jesus (having been born of the Spirit) as a Man on the earth, these disciples are being sent by Jesus (being born of the same Spirit) as men on earth. They received Him (His life) INTO themselves, as Jesus breathed on them. We will see that the Day of Pentecost they waited for was fifty days later, but for now, let's take note that Jesus said, "As the Father has sent Me, I also send you." Up to this point, these men had already heard the Gospel from Jesus, repented of their sins, believed on Him, and left all to follow Him. However, they were not yet born again, because Jesus was not yet raised from the dead (in order to be the firstborn among many brethren). The Holy Spirit had been with them but not yet IN them. Listen to Jesus explain it.

> *It is important to see how Jesus was born of the Spirit AND endued with power from on high. This helps us understand the baptism with the Holy Spirit is biblical, and something Jesus Himself received as a Man.*

📖 *John 14:16-18 NKJV*

"And I will pray the Father, and He will give you another Helper, that He may abide with you forever- the Spirit of truth, whom the world cannot receive, because it neither sees Him nor knows Him; but you know Him, for He dwells with you and will be in you. I will not leave you orphans; I will come to you."

Did you see the word of God distinguish between dwelling "WITH you" and "IN you?" Jesus is telling His disciples of the day He would come to breath the Holy Spirit *into* them, so they can be born again into the family of God. As these men were following Jesus for over three years, the Holy Spirit was indeed with them as Jesus would give them power and send them out to preach the gospel of the kingdom, heal the sick, and cast out demons. He was with them to give understanding and insight into the things Jesus was teaching them. He was with them as they walked with Jesus and witnessed the wonderful works God did through Him. Jesus said they knew Him, but they did not have Him dwelling IN them yet. Jesus was not yet glorified, and the Holy Spirit had not yet been given to dwell in their hearts. John explains this clearly in another place.

📖 *John 7:37-39 NKJV*

"On the last day, that great day of the feast, Jesus stood and cried out, saying, 'If anyone thirsts, let him come to Me and drink. He who believes in Me, as the Scripture has said, out of his heart will flow rivers of living water.' But this He spoke concerning the Spirit, whom those believing in Him would receive; for the Holy Spirit was not yet given, because Jesus was not yet glorified."

📖 *John 7:39 AMP*

"But He was speaking of the [Holy] Spirit, whom those who believed in Him [as Savior] were to receive afterward. The Spirit had not yet been given, because Jesus was not yet glorified (raised to honor)."

Those believing in Jesus WOULD receive the Spirit AFTERWARD. Not that they have received, but would receive, when Jesus would be glorified by God and raised from the dead. For these disciples (and everyone born of the flesh), they needed to be born of the Spirit first of all. The work of Jesus Christ, Him crucified and Him resurrected had to be applied to their own lives. The death of the old man, the cutting away of their sinful nature, and the pouring in of Christ's life (that overcomes death) by the Spirit of God. Jesus needed to die and be raised again before anyone could be born again by receiving the Holy Spirit IN them. God designed it this way so Jesus would be the firstborn from the dead. He would be the firstborn of the new creation man He was bringing forth to dwell on the face of the earth. The firstborn of the congregation of men and women He would use to multiply the life of Christ through, on the earth. God did this so Jesus would have preeminence in all things and be the Head of the body (the church of God).

📖 **Colossians 1:18 NKJV**
"And He is the head of the body, the church, who is the beginning, the firstborn from the dead, that in all things He may have the pre-eminence."

Just as the Father sent Jesus into the world, born of the Spirit, these disciples were also brought forth as a new creation into the world by the indwelling Spirit they received from Jesus. We are studying this to notice the timing of it all. This was on the first day Jesus was resurrected from the dead. However, the Promise of the Father (being endued with power), was going to be fifty days later on the Day of Pentecost. So, let's dig further into the word of God to help us understand and see that these are two entirely different (but necessary) experiences which we also need to have with the Holy Spirit. Experiences like both Jesus and the disciples had.

> **Let's dig further into the word of God to help us understand and see that these are two entirely different (but necessary) experiences which we also need to have with the Holy Spirit.**

📖   **Acts 1:1-8 NKJV**
"The former account I made, O Theophilus, of all that Jesus began both to do and teach, until the day in which He was taken up, after

He through the Holy Spirit had given commandments to the apostles whom He had chosen, to whom He also presented Himself alive after His suffering by many infallible proofs, being seen by them during forty days and speaking of the things pertaining to the kingdom of God. And being assembled together with them, He commanded them not to depart from Jerusalem, but to wait for the Promise of the Father, 'which,' He said, 'you have heard from Me; for John truly baptized with water, but <u>you shall be baptized with the Holy Spirit not many days from now</u>.' Therefore, when they had come together, they asked Him, saying, 'Lord, will You at this time restore the kingdom to Israel?' And He said to them, 'It is not for you to know times or seasons which the Father has put in His own authority. But <u>you shall receive power when the Holy Spirit has come upon you</u>; and you shall be witnesses to Me in Jerusalem, and in all Judea and Samaria, and to the ends of the earth.'"

Luke is laying it out for us in an orderly manner. The first time Jesus presented Himself alive to the apostles, was the night of the same day He was raised from the dead. At that time, He breathed the Holy Spirit *into* them, and they became born again. The resurrected Christ Jesus was then seen by them for forty days, speaking to them of things pertaining to the kingdom of God. After that, the Bible says they were assembled together and Jesus told them to not depart from Jerusalem, but to wait for the Promise of the Father. Jesus said, "you <u>shall be</u> baptized with the Holy Spirit not many days from now." Jesus said this forty days *after* His resurrection (when He gave them the Holy Spirit to dwell IN them). He now said, "you shall receive power when the Holy Spirit has come UPON you." Then, according to Luke 24, Jesus led them out as far as Bethany, lifted His hands to bless them, and as He was blessing them, He was carried up into heaven. The day of Pentecost came ten days later.

In this passage, we also see another reason for needing this power from on high, which is in order to be witnesses to Jesus to all the ends of the earth. The Promise of the Father is being "baptized with the Holy Spirit" by the resurrected Christ, who God gave the authority to do so. This is also called (by Jesus) "being endued with power from on high when the Holy Spirit has come UPON you". It is something every child of God needs in their life. It is something every disciple needs. It is something that Jesus needed. Let's keep searching and look at the actual Day of Pentecost where the word Christ spoke to them was fulfilled.

📖 **Acts 2:1-4 NKJV**

"When the Day of Pentecost had fully come, they were all with one accord in one place. And suddenly there came a sound from heaven, as of a rushing mighty wind, and it filled the whole house where they were sitting. Then there appeared to them divided tongues, as of fire, and one sat upon each of them. And they were all filled with the Holy Spirit and began to speak with other tongues, as the Spirit gave them utterance."

> *In this passage, we also see another reason for needing this power from on high, which is in order to be witnesses to Jesus to all the ends of the earth.*

Did you see that this anointing, the baptism with the Holy Spirit, is specific to individuals, and not corporate? The word says He came and sat upon EACH of them. UPON each of them—the Holy Spirit filled them and gave them utterance to speak with other tongues. This baptism with the Holy Spirit was a *separate* and *secondary* receiving from the Lord, which we've established both Jesus and His disciples experienced. Doesn't that convince you of your own need for such a baptism, in order to be endued with power by God for life and ministry? At the end of this chapter, I will pray a prayer for anyone who wants to receive this baptism with the Holy Spirit.

For now, let's continue to better understand the concept of being *filled with the Holy Spirit*. At Pentecost, we saw the Promise of the Father coming to rest UPON them and fill them to speak in other tongues. But what else can we learn about being filled with the Spirit after we have been born again; after we have been baptized with Him through our faith in Jesus Christ? Let's look at Peter.

Fillings of the Holy Spirit

📖 ***Acts 4:8-10,13 NKJV***

"Then Peter, filled with the Holy Spirit, said to them, 'Rulers of the people and elders of Israel: If we this day are judged for a good deed done to a helpless man, by what means he has been made well, let It be known to you all, and to all the people of Israel, that by the name of Jesus Christ of Nazareth, whom you crucified, whom God raised from the dead, by Him this man stands here before you whole'....Now when they saw the boldness of Peter and John, and perceived that they were uneducated and untrained men, they marveled. And they realized that they had been with Jesus."

Here the Holy Spirit *fills* Peter with what is needed to stand and speak boldly before the rulers and elders of Israel; to preach the Gospel of Christ and be His witness. This enduing with power from the Holy Spirit allows men to be filled with measures of courage and boldness to declare truth, even when the people we are talking with are many levels higher than us according to societal standards. Look at Peter and John, uneducated and untrained men, boldly telling highly educated and highly trained men (to their faces) that they crucified the Son of God. They had no concern for what might happen to them. Do you need this kind of power in your life? Normally, when someone is in a place where they know those around them are smarter or richer or more important than they are (according to the world), then that person will be quiet and not want to do anything to draw attention. The Holy Spirit can change that in your life and give you boldness in the will and purpose of God.

Imagine if the President of the United States came to your house and is sitting in your living room. He is not a follower of Jesus and has come to ask you why you are creating so much trouble in his country by preaching Jesus as the only way to heaven. All of his entourage and security detail have filled your house for the purpose of intimidation, and he intends to demand that you stop preaching in the name of Jesus. Most people would back down for fear, and for not wanting to be the only one in the room who disagrees with everyone else. However, we as true followers of Jesus Christ cannot yield to such pressure and deny Jesus. What we need in that moment is to be filled with the Holy Spirit to stand our ground coura- geously and speak the word of God, regardless of the consequences. We need power to overcome our fears and power to boldly declare the truth. Peter and John were under a similar pressure before the rulers and elders, who were commanding them not to speak or teach in the name of Jesus. They stood their

> *What we need in that moment is to be filled with the Holy Spirit to stand our ground courageously and speak the word of God, regardless of the consequences.*

ground by the power of God. They then departed and went to where the brethren were gathered, and prayed. Listen to their prayer and how God responded.

📖 *Acts 4:29-31 NKJV*

"'Now, Lord, look on their threats, and grant to Your servants that with all boldness they may speak Your word, by stretching out Your hand to heal, and that signs and wonders may be done through the name of Your holy Servant Jesus.' And when they had prayed, the place where they were assembled together was shaken; and they were all filled with the Holy Spirit, and they spoke the word of God with boldness."

Peter and John were born of the Spirit at a certain time; they were baptized with the Spirit at another time; and here they are filled with the Spirit to speak the word of God with boldness particularly. Being born of the Spirit and baptized with the Spirit are both necessary for realization of the full Christian experience—demonstrated by the Spirit and with power. Being filled with the Spirit is something God does as we walk with Jesus (according to His way) and are yielding ourselves to Him. It is the Spirit who decides what to do at a given moment and in a given situation. We do not forcibly bring forth the wisdom of God, or discernment, utterance, healing, or anything else (in our own strength). Those are things only the Spirit of God can do. Being filled with the Spirit is Him enabling us, in a particular moment, for the will of God to be done expressly, as we abide in and obey Jesus.

Even in the Old Testament, when God wanted to speak to His people, He would do it by placing His Spirit UPON the servant of His choice in order to speak the words of God. One day, when the children of Israel were in their wilderness journey, after God delivered them from the slavery of Egypt, the people began complaining to Moses about the food God was providing them. Moses began talking with God about it and the Lord told him what He would do.

> *Being filled with the Spirit is Him enabling us, in a particular moment, for the will of God to be done expressly, as we abide in and obey Jesus.*

📖   *Numbers 11:16-17 NKJV*
"So the LORD said to Moses: 'Gather to Me seventy men of the elders of Israel, whom you know to be the elders of the people and officers over them; bring them to the tabernacle of meeting, that they may stand there with you. Then I will come down and talk with you there. I will take of the Spirit that is UPON you and will put the same UPON them; and they shall bear the burden of the people with you, that you may not bear it yourself alone.'"

Because Christ had not yet gone to the cross, and the Holy Spirit was not yet given to dwell IN men, these were still men who carried the sinful nature they were born with, which they inherited from Adam. God's way of interacting with them and doing work through them was to place His Spirit UPON them. The Spirit enables a man to talk with God, to understand and hear from God, to speak the words of God, and even to bear the burden of people for God's will and purpose. It is the Holy Spirit that bears witness with a man's spirit, even if that man is not born again. Man can never hear or understand anything from God except by the Spirit of God, whether that man knows it or not. In this situation, God's solution to help Moses in dealing with the burden of leading the rebellious people, was to take of that same Spirit He placed UPON Moses and put Him UPON the elders.

📖 *Numbers 11:24-25 NKJV*

"So Moses went out and told the people the words of the LORD, and he gathered the seventy men of the elders of the people and placed them around the tabernacle. Then the LORD came down in the cloud, and spoke to him, and took of the Spirit that <u>was upon him,</u> and placed the same <u>upon the seventy elders;</u> and it happened, <u>when the Spirit rest-ed upon them,</u> that they prophesied, although they never did so again."

> **The Spirit enables a man to talk with God, to understand and hear from God, to speak the words of God, and even to bear the burden of people for God's will and purpose.**

These men were not born again, but WHEN the Spirit came and rested upon them, He enabled them to speak the word of God through prophesying. The Spirit was not IN Moses or IN these elders but UPON them for a particular assignment in the will of God at that moment. He filled them with what was needed. Did you see how the elders never prophesied again? The Spirit rested UPON them for a task; He is the One who determines what is needed to equip a man with power to accomplish any given task. It is not by man's might, or by man's power, but by the Spirit of God alone.

After hearing the word of God, the crowd departed, but two other men, Eldad and Medad, remained. The Bible says the Spirit also rest-ed UPON them and they prophesied in the camp. Then Joshua, Moses' servant, told Moses what they were doing and wanted Mo-ses to forbid them from prophesying. But see how Moses answered.

📖 *Numbers 11:29 NKJV*

"Then Moses said to him, 'Are you zealous for my sake? Oh, that all the LORD's people were prophets and that the LORD would put His Spirit upon them!"

Moses understood the need for the Spirit of God to rest upon a man. He longed in his heart that ALL the LORD's people would be anointed by the Spirit UPON them. This was not available to all people before Christ came to deal with the sinful nature in man. But for you who are now born again by the Spirit of God dwelling in you, this experience of the Spirit resting UPON you is something our God and Father wants to give you, to empower you for life and ministry. He is now equally available to all. Let's keep digging so He can continue to illuminate us with further understanding, wisdom, and increasing desire for this baptism with the Holy Spirit to be our reality.

> *But for you who are now born again by the Spirit of God dwelling in you, this experience of the Spirit resting UPON you is something our God and Father wants to give you, to empower you for life and ministry.*

When God was going to anoint David to be king of Israel. He came and spoke to His servant Samuel, who was still mourning over the downfall of Saul, the current king.

📖 *1 Samuel 16:1,13 NKJV*
"Now the LORD said to Samuel, 'How long will you mourn for Saul, seeing I have rejected him from reigning over Israel? Fill your horn with oil, and go; I am sending you to Jesse the Bethlehemite. For I have provided Myself a king among his sons.'....Then Samuel took the horn of oil and anointed him in the midst of his brothers; and the Spirit of the LORD came upon David from that day forward. So Samuel arose and went to Ramah."

When God wanted to establish His king according to His will, He sent His Spirit to come UPON that man for power to carry out the duties of being the king. This helps us to see another dimension of the necessity to receive power from on high—it's for our life, and for the duties assigned to us by God. Later, this is displayed when, as the king, David wrote down the plans for all the details of the house of the LORD that his son, Solomon, would build. He told Solomon the LORD had chosen him to build the sanctuary.

📖 *1 Chronicles 28:11-12 NKJV*
*"Then David gave his son Solomon the plans for the vestibule, its houses, its treasuries, its upper chambers, its inner chambers, and the place of the mercy seat; and the plans for all that he had **by the Spirit**, of the courts of the house of the LORD, of all the chambers all around, of the treasuries of the house of God, and of the treasuries for the dedicated things;"*

This helps us to see another dimension of the necessity to receive power from on high— it's for our life, and for the duties assigned to us by God.

David continued in great detail and eventually said to Solomon:

📖 *1 Chronicles 28:19 NKJV*
"'All this,' said David, 'the LORD made me understand in writing, <u>by His hand UPON me</u>, all the works of these plans.'"

David could never have known these plans except **by the Spirit** which was UPON him. The Holy Spirit *is* the hand of God that filled him with understanding and ability, enabling him to put elaborate details down in writing for his son to carry out and obey. This is *also* how the Bible was written by God through human hands. The Spirit of God was UPON each vessel, filling them and establishing their thoughts to bring forth His words as they committed themselves to the work the Lord gave them.

📖 **Proverbs 16:3 NKJV**
"Commit your works to the LORD, and your thoughts will be established."

It is the Spirit of God who establishes the thoughts of a man with the will of God. And it is He who enables a person to do what otherwise would be impossible—like write or speak the word of God, heal, love, perform miracles, etc. There are many other examples in the Old Testament of how the Holy Spirit would function in this way, however, we need to move on from here and engage this *receiving of power from on high* from the perspective of after the cross; within the present reality of the new creation life.

When the church, which was at Jerusalem, suffered great persecution, the brethren were scattered throughout the regions of Judea and Samaria. One of those scattered was Philip, who went down to the city of Samaria to preach Christ to the people. They listened to him with great joy, were believing on the Lord Jesus Christ, and were getting baptized in water.

  📖 *Acts 8:12 NKJV*
"But when they believed Philip as he preached the things concerning the kingdom of God and the name of Jesus Christ, both men and women were baptized."

These men and women were baptized for the remission of their sins in order to receive the new life that God has promised for all who repent and believe on the Lord Jesus Christ. They became born again by receiving the word of God. But look at what the Bible reveals next.

  📖 *Acts 8:14-17 NKJV*
"Now when the apostles who were at Jerusalem heard that Samaria had received the word of God, they sent Peter and John to them, who, when they had come down, prayed for them that they might receive the Holy Spirit. For as yet He had fallen upon none of them. They had only been baptized in the name of the Lord Jesus. Then they laid hands on them, and they received the Holy Spirit."

They were only baptized in the name of the Lord Jesus. They heard the Gospel, repented, believed on Jesus, and received Him into their hearts. God, upon their faith, imputed all the work of Christ to them: the forgiveness and cleansing of sin, the death of the old man, the cutting away of the sinful nature, and the pouring in of the life of Christ by the Spirit of God. They were brand new creations and had the Spirit of Christ dwelling in them, but the Bible said they hadn't yet had the Holy Spirit fall UPON them. To understand the space of time between these two baptisms here in Acts 8, we know that the news traveled all the way to the apostles in Jerusalem, which was over 30 miles away from Samaria, a three-day journey by foot. There

> **They were brand new creations and had the Spirit of Christ dwelling in them, but the Bible said they hadn't yet had the Holy Spirit fall UPON them.**

were no cell phones, no wire service, or any other way to transmit the good news that Samaria had received the word of God. So, it was at least six days (and probably more) before Peter and John could make it down to Samaria, to lay hands on them to receive the baptism with the Holy Spirit.

We should note, you do not need someone to lay hands on you to be born again. Whoever hears the Gospel and responds to it, no matter where they are, no matter who they are, and no matter who is with them or not with them, will become born again by God. These Samaritans now needed the Promise of the Father because He had not yet fallen UPON them. That is what compelled the apostles at Jerusalem to send Peter and John to Samaria. It was not because they were concerned about the quality of the Gospel being preached to them. The Gospel Philip preached was fully sufficient for authentic salvation to take place. He himself was a disciple of Christ, a man full of faith and of the Holy Spirit and approved of by the apostles. The new brethren in Samaria had been baptized in the name of the Lord Jesus but not yet baptized with the Holy Spirit—being endued with power from on high. Are you seeing the differences in these baptisms more clearly now? Is this truth dawning upon your heart in a fresh way, and stirring up in your heart the desire to receive this Promise of the Father for your own life? Before we pray, let's look at one last example, with the apostle Paul and this baptism with the Holy Spirit.

📖 *Acts 19:1-6 NKJV*
"And it happened, while Apollos was at Corinth, that Paul, having passed through the upper regions, came to Ephesus. And finding

some disciples he said to them, 'Did you receive the Holy Spirit when you believed?' So they said to him, "We have not so much as heard whether there is a Holy Spirit.' And he said to them, "Into what then were you baptized?' So they said, 'Into John's baptism.' Then Paul said, 'John indeed baptized with a baptism of repentance, saying to the people that they should believe on Him who would come after him, that is, on Christ Jesus.' When they heard this, they were baptized in the name of the Lord Jesus. And when Paul had laid hands on them, the Holy Spirit came <u>upon them</u>, and they spoke with tongues and prophesied."

Here we have all three baptisms on display. The baptism of John which is the baptism of repentance for the remission of sins and faith toward God. The baptism in the name of the Lord Jesus that comes from hearing the Gospel and believing on and receiving Jesus Christ through faith for salvation. And the baptism with the Holy Spirit in order to be endued with power from on high; the Promise of the Father that came as Paul laid his hands on them.

When Paul came across these disciples, he inquired to see if they received the Holy Spirit when they believed. They didn't know what he was talking about; they hadn't even heard about the Holy Spirit. At the time they were baptized into John's baptism only. Then Paul told them about the name of Jesus Christ, and they were baptized into Him. After that, Paul laid his hands on them

But more importantly than that, they were now baptized with the Holy Spirit in order to bring them necessary power for their life and ministry from that point on.

and prayed for them, and they experienced the Holy Spirit coming UPON them. On this particular day, the Holy Spirit enabled them to speak with tongues and to prophesy. But more importantly than that, they were now baptized with the Holy Spirit in order to bring them necessary power for their life and ministry from that point on.

Are you persuaded, from the word of God, that you need to receive from God the Father and the Lord Jesus Christ this baptism? There are a couple things we need to understand before we pray.

First, you must believe God and exercise faith in His word.

📖 *Hebrews 4:2 NKJV*

"For indeed the gospel was preached to us as well as to them; but the word which they heard did not profit them, not being mixed with faith in those who heard it."

The word of God is powerful, but we must mix the word we hear with faith in our hearts, or it will do us no good and bring no value into our lives.

GNT *"it did them no good, because when they heard it, they did not accept it with faith"*

AMP *"the message they heard did not benefit them"*

NIV *"the message they heard was of no value to them"*

TLB *"it didn't do them any good because they didn't believe it"*

The word of God is powerful, but we must mix what we hear with faith in our hearts, or it will do us no good in our lives. God is wanting you to believe Him, and He is wanting you to diligently seek Him for this Promise of the Father to be fully given to you.

📖 *Hebrews 11:6 NKJV*

"But without faith it is impossible to please Him, for he who comes to God must believe that He is, and that He is a rewarder of those who diligently seek Him."

I have witnessed men, whose doctrine strongly opposed the idea of being baptized with the Holy Spirit, come to the knowledge of this Promise and ask God for the gift of the Holy Spirit to rest UPON them. Their previous lack of belief blocked them from receiving this provision God wants to generously give us all. I implore you not to reject the word of God, but to declare to the Lord that you believe

Him, and you want Him to reward you with this enduing with power from on high.

Second, you must ask, and it will be given to you.

   📖 *Luke 11:9-13 NKJV*
"So I say to you, ask, and it will be given to you; seek, and you will find; knock, and it will be opened to you. For everyone who asks receives, and he who seeks finds, and to him who knocks it will be opened. If a son asks for bread from any father among you, will he give him a stone? Or if he asks for a fish, will he give him a serpent instead of a fish? Or if he asks for an egg, will he offer him a scorpion? If you then, being evil, know how to give good gifts to your children, how much more will your heavenly Father give the Holy Spirit to those who ask Him!"

Our heavenly Father is waiting for you to ask Him to be baptized with the Holy Spirit. He is waiting for you to seek Him so you can be endued with power from on high. And He is waiting for you to knock on the door until He opens it and releases to you the Promise of the Father. Jesus (the Baptizer) is waiting to intercede on your behalf to ask the Father to give you this provision. He said:

   📖 *Luke 12:32 NKJV*
"Do not fear, little flock, for it is your Father's good pleasure to give you the kingdom."

Are you satisfied with the experience of the power of God in your life currently, or do you want more? If you are ready to believe God and ask Him for the baptism with the Holy Spirit, let's pray right now.

Our Father in heaven, You are the Father of lights, and it is from You that we receive every good and perfect gift from above. We thank You for the word of God and how Your Spirit dwelling in us has been giving us understanding and wisdom in the knowledge of Jesus Christ and the Way of God in Him. Now Father, You have

brought us to this critical place of decision making for receiving Your Promise of the baptism with the Holy Spirit. Father, I ask You to look upon Your children, who are humbly crying out to You, who are expressing their faith and desire for You, and are asking You to send Your Promise to rest UPON them. The same Promise that came to rest UPON Jesus, and the same Promise that came to rest UPON the disciples, is the same Promise I am asking You to pour out UPON them. Please make it Your good pleasure to give them the Holy Spirit, and to endue them with power from on high for the rest of their life. I ask that the fullness of the calling to which You have called them in Christ will be fully realized, and that You will receive all the glory from their living union with Jesus Christ, and by the anointing You send to remain UPON them for Your purpose. Thank You Father for hearing me. Thank You for Your faithfulness. Thank You for Your mercy and grace toward us. And thank You for enduing us with power from on high. All these things I believe You for, and even abundantly beyond what I am asking or thinking, for I am asking You to do this in the name of Jesus Christ. Amen.

"FOLLOW ME"

N ow that we have come to this blessed point—as you have believed and known these things concerning the treasure of Jesus Christ, concerning the power of the blood and the cross (by which the old, sinful nature was crucified and removed), concerning the resurrection provision of Christ in you; the hope of glory, and concerning the powerful Promise of the Holy Spirit's enduement—**how do you now grow in it**? How do you continue to experience the freedom of this new creation life more and more each day?

To grow in this mystery, there is still one more thing you need to do. Jesus said, "If you want to be my disciple… Follow Me."

📖 *John 8:30-32 KJV*
"As he spake these words, many believed on him. Then said Jesus to those Jews which believed on him, if ye continue in my word, then are ye my disciples indeed; and ye shall know the truth, and the truth shall make you free."

NKJV *"if you abide in My word, you are My disciples indeed"*
MSG *"if you stick with this, living out what I tell you, you are my disciples for sure"*

To be a disciple of Jesus, to experience true freedom in every area of your life, it requires a continuous, concerted, and consistent following of Him. You need to *continue with Jesus* in order to grow in knowing Him, to grow in learning from Him, and to grow in becoming more like Him.

   📖 **Mark 3:13-14 NKJV**
"And He went up on the mountain and called to Him those He Himself wanted. And they came to Him. Then He appointed twelve, <u>that they might be with Him</u> and that He might send them out to preach,"

NLT *"they were to accompany him"*
TLB *"to be his regular companions"*

The first goal of discipleship (for increasing in this new life) is not ministry, but to become a regular companion of Jesus in order to know Him, and to always be with Him and accompany Him everywhere He wants to go. This is the key to advancing and progressing in practically experiencing His life and knowing Him.

   📖 **John 17:3 AMPC**
"And this is eternal life: [it means] to know (to perceive, recognize, become acquainted with, and understand) You, the only true God, and [likewise] to know Him, Jesus [as the] Christ (the Anointed One, the Messiah), Whom You have sent."

You cannot *perceive* a life unless you are with it. You cannot *recognize* a life you are far from. And you cannot become *acquainted* with or understand a life you are not growing in knowing personally. Thus, the first priority for growing this new life is to grow in knowing Jesus. According to Jesus, the process that causes this to happen is "Follow Me."

  📖 **Matthew 16:24 NKJV**
"Then Jesus said to His disciples, 'If anyone desires to come after Me, let him deny himself, take up his cross, and follow Me.'"

  📖 **Matthew 16:24 AMP**
"Then Jesus said to His disciples, 'If anyone wishes to follow Me [as My disciple], he must deny himself [set aside selfish interests], and take up his cross [expressing a willingness to endure whatever may come] and follow Me [believing in Me, conforming to My example in living and, if need be, suffering or perhaps dying because of faith in Me]."

To be a disciple of Jesus, to experience true freedom in every area of your life, it requires a continuous, concerted, and consistent following of Him.

Choosing to follow Jesus is a deliberate action that daily involves setting aside selfish interests and being conformed to Jesus in all aspects of life. If you wish to follow Jesus as His disciple, it's not a sporadic or automatic thing. It requires an immediate abandonment of the old life and a commitment to following Him consistently in the new life, without excuse.

  📖 **Luke 9:61-62 NKJV**
"And another also said, 'Lord, I will follow You, but let me first go and bid them farewell who are at my house.' But Jesus said to him, 'No one, having put his hand to the plow, and looking back, is fit for the kingdom of God.'"

  📖 **Luke 9:61-62 AMP**
"Another also said, 'I will follow You, Lord [as Your disciple]; but first let me say goodbye to those at my home.' But Jesus said to him, "no one who puts his hand to the plow and looks back [to the things left behind] is fit for the kingdom of God.'"

MSG *"No procrastination. No backward looks. You can't put God's kingdom off till tomorrow."*

Being a disciple of Jesus is a total commitment to Him without any procrastination. Your growth and increasing experience of God's provisions for your life in Christ is located in (and accessed by) following Jesus in complete dedication to Him. Now that we are joined to Christ and His life is in us, we must cling to Him, and we must grow; Christ's life must increase in us.

📖 *2 Peter 3:17-18 NKJV*
"You therefore, beloved, since you know this beforehand, beware lest you also fall from your own steadfastness, being led away with the error of the wicked; but grow in the grace and knowledge of our Lord and Savior Jesus Christ. To Him be the glory both now and forever. Amen."

AMP *"but grow [spiritually mature] in the grace and knowledge of our Lord and Savior Jesus Christ"*
TLB *"But grow in spiritual strength and become better acquainted with our Lord and Savior Jesus Christ"*

There is an expectation from heaven that you will grow. The way to grow spiritually mature and become better acquainted with Jesus is to learn how to follow Him in discipleship daily. All who have been born again with this new creation life have been called to grow up into Christ until He is made manifest in you and until you become an aroma of His fragrance everywhere you go.

📖 *Ephesians 4:15 AMPC*
"Rather, let our lives lovingly express truth [in all things, speaking truly, dealing truly, living truly]. Enfolded in love, let us grow up in every way and in all things into Him Who is the Head, [even] Christ (the Messiah, the Anointed One)."

TLB *"and so become more and more in every way like Christ"*
GNT *"we must grow up in every way to Christ"*
NASB *"we are to grow up in all aspects into Him"*

Discipleship with Jesus is God's means for developing and growing the Christ-life in us. It's the lifelong process of intentionally being with Jesus and being conformed to His image and likeness in every way, as we continue daily with Him. This is the highest purpose of God for our life now that we are born again.

📖 *Romans 8:28-29 NKJV*
"And we know that all things work together for good to those who love God, to those who are the called <u>according to His purpose</u>. For whom He foreknew, He also predestined <u>to be conformed to the image of His Son</u>, that He might be the firstborn among many brethren."

AMPC *"to be molded into the image of His Son [and share inwardly His likeness]"*
GNT *"to become like his Son"*

For us to actually become *like* Jesus, we must walk with Him, constantly looking to, learning from, and obeying Him, and growing progressively into His image from one degree of glory to another. This is the work of the Spirit as we continue with Jesus.

> **Discipleship with Jesus is God's means for developing and growing the Christ-life in us. It's the lifelong process of intentionally being with Jesus and being conformed to His image and likeness in every way, as we continue daily with Him.**

And although discipleship is with Jesus first and foremost, God may also appoint someone to disciple us—to help us learn the life and way of Christ more accurately. If He does appoint such a *human discipler* to walk with and learn from, it is only to help us grow this new life that we have acquired in Christ Jesus. It is actually expedient for us to learn Christ under more mature and faithful men who have gone before us, whose lives give evidence of Christ's own likeness. Otherwise, our growth could easily take much longer, and the process of being conformed to His image could be much more arduous. The apostle Paul said it like this:

📖 *1 Corinthians 11:1 KJV*
"Be ye followers of me, even as I also am of Christ."

All that God has helped us to see and experience as we've traveled together through the pages of this book, as good as it is for our lives, for you to grow in it, for you to increase in it, for others to experience the fruit of Christ's life in you, you need to follow Jesus. You need to decide to take His yoke of discipleship for the rest of your time on earth. Jesus said:

📖 ***Matthew 11:29-30 NKJV***
"Take My yoke upon you and learn from Me, for I am gentle and lowly in heart, and you will find rest for your souls. For My yoke is easy and My burden is light."

CEV *"Take the yoke I give you. Put it on your shoulders and learn from me"*
AMP *"Take My yoke upon you and learn from Me [following Me as My disciple]"*

A yoke is a wooden crosspiece that is fastened over the necks of two like animals, joining them together and causing them to go in the same direction to accomplish a unified task. Discipleship is a deliberate, willing choice to come under *that* yoke with Jesus. It is a necessary, lifelong training for those who are born again. In being yoked daily to Jesus, we learn how to let the death that happened at the cross (our sinful nature having been crucified and removed) become an active reality in our lives, so Christ can release His life through us. It is the invitation from Jesus to deny self, take up our cross daily, and follow Him. One day, Jesus was talking to a young ruler who came to ask Him about obtaining eternal life.

📖 ***Matthew 19:21 NKJV***
"Jesus said to him, 'If you want to be perfect, go, sell what you have and give to the poor, and you will have treasure in heaven; and come, follow Me.'"
📖 ***Matthew 19:21 AMP***
"Jesus answered him, 'If you wish to be perfect [that is, have the spiritual maturity that accompanies godly character with no moral or ethical deficiencies], go and sell what you have and give [the money] to the poor, and you will have treasure in heaven; and come,

follow Me [becoming My disciple, believing and trusting in Me and walking the same path of life that I walk.'"

CEV *"come and be my follower"*

Do you want to walk the same path that Jesus is walking? Do you truly want to be His follower, a disciple indeed? If you want to be perfect (complete, mature) and grow in this new life, there is one thing you need to do—follow Jesus in discipleship.

   📖 **Luke 9:23 NKJV**
"Then He said to them all, 'If anyone desires to come after Me, let him deny himself, and take up his cross daily, and follow Me.'"

NLT *"to be my follower, you must give up your own way, take up your cross daily, and follow me"*

If you have discovered the treasure of Jesus Christ living in you, you will now need to give all your attention to Him in this matter. You have found the means of the cross that terminated the old nature, and you have found His life as the only good and proper life to follow. Now, are you willing to deliberately come under His yoke and learn from Him, however He may choose to disciple you?

Let's pray.

✝

Our Father in heaven, thank You for Jesus Christ. Thank You for the Holy Spirit. Thank You for showing me the treasure and work of Jesus, and all the wonderful provisions You have located for my life in Him. Lord Jesus, I see You are inviting me into a lifelong discipleship relationship with You. I want to accept Your offer and come willingly under Your yoke to follow You. I want to know You more and more each day and be conformed to Your image in every dimension of this new life You have given me. God, I want to grow well and grow up into Christ in all things. Please teach me, Lord, and cause me to grow in grace and in the knowledge of

the Lord Jesus Christ. Help me to live in the way that allows Christ's life to be formed in me and released and manifested through me always for the glory of God. And if you have assigned one of your faithful men on earth for me to learn this life from, will you please lead me to them? Thank You for hearing me, Father, for I am praying to You in the name of Jesus Christ. Thank You, Holy Spirit, for revealing Jesus Christ and Him crucified to me. Thank You for giving me understanding as I've undertaken this journey with you. I want You to continue to lead and guide me as I walk with Jesus, and I ask You to help me to always walk the same path He is walking. All glory and praise be to You, God, as I pray these things, believing You will do even more than I ask or think, in the name of Jesus Christ. Amen and amen.

**We have provided you with some additional resource references for a deeper dive into the concepts and ways of discipleship and growing this new life on page 330. You can utilize them to help you progress in your journey with the Lord. May God bless you as you pursue a deeper intimacy with Him in the name of Jesus Christ **

ADDITIONAL RESOURCES

LivingSeed Ministries

These are the brethren who have had the greatest impact in our development in the Lord Jesus. You will do well to visit the website, the YouTube channel or to acquire any of these books for your ongoing discovery and development in the Lord Jesus.

- Understanding the Concept and Conditions for Discipleship — *by Peace House Discipleship Works*
- The Kingdom Lifestyle — *by Gbile Akanni*
- What God Looks For In His Vessel — *by Gbile Akanni*
- Raising Agents of Transformation — *by Gbile Akanni*
- Living Seed Media Gboko — *YouTube channel*
- No More Two — *by Gbile Akanni*
- Battle for the Young — *by Gbile Akanni*

Disciples Storehouse YouTube Channel:
@disciplesstorehouse

We have deliberate Bible studies to help you grow in revelation and understanding of Jesus Christ and Him crucified. Under the "Playlists" we recommend any of these below studies as a next part of your journey. They are meant to go through with your Bible open and your notes ready. They build upon each other, so it is best to start and finish in order.

- Jesus: The Pattern and Example for Life — 16 videos
- The Cross of Christ — 23 videos
- The Word of God — 7 videos
- The Gospel of Christ — 24 videos